Photoshop® 7

VIRTUAL CLASSROOM

Photoshop® 7

VIRTUAL CLASSROOM

Ken Milburn

OSBORNE

New York   Chicago   San Francisco
Lisbon   London   Madrid   Mexico City
Milan   New Delhi   San Juan
Seoul   Singapore   Sydney   Toronto

McGraw-Hill/Osborne
2600 Tenth Street
Berkeley, California 94710
U.S.A.

To arrange bulk purchase discounts for sales promotions, premiums, or fund-raisers, please contact **McGraw-Hill/**Osborne at the above address. For information on translations or book distributors outside the U.S.A., please see the International Contact Information page immediately following the index of this book.

Photoshop® 7 Virtual Classroom

Brainsville.com™
The better way to learn.

1 2 3 4 5 6 7 8 9 0   QPD QPD 0 1 9 8 7 6 5 4 3 2

Book p/n 0-07-222309-X and CD p/n 0-07-222310-3
parts of
ISBN 0-07-222308-1

Publisher	**Acquisitions Coordinator**	**Indexer**
Brandon A. Nordin	Tana Allen	Jack Lewis
Vice President &	**Technical Editor**	**Design & Production**
Associate Publisher	Tom Babcock	epic
Scott Rogers		
	Copy Editor	**Illustrator**
Acquisitions Editor	Mike McGee	Lyssa Wald
Marjorie McAneny		Michael Mueller
	Proofreader	
Project Editor	Nancy McLaughlin	**Cover Design**
Monika Faltiss		Ted Holladay

This book was composed with QuarkXPress™.

About the Author

Ken Milburn is a photographer, author, and fine-artist who uses Adobe Photoshop in both his commercial and fine-art work. This book is his fifth Photoshop title. Ken is also the author of *The Photoshop Bible* (1st and 2nd Editions) and *Digital Photography: 99 Easy Tips to Make You Look Like a Pro!* You can find more Photoshop and digital photography tips at his web site: www.kenmilburn.com.

ABOUT THE TECHNICAL EDITOR

Tom Babcock is trained in biochemistry and music. For many years he has worked as an artist-animator at a small company in Oakland, California. He now resides with his cat, Rusty, in San Francisco where art and music consume his time. He can be reached at tbabcock123@earthlink.net.

Dedication

This book is dedicated to my friend, colleague, and co-author of our upcoming book *Photoshop Elements: The Complete Reference*, Gene Hirsh, and to my son, Lane.

Acknowledgments

I can't tell you how much fun and how invigorating it has been to work with the creative team at Osborne: Roger Stewart, Margie McAneny, Tana Allen, Monika Faltiss, Lyssa Wald, Mike McGee, Eric Houts, and Andrea Reider. They were even supportive and helpful when I inconsiderately landed flat on my back with pneumonia. More importantly, they manage to show their intelligence and sense of humor while they're working like dogs…not an easy thing to do. I also really need and want to thank my friends Bob Cowart and Dan Newman, the geniuses at Brainsville.com. Without them, this book could never have happened. Matthew David, Gene Hirsh, and Winston Steward all made significant contributions to the manuscript, for which I am grateful. I'd also like to thank the beta support team at Adobe, who provided invaluable assistance during the writing of this book. Finally, I want to thank my agent, Margot Maley Hutchison, without whose help I'd be stark raving crazy.

Contents at a Glance

Guild House, Farnsby Street, Swindon X, SN99 9XX
Customer Careline Tel: (0870) 1650255

PLEASE RETAIN

DELIVERY NOTE

MEMBER No: 0026937204

NAME: MR J S MAXWELL

REF: 9109223819

DATE: 14/08/02

YOUR ORDER DETAILS
1465640 Virtual Photoshop 7+CD   Enclosed

THANK YOU FOR YOUR RECENT ORDER
WE HAVE PLEASURE IN ENCLOSING THE GOODS REQUESTED

*"Why not ring 0870 1650165, our account information and Orderline, if
you wish to order, make a payment or for simple account enquiries".*

PICKING SLIP

CM   0026937204

Virtual Photoshop 7+C 1465640 17878 * * * * * *

H14

78510348

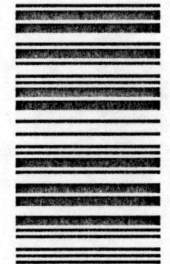

2   PUSSIKESKUS 3   **04**   1   **SI**

If you have to return all or part of your order please enclose this slip

111110

00012365

Please check the contents of the parcel against the details on this Delivery Note. If there is anything missing or incorrect, always contact our Customer Services department who will be pleased to resolve the matter for you. Please enclose the packing slip with any return made. We would also advise you to get a receipt from the Post Office or Carrier.

When do I pay for my books/items?

The total amount due will be shown on your next statement. All payments must be sent to us within 10 days of receipt of your statement.

Please make your cheque or postal order payable to your club quoting your membership number on the reverse. You can also pay by credit card by completing the reverse of the order form.

Contents

Introduction

WHO WILL ENJOY THIS BOOK?

Anyone who's looking for a quick and easy-to-understand visual overview of the essentials of Photoshop Professional 7.0, its most intriguing new features, and the solutions it offers for easing the problems that most often plague its users. I have not even attempted to cover every little nit and pick in this infinitely vast program, but opted to give you the information that you're most likely to find useful...especially if you have a pressing need to produce professional level work from an image-editing program but just don't have the time to preface that with an intense study of all the multiple choices that Photoshop gives you for doing most anything your way.

WHAT MAKES THIS A VIRTUAL CLASSROOM?

The accompanying CD makes this book a *virtual classroom*. Instead of just reading about Photoshop, you can watch and listen as I discuss the different topics examined in each chapter while helpful visuals appear on screen, demonstrating various features and techniques.

It's important to note that the CD is not a visual repetition of the book—not everything discussed in the book is covered on the CD, and some topics broached on the CD are covered in more detail there than in the book. The goal for the CD is to give you the experience of sitting in on one of my classes, allowing me to elaborate on certain topics that can be better expressed and explained in a full-color, moving medium. Topics in the book that wouldn't be any better explained through sound, color, and motion are not found on the CD, whereas topics that couldn't be effectively explained through text and black-and-white images *are* found on the CD.

You can learn a great deal from the book without ever watching the CD. I hope, however, that you'll read the book *and* watch the CD to enhance what you've absorbed through your reading. This approach is the closest match to hands-on classroom training experience, because I typically discuss a topic and then show it to or demonstrate it for the class, inviting the students to work along with me on their computers so that the skills become part of each student's personal experience.

HOW THIS BOOK WORKS

Of course you know how a book *works*: you open it and start reading, turning pages as you go. Not too difficult, right? This book, however, has some useful features that you should be aware of:

▶ **Tips and Sidebars** Whenever I thought of something that I'd present as a quick aside during class, I turned it into a tip. Tips relate to the main topic in the nearby text, but are extra bits of helpful information rather than entire topics unto themselves. Sidebars delve a little deeper, discussing larger topics that relate to nearby text.

▶ **CD references** At the end of chapters containing topics covered on the CD, an "On the Virtual Classroom CD-ROM" notation appears, directing you to the specific CD lesson that relates to the chapter you've just read.

▶ **Glossary** I thought it would be helpful to include an alphabetized list of Photoshop terms. All the terms in the glossary are found in the book, and many are explained in context within the chapters.

I hope you enjoy the book and the CD videos. You'll find additional Photoshop resources at my Web site: www.kenmilburn.com. I invite you to use those resources, and to contact me at the site with specific questions, insights, suggestions, and constructive criticisms.

 # PHOTOSHOP 7 VIRTUAL CLASSROOM CD

This CD contains an exciting new kind of video-based instruction to help you learn Photoshop 7 faster. We believe this learning tool is a unique development in the area of computer-based training. The author actually talks to you, right from your computer screen, demonstrating topics he wrote about in the book. Moving "screencams" and slides accompany his presentation, reinforcing what you're learning.

The technology and design of the presentation were developed by Brainsville.com. The content on the CD-ROM was developed by McGraw-Hill/Osborne, Robert Fuller, and Brainsville.com. Patents (pending), copyright, and trademark protections apply to this technology and the names *Brainsville* and Brainsville.com.

Please read the following directions for usage of the CD-ROM, to ensure that the lessons play as smoothly as possible.

GETTING STARTED

The CD-ROM is optimized to run under Windows 95/98/ME/NT/2000 or a Mac, using the QuickTime player version 5 (or later), from Apple. If you don't have the QuickTime 5 player installed, you must install it, either by downloading it from the Internet at http://www.quicktime.com, or running the Setup program from the CD-ROM. If you install from the Web, it's fine to use the free version of the QuickTime player. You don't need to purchase the full version. If you can't install the QuickTime player, or you prefer to use Windows Media Player, we have provided the lessons in that format as well, primarily as a backup plan. See the Troubleshooting section for details.

To install the QuickTime player from the CD-ROM follow these steps:

On a Windows PC

1. Insert the CD-ROM in the drive.

2. Use Explorer or My Computer to browse to the CD-ROM.

3. Open the QuickTime folder.

4. Open the Windows folder.

5. Double-click on the QuickTime Installer program there.

6. Follow the setup instructions on screen.

On a Mac

1. Insert the CD-ROM in the drive.

2. Open the QuickTime folder.

3. Open the Mac folder.

4. Run the QuickTime installer file there.

RUNNING THE CD IN WINDOWS 95/98/ME/NT/2000/XP

Minimum Requirements

▶ QuickTime 5 player

▶ Pentium II P300 (or equivalent)

▶ 64MB of RAM

▶ 8X CD-ROM

▶ Windows 95, Windows 98, Windows NT 4.0 (with at least Service Pack 4), Windows ME, Windows 2000, or Windows XP

▶ 16-bit sound card and speakers

Photoshop 7 Virtual Classroom CD-ROM can run directly from the CD (running the videos from the hard drive for better performance is explained in the "Improving Playback" section below) and should start automatically on a PC when you insert the CD in the drive. If the program does not start automatically, your system may not be set up to automatically detect CDs. To change this, you can do the following (but read the next section first):

1. Choose Settings, Control Panel, and click the System icon.

2. Click the Device Manager tab in the System Properties dialog box.

3. Double-click the Disk Drives icon and locate your CD-ROM drive.

4. Double-click the CD-ROM drive icon and then click the Settings tab in the CD-ROM Properties dialog box. Make sure the "Auto insert notification" box is checked. This specifies that Windows will be notified when you insert a compact disc into the drive.

If you don't care about the auto-start setting for your CD-ROM, and don't mind the manual approach, you can start the lessons manually, this way:

1. Insert the CD-ROM.

2. Double-click the My Computer icon on your Windows desktop.

3. Open the CD-ROM folder.

4. Double-click the startnow.exe icon in the folder.

5. Follow instructions on the screen to start.

RUNNING THE CD ON A MAC

Minimum Requirements

▶ A PowerPC processor–based Macintosh computer

▶ At least 64MB of RAM

▶ Mac OS 7.5.5 or later including the latest version of OS X

To run the CD:

1. Insert the CD-ROM.

2. Double-click on the file INlesson to start the introduction.

THE OPENING SCREEN

When the program autostarts on a PC, you'll see a small window in the middle of your screen. Simply click the indicated link to begin your lessons. This will launch the QuickTime player and start the introductory lesson.

On some computers, after the lesson loads you must click the Play button to begin. The Play button is the big round button with an arrow on it at the bottom center of the QuickTime player window. It looks like the play button on a VCR. You can click on the links in the lower left region of the presentation window to jump to a given lesson.

The QuickTime player will completely fill a screen that is running at 800x600 resolution. (This is the minimum resolution required to play the lessons.) For screens with higher resolution, you can adjust the position of the player on screen, as you like.

If you are online, you can click on the Brainsville.com logo under the index marks to jump directly to the Brainsville.com web site for information about additional video lessons from Brainsville.com.

IMPROVING PLAYBACK

Your Virtual Classroom CD-ROM employs some cutting-edge technologies, requiring that your computer be pretty fast to run the lessons smoothly. Many variables determine a computer's video performance, so we can't give you specific requirements for running the lessons. CPU speed, internal bus speed, amount of RAM, CD-ROM drive transfer rate, video display performance, CD-ROM cache settings, and other variables will determine how well the lessons will play. Our advice is to simply try the CD. The disk has been tested on laptops and desktops of various speeds, and in general, we have determined that you'll need at least a Pentium II-class computer running in excess of 300MHz for decent performance. (If you're doing serious web-design work, it's likely your machine is at least this fast.)

CLOSE OTHER PROGRAMS

For best performance, make sure you are not running other programs in the background while viewing the CD-based lessons. If you want to have the program you're learning (in this case, Photoshop) open so you can switch to it to try new techniques as you learn them, that is perhaps the one exception. Rendering the video on your screen takes a lot of computing power, and background programs such as automatic e-mail checking, web-site updating, or Active Desktop applets (such as scrolling stock tickers) can tax the CPU to the point of slowing the videos.

ADJUST THE SCREEN COLOR DEPTH TO SPEED UP PERFORMANCE

It's possible the author's lips will be out of synch with his or her voice, just like web-based videos often look. There are a couple of solutions. Start with this one. Lowering the color depth to 16-bit color makes a world of difference with many computers, laptops included. Rarely do people need 24-bit or 32-bit color for their work anyway, and it makes scrolling your screen (in any program) that much slower when running in those higher color depths. Try this (on a PC):

1. Right-click on the desktop and choose Properties.

2. Click the Settings tab.

3. In the Colors section, open the drop-down list box and choose a lower setting. If you are currently running at 24-bit (True Color) color, for example, try 16-bit (High Color). Don't use 256 colors, since video will appear very funky if you do.

4. Click OK to close the box. With most computers these days, you don't have to restart the computer after making this change. The video should run more smoothly now, since your computer's CPU doesn't have to work as hard to paint the video pictures on your screen.

On a Mac, use the Control Panels, then Monitors, to adjust the color depth. On OS X changes are made in System Preferences, Displays. Choose Thousands.

If adjusting the color depth didn't help the synch problem, see the section about copying the CD's files to the hard disk.

TURN OFF SCREEN SAVERS, SCREEN BLANKERS, AND STANDBY OPTIONS

When lessons are playing you're not likely to interact with the keyboard or mouse. Because of this, your computer screen might blank, and in some cases (such as with laptops) the computer might even go into a standby mode. You'll want to prevent these annoyances by turning off your screen saver and by checking the power options settings to ensure they don't kick in while you're viewing the lessons. You make settings for both of these parameters from the Control Panel. (You can, if you prefer, just press the SPACEBAR or the SHIFT key to wake up the screen if it blanks.) For PCs (only):

1. Open Control Panel, choose Display, and click on the Screen Saver tab. Choose "None" for the screen saver.

2. Open Control Panel, choose Power Management, and set System Standby, Turn Off Monitor, and Turn Off Hard Disks to Never. Then click Save As and save this power setting as "Brainsville Courses." You can return your power settings to their previous state if you like, after you are finished viewing

the lessons. Just use the Power Schemes drop-down list and choose one of the factory-supplied settings, such as Home/Office Desk.

COPY THE CD FILES TO THE HARD DISK TO SPEED UP PERFORMANCE

The CD-ROM drive will whir quite a bit when running the lessons from the CD. If your computer or CD-ROM drive is a bit slow, it's possible the author's lips will be out of synch with his or her voice, just like web-based videos often look. The video might freeze or slow down occasionally, though the audio will typically keep going along just fine. If you don't like the CD constantly whirring, or you are annoyed by out-of-synch video, you may be able to solve either or both problems by copying the CD-ROM's contents to your hard disk and running the lessons from there. To do so on a PC or Mac:

1. Check to see that you have at least 650MB free space on your hard disk.
2. Create a new folder on your hard disk (the name doesn't matter) and copy all the contents of the CD-ROM to the new folder (you must preserve the sub-folder names and folder organization as it is on the CD-ROM).
3. Once that is done, you can start the program by opening the new folder and double-clicking on the file startnow.exe (on a PC) or Inlesson (on a Mac). This will automatically start the lessons and run them from the hard disk.
4. (Optional in Windows) For convenience, you can create a shortcut to the start-now.exe file and place it on your desktop. You will then be able to start the program by clicking on the shortcut.

UPDATE YOUR QUICKTIME PLAYER

The QuickTime software is updated frequently and posted on the Apple QuickTime web site, www.quicktime.com. You can update your software by clicking Update Existing Software, from the Help menu in the QuickTime player. We strongly suggest you do this from time to time.

MAKE SURE YOUR CD-ROM DRIVE IS SET FOR OPTIMUM PERFORMANCE

CD-ROM drives on IBM PCs can be set to transfer data using the DMA (Direct Memory Access) mode, assuming the drive supports this faster mode. If you are experiencing slow performance and out-of-synch problems, check this setting. These steps are for Windows 98 and Windows ME.

1. Open Control Panel and choose System.

2. Click on the Device Manager tab.

3. Click on the + sign to the left of the CD-ROM drive.

4. Right-click on the CD-ROM drive.

5. Choose Properties.

6. Click the Settings tab.

7. Look to see if the DMA check box is turned on (has a check mark in it).

If selected, this increases the CD-ROM drive access speed. Some drives do not support this option. If the DMA check box remains selected after you restart Windows, then this option is supported by the device.

In Windows 2000, the approach is a little different. You access the drive's settings via Device Manager as above, but click on IDE/ATAPI Controllers. Right-click the IDE channel that your CD-ROM drive is on, choose Properties, and make the settings as appropriate. (Choose the device number, 0 or 1, and check the settings. Typically it's set to DMA If Available, which is fine. It's not recommended that you change these settings unless you know what you are doing.

TROUBLESHOOTING

This section offers solutions to common problems. Check www.quicktime.com for much more information about the QuickTime player, which is the software the Virtual Classroom CDs use to play.

THE CD WILL NOT RUN

If you have followed the previous instructions and the program will not work, you may have a defective drive or a defective CD. Be sure the CD is inserted properly in the drive. (Test the drive with other CDs, to see if they run.)

YOU ARE RUNNING WINDOWS XP AND THE LESSONS WON'T START

Due to strange interactions between Windows XP and QuickTime 5, QuickTime movies may not run when the link on the splash screen is clicked on. This appears to have to do with the .MOV file association not being made correctly during installation of QuickTime. Here is the workaround to get things going:

1. After installing QuickTime (which I assume you have done), run QuickTime Player (from the Start button).

2. In the QuickTime Player window, click File/Open Movie.

3. Browse to the CD-ROM drive using the resulting dialog box.

4. Open the movie called INlesson.mov.

5. The introductory lesson should now play. Now you can open other lessons by clicking on the navigation menu within the lessons.

THE SCREENCAM MOVIE IN A LESSON HANGS

If the author continues to talk, but the accompanying screencam seems to be stuck, just click on the lesson index in the lower left region of the QuickTime window to begin your specific lesson again. If this doesn't help, close the QuickTime window, then start the Virtual Classroom again.

VOLUME IS TOO LOW OR IS TOTALLY SILENT

1. Check your system volume first. Click on the little speaker icon next to the clock, down in the lower right-hand corner of the screen. A little slider pops up. Adjust the slider, and make sure the Mute check box is not checked.

2. Next, if you have external speakers on your computer, make sure your speakers are turned on, plugged in, wired up properly, and the volume control on the speakers themselves is turned up.

3. Note that the QuickTime player also has a volume control setting. The setting is a slider control in the lower left of the QuickTime Player window.

4. The next place to look if you're still having trouble, is in the Windows volume controls. Double-click on the little speaker by the clock, and it will bring up the Windows Volume Control sliders. Make sure the slider for "Wave" is not muted, and it's positioned near the top.

BACKUP LESSONS This CD includes alternate files for all of the lessons, in the Windows Media format, for playing in the Windows Media Player. We've supplied these extra files in case you have trouble running the lessons in the QuickTime player. These files, though of a somewhat lower-quality appearance than the QuickTime files, may still be useful if you have trouble running the QuickTime files. Note also that the navigation links that appear beneath the author's face will not work in the Windows Media Player files. This is due to limitations in the Windows Media player.

To view the backup lessons:

Windows users can click on the Windows Media Files link in the normal startup screen for this CD. (If the startup screen didn't appear when you inserted the CD, double-click the startnow.exe icon.) Use the resulting browser window for starting your lessons. When a lesson ends, return to the browser window and click on the next lesson you want to run.

Mac users can double-click the HTML file called WMfiles.html. Use the resulting browser window for starting your lessons. When a lesson ends, return to the browser window and click on the next lesson you want to run.

In Media Player, we suggest you set the skin to Classic, then switch to Compact Mode and then set the view to 100%. The picture will be much clearer that way.

As an alternative approach to running the Windows Media files, you can simply use Windows Explorer or the Mac Finder to navigate to the Windows Media folder on the CD. Then open the Windows Media folder and double-click on the lesson name you want to see. For example, 01lesson.wmv is lesson 1.

To view the Windows Media files, you will need the Windows Media player. (This player is available for both the PC and Mac platforms.) It is likely to be installed on your Windows PC already. If you're on a Mac, or if you don't have the latest Windows Media player (you'll need version 6.4 or later), you can download the latest Windows Media Player for free from www.microsoft.com/windowsmedia.

FOR TECHNICAL SUPPORT

▶ Phone Hudson Software at (800) 217-0059

▶ Visit www.quicktime.com

▶ Visit www.brainsville.com

1

Welcome to Photoshop 7

This chapter will acquaint you with all the

functional elements unique to Photoshop, with emphasis

on those features new to Version 7.0. Its aim is to bring you

realistic expectations of the results you can get from the

program, and how quickly you'll get those results. You're also

likely to learn that Photoshop is well suited for a number of

jobs you didn't expect of it. Later chapters will give you more

detailed descriptions of how to use these features to achieve

specific tasks or solve problems.

How Photoshop Differs from Other Graphics Programs

If you're using Photoshop in a professional setting, you probably already know there are two basic types of computer graphics programs: painting and drawing programs.

Painting Programs

The most common type of paint program is a photo editor. The leading photo-editing program (to the extent that it can now be called the de-facto standard and the product against which all others are judged) is—you guessed it—Adobe Photoshop.

Paint programs are also known as bitmapped programs because their images are composed of uniform-sized dots, each of which is one of 16.8 million possible specific shades of color. (In computerese, each individual shade is referred to as a "color"—the word shade is rarely mentioned.) In other words, the picture is really a map (or, more accurately, a mosaic of these dots or "bits". It is the way these dots are grouped that determines the shapes and shades you see in the picture. Since the dots are of a fixed size, if you enlarge the picture, you enlarge the dots.

Modern paint programs attempt to work around this size restriction by employing a process known as *resampling*. Resampling enlarges bit maps by moving the *pixels* (a hybrid of the term *picture element*—a single square of color that composes the smallest unit of color in a digital photograph or painting) further apart, rather than by resizing them. Resampling then uses one of several methods to *interpolate*—that is, fill in and recolor—as many pixels as it takes to refill what would otherwise be white space between the moved-apart pixels. The usual methods are *bicubic* and *bipolar*. The filled-in pixels are made to graduate the color shading between the two original pixels. The result is that the enlarged image seems to have as good a resolution as the original because there are just as many pixels per inch. However, there are two problems with resampling:

▶ No program can invent detail where there was none before. So if you want the image larger in order to see more of the eyebrow hairs on a model's face or the bluebonnets in the valley meadow, you're out of luck.

▶ None of the edges will be truly sharp. In fact, if the enlargement is much more than 100 percent of the original size, the picture will look slightly out of focus.

Paint programs are what you use when you're working with images that have been digitized (copied with a scanner or photographed with a digital camera), because a bitmap is the native form of the original image, and because it's much easier to change specific areas of the image according to such characteristics of the photo as brightness, contrast, and color saturation. It is also much easier to work on specific areas of the images (as opposed to physical object shapes) because you can enclose them within freehand selections.

> **NOTE** If you care to invest a bit more money, there are a couple of third-party filters that are sophisticated enough to find the points between the two original pixels and then redraw a sharp-edged but *anti-aliased* (smoothed) line to re-create a sharp edge. One is Genuine Fractal's Print Shop Pro. The other is S-spline.

> **WHAT ARE PAINTING PROGRAMS?** Painting programs obviously include those programs that act like a brush and canvas and are primarily meant as a means of creating something that looks more like a painting than a photograph—though most painting programs can also do basic photo editing. Bitmapping is the best way to implement this feeling, precisely because it isn't as exact and "mechanical" as geometric vectors. The most widely used natural media painting program is Corel Painter 7. A Macintosh program known as Studio Artist and a biplatform program called Deep Paint (which also acts as a Photoshop plug-in) have also recently been attracting a lot of well-deserved attention.

The major difference in how you use bitmapped paint programs and vector shape drawing programs has to do with how you edit specific objects or shapes within the painting. Because the bitmapped shape is defined only by an otherwise unrelated group of adjacent pixels of different colors, you have to define that shape by indicating its boundaries. It has become traditional in paint programs to define those boundaries with a *marquee* (a blinking dashed line resembling a queue of marching ants). The pixels within that marquee are called a *selection*. In order to select a shape in a drawing program, you simply click its outline(s), because all shapes are geometric entities.

DRAWING PROGRAMS

Drawing programs work by defining formulas that specify geometric shapes, line color and thickness, and fill colors and gradients. The finished picture is a combination of these shapes. Since the shapes can be resized by recalculating the formulas, the completed picture is always as well-defined as the target output device (screen, printer, printing press) is capable of making it. Size does not matter. Dots, pixels, grains—or whatever you want to call them this week—only come into play as a characteristic of the device on which they are printed or displayed. So you can scale the combination of shapes that make up a picture in an illustration program (such as Adobe Illustrator, Macromedia Freehand, or CorelDraw!) to any size you like without losing a single smidgeon of definition. Then you can even add your own additional definition if you like—especially since you were probably the one who drew the original art.

The resolution independence I just described may sound like heaven, but there are serious drawbacks with using this kind of program. The biggest drawback is that there's no practical way to create a picture with nearly as much detail as even very low-resolution digital cameras can provide. Even if you did have the creative capacity to fashion such an image, it would take you weeks to draw. Furthermore, because the illustration would have to employ different formulas to match every few pixels in a digital photo, the resulting file would be several times the already-huge file size of the typical high-resolution digital photo.

As you'll learn—if you don't already know—there are still many uses for the drawing tools that create vector paths (or, as they're called in Photoshop, just plain *paths* or *shapes*) provided in an image editing program. Photoshop's Pen and Shape tools constitute a set of drawing tools that have the same look, function, and user interface as similar tools in its sister product, Adobe Illustrator—the leading drawing program. However, you're much more likely to use them for making smooth-edged and precise selections and clipping paths (see Chapter 7) than for straight drawing. To be sure, you can easily draw shapes in Photoshop, but if you're planning to create eye-grabbing posters and web graphics, you're better off with the vastly more versatile capabilities of a real illustration program. On the other hand, if your need for drawing capabilities is only occasional, Photoshop certainly gives you enough to ensure that you won't need to look elsewhere unless you need high-end capabilities.

HOW PHOTOSHOP DIFFERS FROM OTHER IMAGE EDITING PROGRAMS

I'm going to get into some trouble for saying this, but the main difference between Photoshop and the covey of geese following the gander is that Photoshop is the gander. Virtually no professional photographer, image editor, graphic artist, or ad agency art director would dare be without it. That's almost as true of graphic artists in every profession, from motion picture set and makeup designers (such as Thomas Knoll of Industrial Light and Magic, who invented the program) to animators to interior decorators. I can't begin to tell you what a relief it is to know that there's almost a 100 percent chance that the person who gives you the picture and the person you pass it on to will use the same product. In addition, almost every program that makes a contribution to the image editing process—particularly special purpose and special effects programs (a.k.a. *filters*), called *plug-ins*—are required to be Photoshop-compatible.

In fact, one way to acquire Photoshop-compatible plug-ins is to buy other image editing programs that come with suites of their own customized plug-ins. It's a sure bet that, because these programs want to be able to accept the hundreds of third-party plug-ins made for Photoshop, their own plug-ins will also be Photoshop-compatible.

The other thing that really sets Photoshop apart from the competition is experience. Adobe has been on top of the market for so long that they've had the time and money to make this an almost endlessly versatile product. For instance, the program not only makes selections, it has tools such as the Magnetic Lasso that automate the process, and a built-in plug-in filter that allows you to (more or less) automatically divorce shapes with very complicated edges from their backgrounds.

You'd think that if what I said in the previous paragraph were true, other image editing programs simply wouldn't be selling. Truth is, several competitors do quite well, thank you. Some reasons for this are

▶ Each program tends to have a few valuable and unique brushes, effects, or routines.

▶ Over time, people tend to collect image-editing programs because each has special personality traits. After a while, too, one acquires competitive programs because they come bundled with other software. (For example, Corel PhotoPaint 10 is included with CorelDraw! 10, and Macromedia Fireworks can be had hugely discounted when bought with "Studio" bundles that include other Macromedia web or drawing software.)

It would be tedious, time-consuming, and possibly pointless to detail the differences in features between even the three or four most directly competitive programs and

Photoshop. Suffice to say, each has particular strong points that are especially useful to a specific artist profile or special situation. However, nothing has the same range of power and versatility as Photoshop—especially now that you can even program it to do things Adobe didn't even think of. Of course, this means that shortly you'll be able to buy programs (called *scripts*) written by independent programmers to do things neither you nor Adobe ever imagined as useful. Finally, no other image editing program is as businesslike as Photoshop. By businesslike, I mean that it has the built-in ability to manage project workflows, build accurate (even expensive and elaborate) image calibration and device profiling systems, and create material for professional output for offset printing.

NEW CAPABILITIES IN PHOTOSHOP 7.0

Photoshop 7 has a new look that is much "prettier" and more modern than past versions of the program. In other words, the look of Photoshop 7 is much more in keeping with the graphical design of new operating systems such as Mac OS X and Windows XP. There are also innumerable interface tweaks and options. Most of these modifications are improvements over previous versions, but some—such as having to now access the Brushes palette in the much less obvious Options Bar—are just darned annoying.

All these small cosmetic changes are too numerous to mention here, and most of them are too difficult to explain out of context.

The new features are listed here:

▶ The File Browser
▶ Greatly expanded painting control
▶ The Healing Brush
▶ New Blend modes
▶ Auto Color Correction
▶ Workspace presets
▶ PDF security
▶ Tool presets
▶ An enhanced Liquify interface
▶ Picture packages

▶ The Web Gallery

▶ An expanded Save for Web command

▶ Pattern Maker

▶ Spell checking

The rest of this section will explain what each of these features does.

FILE BROWSER

The File Browser was actually introduced with Photoshop Elements. This newer version, however, is much faster and does more to help you manage your images. By default, the File Browser is located in the palette well. However, once this palette is opened, it will cover most of your work area (unless you have a two-monitor setup), so you'll probably click it off before you remember to return it to the palette well. If that happens, just choose either File | Browse or Window | Show File Browser. You can see an example of the File Browser in Figure 1-1.

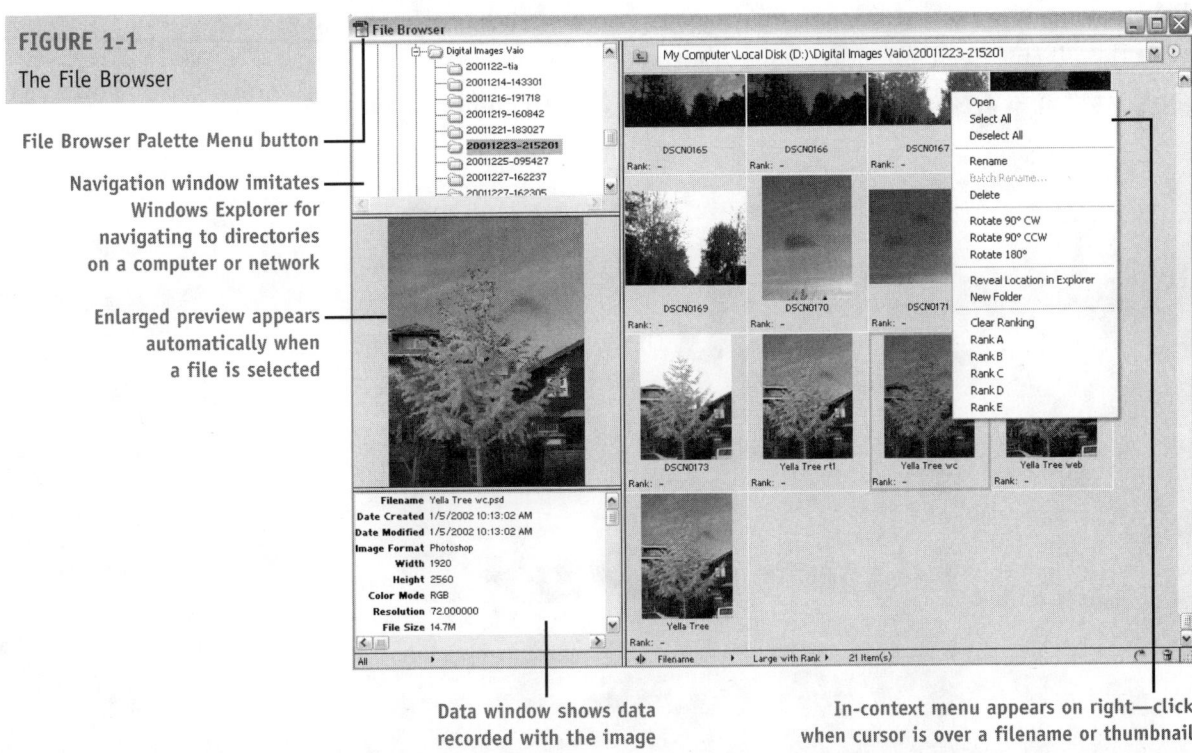

FIGURE 1-1
The File Browser

File Browser Palette Menu button

Navigation window imitates Windows Explorer for navigating to directories on a computer or network

Enlarged preview appears automatically when a file is selected

Data window shows data recorded with the image

In-context menu appears on right—click when cursor is over a filename or thumbnail

Not only is Photoshop 7's File Browser faster than Photoshop Elements', it is significantly handier and more useful. Besides being able to visually preview the files you're going to open, you can also

▶ Choose the size of the image thumbnails

▶ Choose the size of the image preview

▶ Rename a file

▶ Batch rename all the files

▶ Rank files

▶ Rotate thumbnails without resampling

▶ Choose the size of thumbnails and whether to display ranking

▶ Eject the disk you're browsing if it's removable (CD, floppy, Zip).

CHOOSE THE SIZE OF THE IMAGE THUMBNAILS

By choosing the size of the image thumbnails, you can decide whether it is more important to see detail in images (very useful when trying to choose between small differences in similar images) or to get a quick overall view of the variety of images in your current folder. To choose the size of the image thumbnail, from the File Browser Palette menu choose Small, Medium, or Large Thumbnail. If you are going to rank your thumbnails (see the following illustration for your choices—*small*, *medium*, *large*, *large_rank*, and *details*), you will want to choose Large Thumbnail with Rank.

CHOOSE THE SIZE OF THE IMAGE PREVIEW

As soon as your cursor passes over one of the thumbnails, the same thumbnail appears in the image preview window. You can decide how large this preview image will be by dragging the bars at the top, bottom, and right side of the window. The image automatically resizes to fill the window.

RENAME A FILE

In Windows XP, a single click often causes something to execute, so you can't always rename a file by double-clicking the filename as you can in the pre-XP versions of Windows.

To Rename A FILE:

1 Select a thumbnail (click it—not the name) and click the File Browser Palette Menu button or CTRL-click/right-click while the cursor is over a thumbnail. Either way, a menu pops up, as shown here:

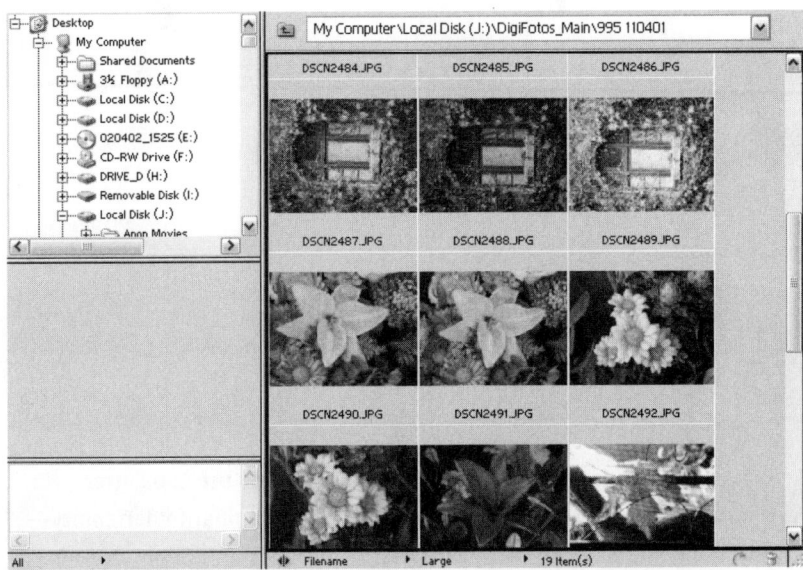

2 Choose Rename. The filename is highlighted without the extension, so you can just enter a new filename. This is a bit of a safeguard against entering the wrong file type, which would cause the file to refuse to open.

10   CHAPTER 1
    WELCOME TO PHOTOSHOP 7

BATCH RENAME ALL THE FILES

Batch renaming is a good way to rename all the digital images from a roll of scanned film or from a camera's memory card to a general subject category. For instance, Sue Bday, Ronna Lee (for a series of pictures of a model), and Sunsets (for a picture category). I find it very useful and a big time-saver to name a whole series of shots this way. You could also then sort the images into subfolders and rename the files by the names of the subfolders. These are the sorts of file management tricks that allow you to meet deadlines and please the client by finding and delivering exactly the right picture. If there are a few shots that don't belong in the category, it is then much easier to go back and rename a few.

To Batch RENAME:

1   In the File Browser, navigate to the folder that contains the files you want to rename.

2   Make sure no individual thumbnail is selected (highlighted), then choose Batch Rename from the File Browser Palette menu. The Batch Rename dialog appears, as shown here:

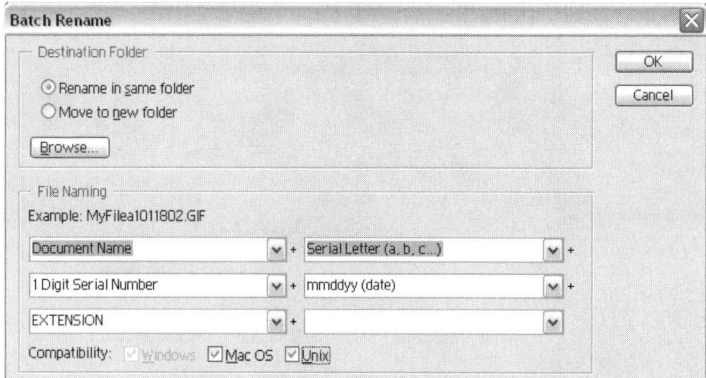

3   You can either create a new folder for the renamed files or simply use the current folder. Creating a new folder will move the files and leave the original folder empty— so don't mistakenly think you've erased all your files.

4   In the lower part of the dialog, you see a matrix of six pull-down menus. In between each pair of menus (save the last pair) is a plus sign. What this means is that the choice you make on each menu is added (in the order in which you choose it) to the new filename. Only the three variations of one of these choices, document name, will let you type in your own entry. The others are entered automatically by Photoshop 7.

5 In the first menu's entry field, type the name you want all your image files to start with. (By the way, don't ask me why the industry calls images *documents*—just know that that's the way it is.)

6 Use the next button to the right to add to your filename. You should add a number or letter that makes the name of this file unique and makes it easy to specify exactly which of these images with the same starting name will be the one(s) you want to do more with. You can choose a lowercase or capitalized letter, or a 1-, 2-, or 3-digit number. You can even add more than one of these in sequence by choosing another variant from the next menu to the right.

7 If you want to add the date, choose the preferred date format variant from the next menu to the right. I prefer putting the date just before the extension so it's easy to distinguish from the sequence numbers. Also, when using the date, it's better to use letters for sequencing.

8 You should always use the file extension in your image filenames. It makes them much more compatible with other programs, computers, and the Web. It also ensures that you won't overwrite the original JPEG file when you save your opened file in another, lossless format.

9 It's your choice, but it's a good idea to keep your files in a format that is compatible with as many other computers as possible. Keeping this in mind, at the bottom of the palette, check the two boxes that aren't grayed for other operating systems.

> NOTE You have to batch rename *all* the files in a folder. There's no way to select just a few files—unless, of course, you move them temporarily into their own folder. Then you can rename them and move them back.

10 Click OK and wait. After a minute (or after several minutes, depending on how many files are in the folder and the speed of your computer), the thumbnails will reappear with their newly assigned names, as shown in the following illustration.

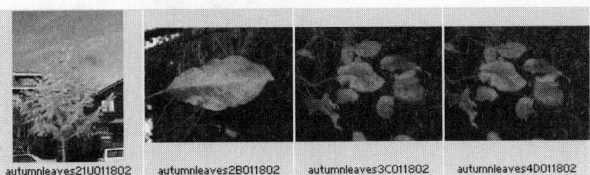

autumnleaves21U011802   autumnleaves2B011802   autumnleaves3C011802   autumnleaves4D011802

RANK FILES

Ranking files makes it easier to find the files you consider to be the best candidates for further work, or the ones you're most likely to need to reuse, or the ones your client or subject likes the best. You can rank them by any of the letters from A through D. From either the in-context menu or the File Browser Palette menu, choose the letter by which you wish to rank the highlighted image. If you want to give several images the same rank, simply press SHIFT and individually click the files you want to give the same ranking. Their positions needn't be contiguous. Then follow the same procedure as if you were ranking a single image. The following illustration shows files ranked in the Browser.

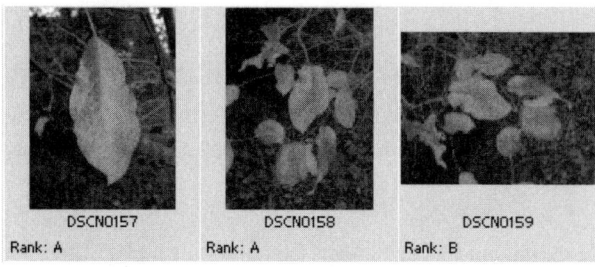

ROTATE THUMBNAILS WITHOUT RESAMPLING

Rotating thumbnails is also done by choosing a menu item. When you rotate a thumbnail, Photoshop does not actually rotate the image itself. Therefore, you won't lose data from the original image by opening it, making a change, and then recompressing it to a lossy format when you save it.

> **NOTE** Rarely is it a good idea to open a JPEG image and then resave it to the same filename and type. Each time you repeat the process, you lose more image quality because the file is recompressed. The most legitimate reason is that you are going to rescale it and then set a compression level that is the best compromise between the resulting quality loss and the smallest file size (so your files will load faster onto web pages).

PAINTING

Photoshop's painting capabilities have suddenly opened new possibilities for creating artwork that resembles traditional painting. The new Brushes palette allows for creation of an infinite number of brush styles, and includes the ability to paint with canvas textures, brush shapes and sizes, tilt, spacing, scatter, jitter, number of brush tips, colors, and wet edges.

The new painting capabilities are associated with a pair of new palettes: the Brush Presets palette and the Brush Styler palette. Chapter 8 of this book covers all the new painting palettes and describes how to put them to use. In the meantime, the following illustrations will give you a glimpse of the power you now have at your brush tips.

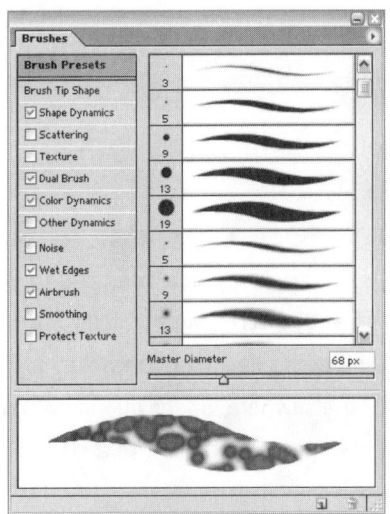 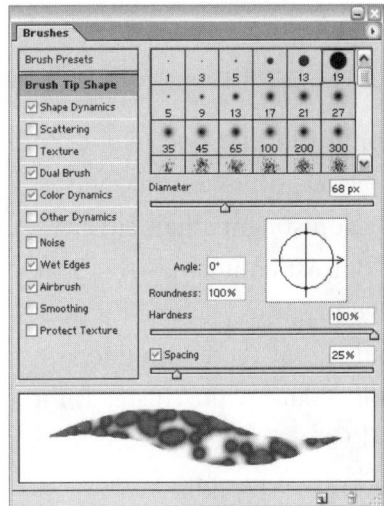

THE HEALING BRUSH

The Healing Brush could be the big surprise winner amongst all of Photoshop 7's unique features. That's because this silly looking Band-Aid icon can eliminate about 75 percent of the time you spend retouching. Much like the Clone tool, it picks up the texture from another area of the image. Then you paint over the area that has a mole, blemish, pit, scratch, or dust spot. For a moment, the painted-over area looks like it is the wrong brightness or color; then it magically blends with its surroundings. What a cool tool. The following illustration shows the same area before and after being treated with the Healing Brush.

NEW BLEND MODES

Photoshop 7 sports some very interesting new Blend modes—especially in the Layers palette. In Figure 1-2, I have placed a gradient layer above the background layer in each example, and assigned the labeled Blend mode to the gradient layer in each square. After all, a picture is worth a thousand words.

AUTO COLOR CORRECTION

This is a single-click command that does wonders fixing photos shot in mixed lighting. It also does a better job of autofixing the brightness and contrast adjustments than either the Auto Levels or Auto Contrast command—both of which still exist. I'd love to show you what a neat trick this new command is, but there's no good way to illustrate it in black and white. Instead, I'll show you in the Virtual Classroom…and it'll take all of two seconds. (Okay, two minutes.)

> **NOTE** This is a great command to use when you're scripting a batch routine for downloading documentary pix to be transferred elsewhere, or for making a contact sheet-type presentation to a client.

WORKSPACE PRESETS

If you have a favorite way of setting up your palettes and toolboxes—particularly if you have a dual-monitor system—you can save it and then come back to it any time you like. You can even save several such workspace layouts. You could have

FIGURE 1-2
Effects of the new Layer Blend modes

different workspace layouts for different types of jobs, or you could have different workspace layouts for use by different people who use the same computer (though there's nothing to keep one of those people from using another's layout).

To create a new layout, simply use the Windows menu to open the palettes you want to use, then use the cursor to size and place the open palettes. If you want some palettes in the Palette Well, choose Dock to Palette Well from any palette's menu.

To Save THE LAYOUT SO YOU CAN USE IT AGAIN:

1 Choose Window | Workspace | Save Workspace. The Save Workspace dialog appears, as shown in the following illustration:

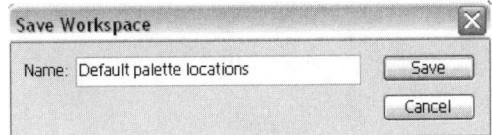

2 In the Name field, enter a name that will cause you to remember the purpose of the workspace layout, or the user for whom it's intended, and click OK.

To Retrieve THE LAYOUT:

▶ Choose Window | Workspace | The Name of Your Workspace. The palettes automatically rearrange themselves.

PDF SECURITY

For now, suffice it to say that you can assign a password to a PDF file. Thereafter, whether you attempt to open the file in Photoshop or Acrobat, the password will be required for access.

TOOL PRESETS

You can now save any set of tool options that you've set in that tool's Options Bar by a unique name. After that, you can retrieve the tool with exactly that set of options by simply choosing the name you've assigned from the Options Bar's Tool flyout.

To Save A SET OF TOOL OPTIONS:

1 Choose the tool you want to use.

2 In the tool's Options Bar, make all the settings you think you'd need to frequently reuse.

3 Click the Tool flyout button. The Tool dialog appears.

4 From the Tool dialog menu, choose New Tool Preset. The New Tool Preset dialog appears.

5 In the Name field, enter a name that will cause you to remember the use of this particular group of settings and click OK.

When you next want to use this group of settings, simply choose the name you entered from the Tool flyout in the Options Bar.

ENHANCED LIQUIFY INTERFACE

As you can see in Figure 1-3, the Liquify command interface has been given a new look in keeping with the X/Windows XP redesign of the overall interface. There are also some nice new features, including a new tool that "makes waves" (it's called the Turbulence Brush). The most important new feature in Liquify is the ability to save the Mesh. The Mesh can then be recalled in order to place the same distortion effects on another image.

PICTURE PACKAGES

Hooray! You can now include different pictures on a picture package page. This means that you can make up a storyboard or album pages.

For those who aren't familiar with a picture package, its name is derived from the practice of wedding and portrait photographers who offer their clients several sizes of prints (usually of the same photo) on a single sheet of paper at a lower price than the prints would cost individually.

FIGURE 1-3

The new Liquify interface and tools

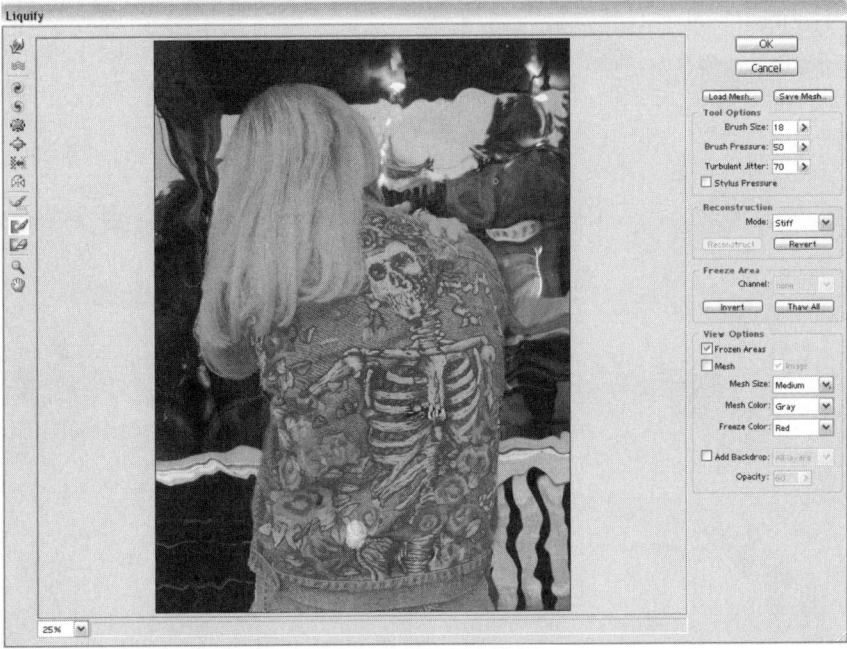

To Print A PICTURE PACKAGE WITH DIFFERENT PICTURES IN EACH SQUARE:

1 (Optional) Place all the images you want to print on the picture package into the same folder.

2 Choose File | Automate | Picture Package. The Picture Package dialog box appears (see Figure 1-4).

3 From the Page Size menu in the Document area, choose the page size closest to a page size used by your printer. The page sizes stated on the menu don't include the border— so, for instance, an 8x10-inch overall layout fits on an 8.5x11 sheet of paper.

4 From the Use menu in the Source area, choose File.

5 Click the Browse button and navigate to the folder in which you have placed the images you want to use on the preview page.

6 From the Layout menu in the Document area, choose the layout you want to use.

FIGURE 1-4
The Picture Package dialog

7 You will have to remember that some layouts will rotate pictures in one direction, and others in another. That's all right if you're going to cut the pictures apart, but if you're making album pages, your choices will be limited to certain layouts. Also, you may want to crop and rotate some pictures in advance so they fit the layout. For that reason, I suggest placing copies of the original files in the target folder.

8 Click in the preview square for the first image. A Select an Image File Browser will appear. Double-click the file you want to place in that particular square.

9 Repeat step 8 for each of the other squares on the preview page.

10 If you want a title for the page (or a caption for the whole group of pictures), choose Custom Text from the Content menu; then enter the text you want to use, and make the rest of the choices in the Label section according to your preferences.

WEB GALLERY

One truly important improvement eliminates the danger, in version 6, that your original .PSD files could get damaged if they weren't first converted and optimized as JPEGs. In version 7, the Web Gallery images are automatically created as JPEG duplicates of the original images, so there is no longer any danger of losing your originals.

SAVE FOR WEB

The Save For Web command, introduced in Photoshop 6, allows you to compare the settings made for an optimized web image to the original and, simultaneously, to as many as three different optimizations. When you change the settings, you immediately see the result before you commit to it. In version 7, there are two new GIF transparency options, Dithered Transparency and Remap Transparency. You can also save a black-and-white WBMP (Wireless BitMaP) file—a format used especially for wireless web phones.

PATTERN MAKER

Pattern Maker joins Extract and Liquify as full-screen plug-in interfaces that accomplish a specialized imaging task. Pattern Maker lets you select part of the image that will become a tile in a textured background; then, when you click OK, it fills the entire image with the seamless tile. You can use this technique to make some pretty bizarre textures in any image size. Figure 1-5 shows the Pattern Maker dialog, while the illustration here shows the texture generated by the settings shown in the dialog.

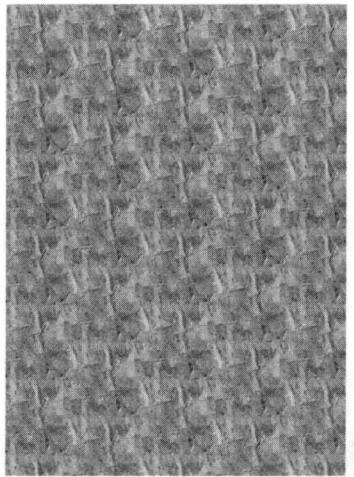

SPELL CHECKING

You can now check the spelling of any text in your image document that hasn't been *rasterized* (converted to a bitmap from vector text). You don't need to highlight a block of text in order to spell check it. All you do is choose Edit | Check Spelling and the Check Spelling dialog appears, as shown here. If you check the Check All Layers box, all the spelling in the document will be checked.

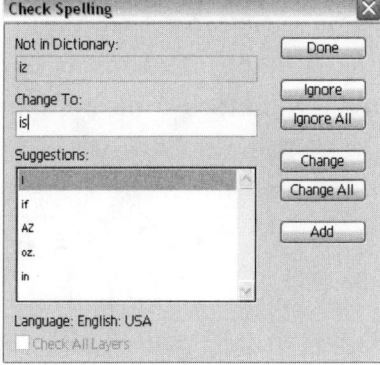

FIGURE 1-5

The Pattern Maker dialog

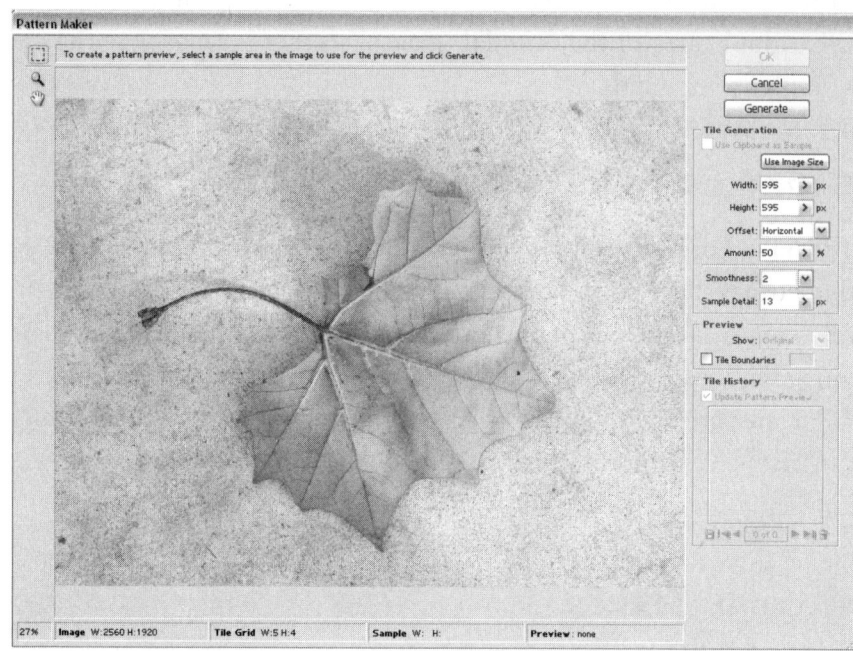

NEW CAPABILITIES IN IMAGEREADY 7.0

Like Photoshop, ImageReady boasts the same new look in its interface in version 7. Figure 1-6 illustrates the interface and all its functional areas.

NEW ROLLOVER PALETTE

The Rollover palette now shows each rollover state as a separate item that can be selected and modified from the palette. This makes it much easier to tell what state the document and its rollovers are currently in. There are also more choices on the menu: Duplicate State, Rollover State Options, and the ability to check (toggle on/off) the visibility of new layers in all states and frames. Finally, there are new buttons at the bottom of the palette—Create Layer Based Rollover and Create New State—that accelerate the creation of rollovers.

PROTECT VECTORS AND TEXT

There's a new button in the Optimize palette that brings up the Modify Lossiness Setting dialog, giving you the chance to drag a slider to indicate the quality of the post-optimized (and, therefore, rasterized) text and vectors that are still active in

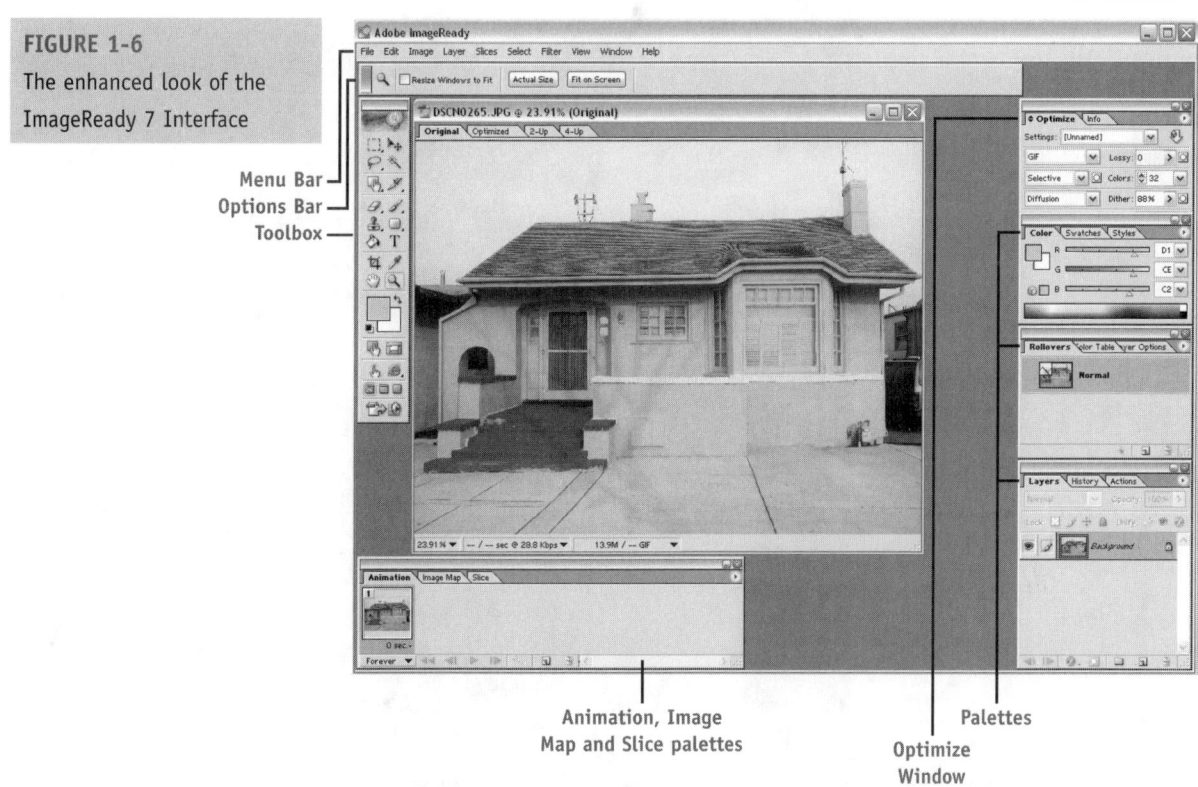

FIGURE 1-6

The enhanced look of the ImageReady 7 Interface

Menu Bar
Options Bar
Toolbox

Animation, Image
Map and Slice palettes

Optimize
Window

Palettes

the original Photoshop 7 file. You can see the new button and the new dialog in Figure 1-7.

REMAP TRANSPARENCY

If you are optimizing a GIF file, you can designate any color(s) in the image as transparent. Simply select a color in the Color Table palette and click the Map/Unmap Selected Colors To Transparent button at the bottom of the Color Table palette, as shown in the following illustration.

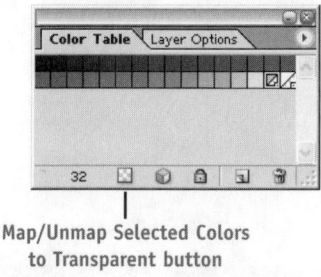

Map/Unmap Selected Colors
to Transparent button

FIGURE 1-7

The new ImageReady
Optimize palette and Modify
Lossiness Setting dialog

DITHERED TRANSPARENCY

Transparent effects can now be dithered so that effects such as drop shadows can fade into the nontransparent background. To do this, choose Show Options from the Optimize palette's menu, then select any of the dithered options from the Choose Transparency Dither Options menu, shown here:

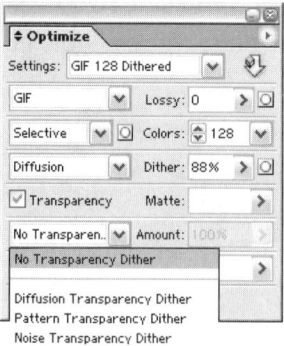

Personalizing Your Photoshop Workflow

Before getting started, you need to choose the settings for your display that give you the best chance of publishing the image you see onscreen. If you spend more than an hour a day at it, you'll also want to make sure you've set up your computer and Photoshop in such a way that you get the job done in the least amount of time. After you've done that, you should make sure you don't accidentally lose your valuable images—or any of the information they contain—during the work process. You can do this by learning to organize, visually catalog (on both paper and disk), name, and annotate your images. You also need to know how to experiment with duplicate images so you don't lose any information from your originals. Finally, you need to understand what file format options are available to you when saving your files, and the advantages and dangers inherent in each.

MAKE PHOTOSHOP SCREAM

Let's face it: The best way to make Photoshop give you the most productivity is to spend money on optimizing your computer.

If you plan to make a living (or a good part of it) working in Photoshop, keep upgrading your computer with more and more memory. You should have between five and six times as much RAM (volatile computer memory) as the size of the file you typically work on. Most professionals consider a gigabyte of RAM a minimum these days. You'll also want the quickest processor you can afford, as well as a very fast CD recorder so you'll be encouraged to permanently archive your work on a project-by-project basis and also have a way to send large image files to clients, print shops, and other outside resources. Get a high-performance color card (especially if you're going to work with video and multimedia) and a large (bigger is better, but 17 inches is a practical minimum) single-gun, shadow-masked monitor (a.k.a. Trinitron) made or licensed by Sony and assembled by a manufacturer of known quality. If you insist on one of the flat-panel LCD monitors, make sure it's one that responds well to instrumented calibration (because that's where you'll eventually want to head). Now, here's the big surprise: If you shop carefully, you can buy everything mentioned here for less than $2000.

> **NOTE** You do not need nearly as much computer horsepower as I'm suggesting to run Photoshop 7. The minimum requirements recommended by Adobe are an Intel Window 98+ Pentium or Mac OS 8.5 + PowerPC-based system, 64MB of RAM, 125MB of hard disk space, a color monitor with 800x600 resolution and at least 256 colors, and a CD-ROM drive.

> **TIP** Use a dual-monitor system. It will boost your productivity greatly because you can put all your palettes and dialogs on one monitor while you have the entire screen on the other dedicated to full-time image editing. Very quick and slick. The usual way to do this is with two cards (supported in Windows only by 98SE, Me, XP, and 2000), which must have identical chip sets. However, at least one manufacturer makes a display card that supports two monitors. By the time you read this, there may be others.

If you're more the hobbyist type of Photoshop user, you can certainly get by with a lot less computer. You should make sure your Pentium 3 or G3-equivalent processor is running at 400+ or 160+ MHz, respectively. Consider 256MB of RAM and a 20GB hard drive a minimum. At least 5GB of your hard drive space should be free for memory swapping. Finally, be sure your monitor is capable of displaying all 16+ million visible shades of color.

Hardware questions aside, there are some settings you can make in your operating system as well as others within Photoshop that will ensure you get the most of what your machine has to offer.

First, set your operating system's virtual memory (the hard-drive space that kicks in when you run out of RAM) to be as *small* as possible. You want to do this because you want Photoshop to use it as *little* virtual memory as possible. This is because Photoshop has its own scheme for using virtual memory that's much more efficient.

To Set VIRTUAL MEMORY TO A MINIMUM ON THE MAC:

1 From the Apple menu, choose Control Panels | Memory. The Memory dialog appears.

2 There are three sets of radio buttons. Click the Off buttons under Virtual Memory and RAM Disk.

3 Click the Close button in the upper-left corner of the window to hide it.

4 Restart your Mac.

To Set VIRTUAL MEMORY TO A MINIMUM IN WINDOWS XP:

1 On your Windows XP system, open the Start menu located in the lower right-hand corner of the screen. Choose the Control Panel. Find the System icon and select it. The System Properties dialog appears.

2 Choose the Advanced tab and the Advance Properties dialog appears.

3 Choose Performance | Settings Button. The Performance Options dialog appears.

4 Choose the Advanced tab. The Advanced Performance Options dialog appears.

5 Choose Virtual Memory | Change Button. The Virtual Memory dialog appears, as shown here.

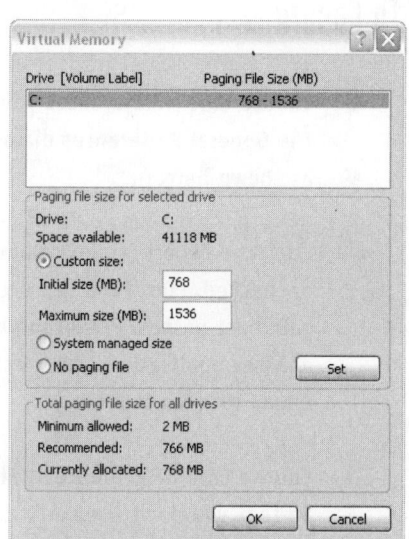

6 Click the Custom Size radio button.

7 Enter the minimum and maximum fields to exactly equal the amount of RAM installed on your computer.

8 Choose OK in all dialogs to close the System Properties.

Regardless of whether you're using Photoshop on a Mac or in Windows, you can also ensure peak performance by choosing the manner in which your hard drive is partitioned and formatted. Windows users should be sure their drives are formatted as FAT 32, the default for all post-Windows 95 versions. Mac users, on the other hand, should be sure they format as HFS+, the default for all OS 8 and later versions. When it comes to partitioning, some folks feel they save file space if they split their drives into several partitions or "virtual drives." Since Photoshop files tend to be quite large, you're probably better off keeping your drives as one large partition so you don't have to split the files that fit into a specific category or project across drives.

SETTING THE PHOTOSHOP PREFERENCES DIALOGS

Once you've got your operating system and hard drive prepared for Photoshop, there are a few things you can do within the program to ensure maximum performance.

To Ensure MAXIMUM PERFORMANCE:

1 Choose Edit | Preferences | General. The General Preferences dialog appears, as shown here.

2 Click the Export Clipboard box until it is unchecked. (On those few occasions when you must paste a Photoshop selection into another application, you'll have to remember to recheck this box.)

3 Choose Edit | Preferences | File Handling. So that you don't inadvertently slow

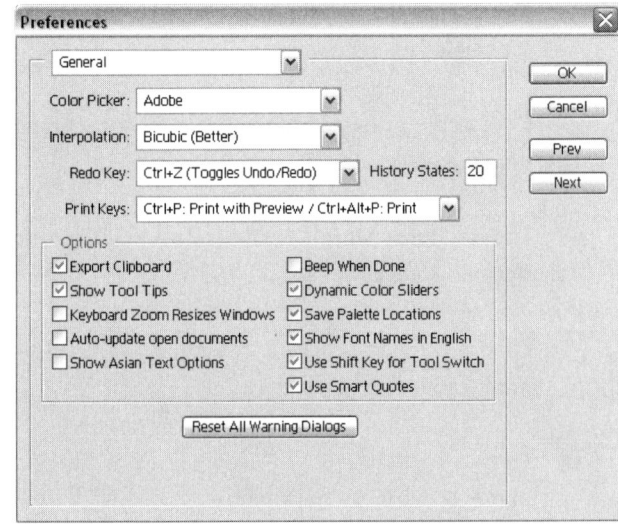

downloads by saving files meant for web display with a preview image, do the following:

4 Choose Ask When Saving from the Image Preview menu. Also, on the Mac, be sure to choose Always from the Append File Extension menu and check the Use Lowercase box. This will ensure that your image files are both web and cross-platform compatible. Finally, check the Maximize Backwards Compatibility In Photoshop format box. (Though all of the choices in this step produce a small increase in file size, productivity is enhanced by ensuring that your files will be compatible to the greatest possible degree.)

5 Choose Edit | Preferences | Displays & Cursors. Click the Brush Size radio button. To increase the speed of filter previews, check the Use Pixel Doubling box in the Display area of the Display & Cursors dialog (shown here).

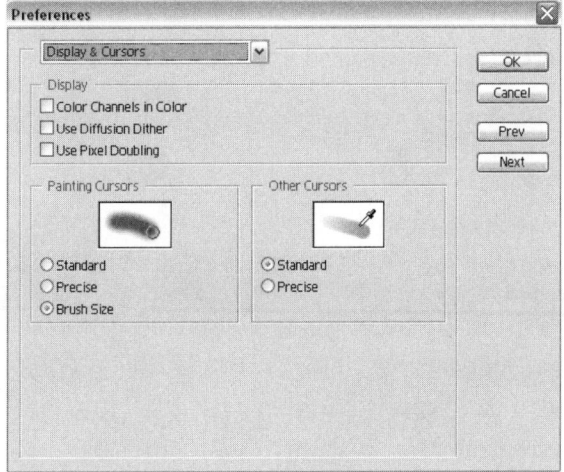

6 Choose Edit | Preferences | Plug-Ins & Scratch Disks. As I mentioned earlier, Photoshop's built-in virtual memory is much more efficient than your operating system's. You've already set up your OS to let Photoshop take advantage of that fact. Now's your chance to set up Photoshop to use its own virtual memory to maximum advantage by specifying your fastest drive as the scratch disk (but be sure it has at least 2 to 5GB of free space on it at all times). From the First Scratch Drives menu, choose the drive letter for your fastest drive. Make sure you also list all your other drives, in order of speed, using the second, third, and fourth menus. If you don't know the speed of your drives, you might try looking inside your computer case. You can usually see the model numbers on the drives, and you may also be able to see the drive's rotational speed (usually either 5400 or 7200 RPM). If you can't see the drive speed, look it up by the model number on the manufacturer's web site.

7 While still in the Plug-Ins & Scratch Disk dialog, you should point to a directory where you have installed all your non-native Photoshop plug-ins. Then, if you are using more than one version of Photoshop (such as Photoshop Elements) or another program that's compatible with Photoshop plug-ins, you can specify the same directory from each and thus avoid wasting time and disk space, because you won't have to configure each individually.

8 Choose Edit | Preferences | Memory and Image Cache. Enter 1 in the Cache Levels field, and uncheck the Cache Histograms box. Although caching will speed up keystroke zooming, it does nothing for zooming with the Magnifier tool. Likewise, it has no effect in the Navigator when you drag a marquee to show the level of zoom. What caching does do is use RAM that you may need for complex image processing. The Memory & Image Cache Preferences dialog is shown here:

> **NOTE** Be sure that when you install the third-party plug-ins, you specify this directory rather than accept the program's default directory. I do this by creating a directory called PS-comp Plug-ins on my computer's most capacious drive. (There are hundreds of free plug-ins available on the Internet—not to mention amazing third-party plug-ins from Corel, Andromeda, Extensis, Alien Skin, and others.)

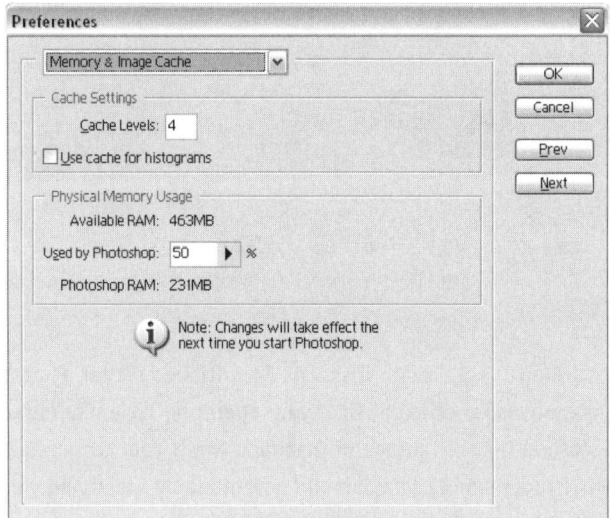

OTHER PHOTOSHOP PERFORMANCE TWEAKS

Aside from the settings in Preferences dialogs, there are a number of other adjustments that can hype your Photoshop performance:

► History palette settings
► Layers palette settings

▶ Channels palette settings

▶ Using the Purge command

HISTORY PALETTE SETTINGS

You can change the number of steps saved in the History palette at any time (see the exercise that follows). Try to work with as few saved states as is practical for the editing stage you are in at any given moment. The reason: each state can, potentially, use as much RAM as the main image (something that's always true of Snapshots, by the way). So, the more RAM you use for History states, the less you will have left over for image processing, and the slower your other operations will become. Be warned, however, that there are no hard and fast rules. If you're doing an operation that requires making many small brush strokes, or you want to have a variety of image states ready for an instant preview by your client, then the advantages of being able to instantly revert to a given state will rapidly outweigh the disadvantages. Just be sure you've installed plenty of RAM.

To Change THE NUMBER OF HISTORY STATES (UNDO LEVELS) ON THE FLY:

1 Press CMD/CTRL-K. The General Preferences dialog should appear. If not, choose it from the Preferences menu in the dialog that does appear.

2 Enter the number of Undo Levels you prefer at the moment in the Undo Levels field.

3 Click OK to return to your image editing chores.

You can repeat the preceding process at any time. Just remember that if you change from a larger number of states to a smaller number, all the steps prior to that smaller number will disappear from the palette, and you will no longer be able to undo them or paint from them.

But wait! There's more: you can also make a couple of other adjustments to the behavior of the History palette from the History palette menu.

To Reach IT:

1 Choose Window | History (or click its tab in the Palette Well in the Options Bar, if it's there). The History palette appears.

2 Click and drag from the small encircled arrow at the top right of the palette. This will cause the menu (for any palette) to appear. The History Palette menu is shown here.

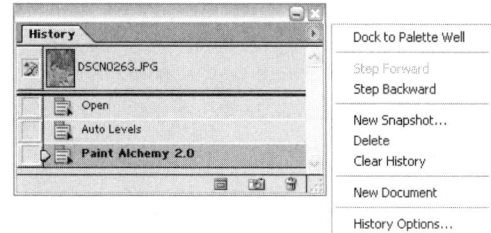

3 From the History Palette menu, choose History Options. The History Options palette appears.

4 Uncheck Automatically Create First Snapshot. It uses more RAM and, if you've started your operations by making a duplicate of the original (Image | Duplicate), you don't need it anyway. You can always clone from the original instead of painting with the History Brush. If you want to paint with the Art History Brush, take a snapshot at the point you really want to paint from, then use the History Brush at the point where you think you might need it.

> **NOTE** Honestly, you should use the preceding technique *only* when you need to save as much RAM and storage space as possible. Otherwise, the automatically taken snapshot is always there when you unexpectedly need to paint back in some part of the original.

LAYERS AND CHANNELS PALETTE SETTINGS

You can speed things up a little bit by turning off all the thumbnails in the Layers and Channels palettes. The trade-off is not being able to visually identify the contents of a layer. However, if you're conscientious about naming your layers accurately, this won't be much of a problem, and Photoshop will run faster by a percentage or two. Tweaks like this may seem petty, but don't think that Steve Jobs doesn't know all these tricks when he demonstrates how much faster Photoshop runs on a Mac than in Windows.

To Turn Off THE THUMBNAILS IN EITHER PALETTE:

1 Choose Window | Layers, or Window | Channels to bring the named palette to the fore.

2 From the menu of the palette, choose Palette Options. The Options dialog for whichever palette you are setting will appear. Shown here is the Layers Palette Options dialog.

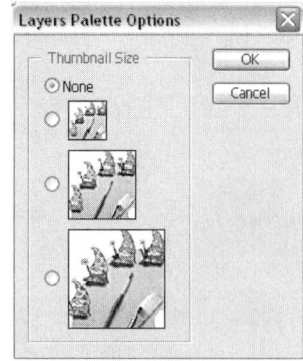

3 Click the None radio button to turn off all the thumbnails, then click OK to confirm the setting.

MAKE LIBERAL USE OF THE PURGE COMMAND

Photoshop saves copies of much of what you do (an Undo step, a copy of a selection, and every History State) in RAM. Before you know it, you won't have much RAM left for doing heavy image processing (such as applying a filter or resampling the image). So, the program has to start swapping what should be processing in RAM to the hard disk. Then things get r-e-a-l-l-y s-l-o-o-o-o-w. You can avoid that particular slowdown by forming a good habit—frequently dump whatever might be stuck in RAM by purging it.

To Purge YOUR RAM:

1 Choose Edit | Purge

2 From the submenu, choose Undo, Clipboard, Histories, or All.

If you do all of the things I've specified in this section, you may be running Photoshop more quickly than some people with extra RAM and faster processors. However, it takes a bit of experience to know when it's more productive to let one of the previous settings do its thing and when it's best not to. Also, if you have a super-fast computer, you may find it far more convenient to leave these settings at their defaults. Try it both ways before making your decision.

CALIBRATE AND MANAGE COLOR

Now that you've got Photoshop running lickety-split, your next job is to make sure it hasn't all been for naught because the image you carefully processed and edited on your monitor isn't an acceptable representation of what will emanate from your printer, web site, or printing press. The only way you can avoid this trap is through careful and thorough color management—including making sure you've done the best job you can in calibrating your monitor and (ideally) your input devices (such as cameras and scanners).

The first, and most important, ingredient in the recipe is monitor calibration. If you're really serious, you should invest in Trinitron monitors (technology that's often licensed by Sony to other monitor makers that have names ending in –tron) and a third-party hardware/software calibration system. (If your monitor's not a

Trinitron and you can't afford to replace it with one, don't give up. Calibrating whatever you've got will work; you just won't have the sharpness, contrast, or color accuracy of a Trinitron.) If you're really demanding, the sky's the limit for what you can spend on hardware calibration systems. On the other hand, I can personally recommend both Monaco EZ-color (which also comes in a version that does device profiling) and the Pantone/ColorVision Opti/PhotoCal and Spyder. At this level, expect to spend between $300 and $450 for the software and hardware. Since this is a Photoshop book, I won't dwell on the step-by-step procedures necessary for setting up these third-party systems. I can, however, promise you that both the procedures and the instructions for following them will take you well under an hour.

> **NOTE** It's a very good idea to place your monitor in a windowless room or, at least, to do your serious Photoshop work after sunset. That's because you should recalibrate your monitor every time there's a significant change in the quality and intensity of the surrounding room light. If you're in a room that gets lots of outside light, this means you'll spend a truly annoying amount of time re-calibrating your monitor.

If you don't have or want to spend the $300 or so for a hardware calibrator, here's the good news. Photoshop comes with a utility called Adobe Gamma that, on the Mac and in Windows versions post-98SE, calibrates your monitor for all graphics applications. It's also simple to use. The utility does an easy-to-understand job of coaching you through each of the necessary steps. Shown here is the Adobe Gamma Wizard screen.

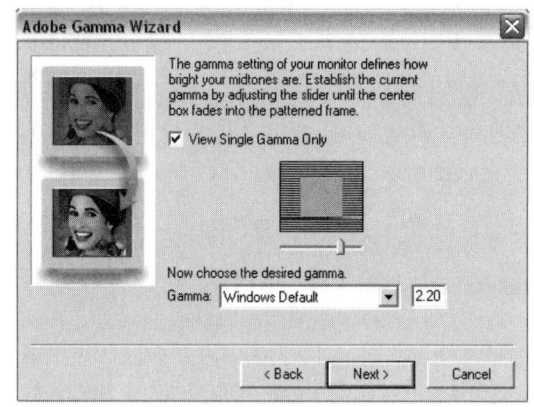

Once you've calibrated your monitor, be sure to save the profile in Photoshop. Then, when you print, the printer will translate the monitor profile to its own profile (that profile should be whatever you create in the process of profiling your printer/ink/paper combination; see the next section).

PROFILING YOUR PRINTER'S INK AND PAPER COMBINATIONS

Once you've calibrated your monitor, the next step is setting up your printer to do the most accurate (or pleasing, if you'd rather be subjective about it) job of printing the file that Photoshop sends it. Various combinations of ink and paper will dramatically affect your printed results. For this reason, you'll want to create your own profile by printing a color test chart until you get a result that looks like the original. Most color printers will let you choose between profiles, so you can come back to your results at any time. If you buy your ink and paper from the same reputable resource (preferably a dealer that specializes in supplying professionals, such as Inkjet Mall or Digital Art Supplies), they will either give you or sell you a profile for your printer. These are called "canned" profiles, and they are the easiest way to ensure reasonably accurate printing. If you're sending your output to a professional print shop or publication, ask for their profiles. If you then save to their profiles, you're more likely to get the results you expect.

PROFILING A DIGITAL CAMERA OR SCANNER

Profiling cameras and scanners requires that you photograph or scan a test chart—unless your hardware's software comes with one. You then use either the Image | Adjust controls in Photoshop or a third-party profiling system (such as Monaco EZ-color) to measure and calibrate the chart and then create a profile. Once you've created the camera or scanner profile, be sure to save it as a profile under a name that you will recognize when you are planning to use that device again. A typical test chart is shown in the following illustration.

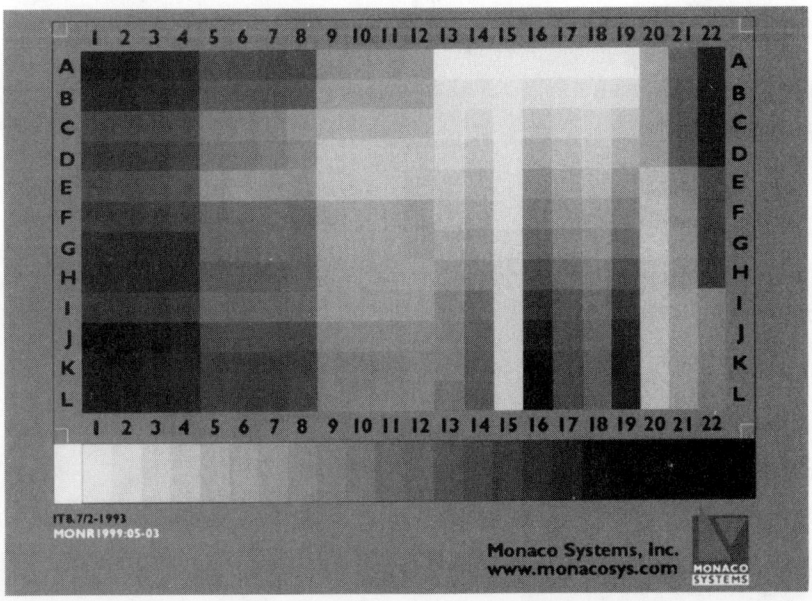

CATALOGING AND MANAGING YOUR IMAGES

Actually, the title for this section is a bit redundant. The primary task in managing your images lies in properly cataloging them. In other words, give them names you can quickly recognize later, organize them into categorical file folders, and archive them to removable media.

NEVER OVERWRITE YOUR ORIGINAL FILES

If you do anything in Photoshop to a file after you've opened it, then save it to its original name, you will have permanently changed (and, therefore, lost) some of the data in the original. This is especially true if your original file was saved in a "lossy" file compression format, such as JPEG, the file format used by most digital cameras.

To Save AN IMAGE FILE THE FIRST TIME YOU OPEN IT IN PHOTOSHOP:

1 Choose Image | Duplicate. Photoshop will automatically open a second copy of the file and will append the word "copy" to the original filename.

2 Close the original file without saving it.

3 Proceed to do whatever you are going to do in Photoshop—even if it's just looking at the file.

4 Save the file to a lossless file format. Choose File | Save As (CMD/CTRL-SHIFT-S). The Save As dialog appears.

5 From the Format menu, choose Photoshop or (at the very bottom of the menu) TIFF. Shown here is the Save As dialog.

6 Choose the folder where you want to save your work in progress from the Save In drop-down list.

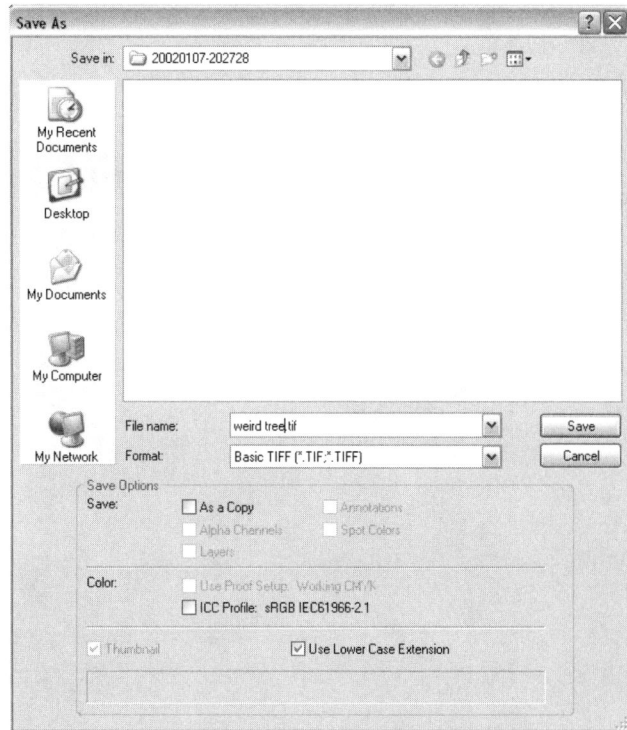

7 Enter the new filename. (See my suggestions in "Establishing File Naming Conventions" later in the chapter.) Proceed according to the Save Options (outlined next) for Photoshop and TIFF files; then click OK to save.

Photoshop (.PSD) and TIFF (.TIF) are the most commonly used cross-platform formats. TIFF files are safer if there's a chance you (or someone else) may want to open the file in another graphics application that doesn't read Photoshop files.

File Save Options to consider for Photoshop (.PSD) and TIFF (.TIF) files are

▶ **As a Copy** Check if you want to save the file as a duplicate of the file you started working on. This is a very handy option if you forgot to duplicate your original file before you started changing it.

▶ **Alpha Channels** These are saved selections and edited masks. You'll save file space if you leave this unchecked, but will, in the end, waste valuable time if you're likely to need these masks/selections at some future date.

▶ **Layers** Pretty much the same story as the preceding option. If you leave Layers unchecked, the file will be flattened as you save, so you'll conserve oodles of disk space, but you won't be able to change layer transparencies, blend modes, or do any further editing on the individual layers.

▶ **Annotations** Annotations were a new feature in Photoshop 6. They're very handy while work is progressing on a file, or for reference later when you're trying to remember how you did something. They don't take up a lot of disk space, either. On the other hand, you sure don't want to keep them (or any of the other boxes here that you can leave unchecked) if your files are web-destined, because annotations will (sometimes dramatically) slow the time it takes for the files to appear on the web page.

▶ **Spot Colors** Spot colors (very specific colors designated to print separately on a printing press) have to reside on their own layer. Leave this box checked if the file is going to be published, or if you might want to change a spot color later; otherwise, you'll be bloating file space.

ROTATING DIGITAL CAMERA IMAGES

If you use a digital camera, it may or may not automatically rotate images that you shoot in portrait (vertical) orientation. If your digital camera doesn't automatically rotate, then it's probable that about half your pictures are lying on one side or another. Therefore, the very first Photoshop Action that I record is one that rotates the picture—either 90 degrees to the left or 90 degrees to the right. I'll show you how to do that in a second, but first, let's think about what happens when you rotate an image—a lot of resampling, that's what. In fact, Photoshop does a superb job of this resampling, but there's still bound to be some data lost in the process. So you don't want to compound the problem even more by resaving the image as a JPEG file. Therefore, keep the original as it is and rotate a *copy* of the image, then save it to a lossless format, such as TIFF, but at lossless compression. Better yet, always use the Photoshop Browser so you can rotate the thumbnail. Photoshop then performs a really neat trick: it rotates the thumbnail without rotating the image. At the same time, it instructs Photoshop to rotate the image when it opens it. Just be sure you save that image to another, lossless file format—otherwise the image will be resampled.

> **NOTE** Some digital camera software and third-party image cataloging software will rotate the image thumbnail without rotating the image itself. The latest software that comes with Nikon and Olympus digital cameras for instance, does this. If you have such software, you'll find it quicker and easier to rotate and rename the images as you transfer them.

To Rotate AN IMAGE SO THAT ONLY THE THUMBNAIL IS ROTATED, AND THEN RENAME THE IMAGE WITHOUT RESAVING THE FILE:

1 In Photoshop, choose File | Browse or (if your screen resolution is higher than 800x600) just click the File Browser tab in the Palette Well. The File Browser dialog appears, as shown in Figure 2-1.

> **NOTE** You can rotate several images at the same time. Press SHIFT while right-clicking each image that you wish to rotate. (They needn't be next to one another.) Then continue with the instructions in step 3.

2 Use the Explorer interface in the left window of the file browser to navigate to the folder that contains the images you want to edit. Click the folder to open it.

3 CTRL-right-click the image you want to rotate. The in-context menu appears. To rotate the image to the left, choose Rotate 90 Degrees CCW (counterclockwise). The thumbnail will be immediately rotated. Note that you can also choose to rotate the image clockwise by 90 degrees or 180 degrees.

4 To rename the image without first loading it (which would require resaving using the Save As command), CTRL-right-click the highlighted image(s) and choose Rename from

FIGURE 2-1
The File Browser dialog, with the in-context menu displayed

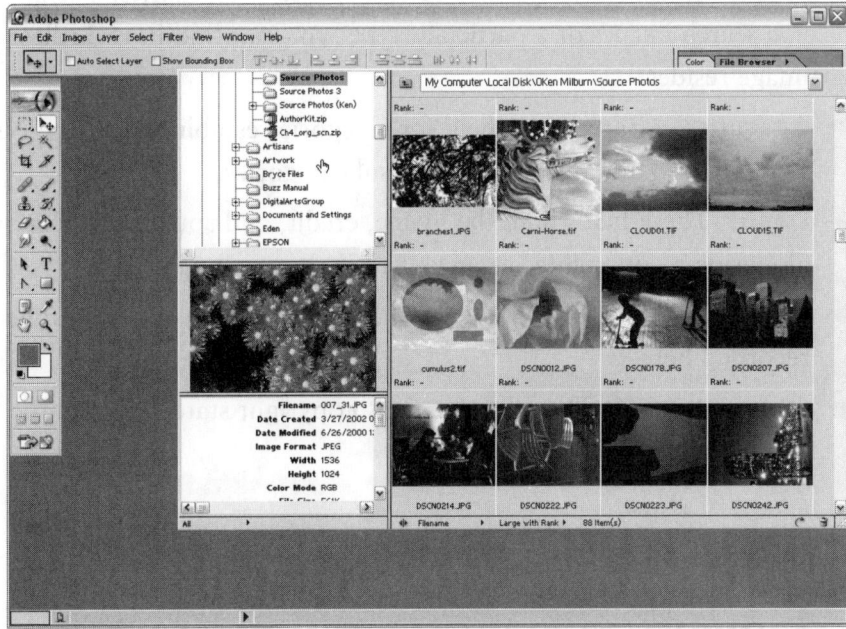

the in-context menu. You'll see that the filename (without the extension) is highlighted. Simply enter the new filename, and the file is renamed without being resaved.

ADD TEXT INFORMATION TO EACH IMAGE

If you're a professional photographer, or if you use your photos in a business where it pays to have as much information as possible about each photo, you'll be glad to know that Photoshop supports all the information fields specified by the Newspaper Association of America (NAA) and the International Press Telecommunications Council (IPTC) for identifying transmitted text and images. You can add this information to any file format supported by Photoshop if you're a Mac user. Windows users are limited to Photoshop, TIFF, JPEG, EPS, and PDF formats. There are many categories of information you can enter, each of which gives you several information fields. These include:

▶ **Caption** The information you want printed under an image, should it appear in a publication.

▶ **Keywords** Single words that describe some aspect of your image. Since images can often fit in multiple categories, it's a good idea to assign numerous words to your image that describe each of these possible categories. Then, when you search images of a particular type, you can find it, regardless of where the image resides.

▶ **Categories** A three-letter field for categories established by the NAA and IPTC. You can also add information for subcategories.

▶ **Credits** These fields hold the byline, credit, and source info that is required alongside a copyrighted image when it appears in print.

▶ **Origin** The name of the subject and the date it was photographed are recorded here.

▶ **Copyright & URL** This is the owner's copyright statement and the URL of the copyright owner.

To Enter THE FILE INFO DATA:

1 Choose File | File Info. The File Info dialog appears, as shown here:

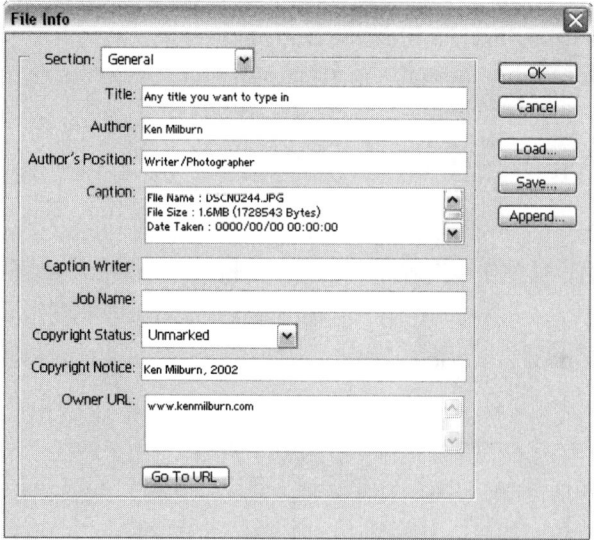

2 The Caption section is shown first. Enter the appropriate information, as described earlier, for each of the fields in this section (category).

3 To move to another section, you can either click the Prev or Next button to move backwards or forwards by one category, or you can choose a category from the Section menu at the top of the dialog.

4 When you have finished entering information in as many category sections and fields as you like, click Save. A Save dialog appears.

5 In the Save dialog, navigate to the folder where your image resides. In the Filename field, enter the name of the file with which you want to associate the information. Don't add a file extension...Photoshop will add the .ffo for you. Click Save. A text file with the .ffo extension is saved to the specified file folder.

You can view the File Info for a file once you've entered the information and stored it, as long as you've opened Photoshop. Just choose File | File Info. As long as the file has the same name, the information you've previously entered will be right there. If you're using Windows, you can also get File Info by right-clicking the file's title bar, then choosing File Info from the in-context menu.

ADDING ANNOTATIONS

You can also make annotations to remind yourself that you've performed certain operations on various parts of the photo. These annotations can be either textual or vocal. Once you've made an annotation, an icon stays atop the image. To read or listen to an annotation, just double-click its icon. If the annotation is text, a Post-It type window opens and reveals the text. If the annotation is vocal, it plays back over your computer's sound card and speaker system. Of course, you have to have a microphone attached to the computer if you plan to use voice annotations.

To Record A TEXT ANNOTATION:

1 Click the Notes tool. The cursor will change to a Note icon.

2 Drag the Note icon to the spot on the photo that you want the annotation to reference. Click. A Note window that resembles a Post-It appears.

3 Type the information you want to note.

4 Close the Note window by clicking the close box in the upper-right corner. (Yes, that's where it is for Windows users, too.)

Unfortunately, there is no way to hide annotation icons without deleting them. However, you can create a proxy document just for annotations: Duplicate the image and change it to a small size (the note icons will maintain their original relative locations), then choose File | Save As. When the dialog opens, change the file format to JPEG and double-click the word "copy" in the filename to highlight it. Next, type **notes** to replace "copy." Now you have an annotated visual reference to the image that doesn't take up much drive space, but you can reference it if you want to remember how you got the results you've produced, or if you want to point out certain details to someone else. (Your client?)

Annotations (both types) can also be dragged off the image space into the gray area surrounding the image (revealed by opening the window so it's larger than the image itself). If the image is very large, then zooming in until the image fits within the monitor space before expanding the window will work.

ORGANIZING YOUR FILE STORAGE

If you're going to keep your files organized, you should start the process long before you even start using Photoshop. Think of it this way: You may have dozens (or even hundreds) of photographs that you've collected over the years. Although it's not imperative, you may want to start by scanning and organizing all those files. You may also have files loosely scattered over a number of drives, CDs, and removable disks. As your collection grows, you will want to keep it organized. Otherwise, you're almost guaranteed to misplace some wonderful memories or important work.

I suggest you start by making a directory called Photos (or, if you're a Windows user, use the My Photos subdirectory in the My Documents folder). Next, make folders for each of your major categories of photos. Mine are: Events, Locations, People, and Type. The Events folder has subfolders for each occasion that deserves to have its pictures kept within one collection. The Locations folder, meanwhile, has subfolders for each specific geographical location. The People folder is organized into folders named after their subjects. I'm sure you get the idea.

If you don't do a lot of events, just name folders for the ones you do cover. If you do lots of events within several different categories (for example, weddings, company parties, graduations) then name a folder for each. Otherwise, just put each event in its own folder. My Locations folder contains subfolders for images that portray a given place with geographical locations that can be broad or narrow in scope; for example, Alameda, Marin, Europe, or Covent Garden.

If I take lots of pictures of a particular subject on different occasions, I create a subfolder named for the subject (Jane Doe, for instance) and put subfolders in it whose elements—events, clothing, or expressions—will help me find related images as quickly as possible.

ESTABLISHING YOUR FILE NAMING CONVENTIONS

When it comes to naming individual images, I try to name them in a way that will make the subject most recognizable to me. These days, you can pretty much count on being able to use at least 32 characters in a filename (not including the drive, folder, or file-type extension), so I create names such as sue_whblouse_smile1.psd.

SAVING TO THE SAFEST FILE FORMAT

As stated previously, don't resave when renaming. Do it in the OS. Don't save a file to JPEG or GIF format unless you need to use it for a specific purpose, such as inclusion in a multimedia slide show or publication on the Web. Even then, make sure you are saving a *copy* of your file to one of those formats. Why? Because those file formats use *lossy* compression or (in the case of GIF) reduce the number of colors in the image. Lossy compression makes very small files with (usually) negligible loss of image quality. This means that you can get more images on your camera's memory card, lots of pictures that open and animate quickly into a PowerPoint slide show, and web images that pop into view on a modem user's computer almost immediately. BUT, it also means that each time you resave an image to the same, or another, type of lossy file format, more image quality is lost.

KEEP SEPARATE FOLDERS FOR WORKS IN PROGRESS

When working on a specific project, you'd be wise to keep different versions of the file as your work progresses. For one thing, you'll be amazed at how much you learn by going back over the different stages you've put a successful image through. Otherwise, it's inevitable that you'll forget how you did some of your best work. Believe me, I've learned that lesson the hard way.

But there's another, even better reason for keeping a separate folder for each work in progress: You can always return to a given stage more quickly—even if you've closed the file—because you don't waste time browsing through flocks of nonpertinent filenames in order to find those that matter. You can also number each progressive stage that the file was saved in, so it's easy to show or re-create the logical progression of your work.

> **NOTE** Photoshop's History palette will let you revert to something you did several steps ago. But remember that the contents of the History palette disappear when you close the file, regardless of whether or not you save the image before closing it.

WINDOWS USERS:
UPGRADE TO XP

One of the Macintosh's strong points in dealing with graphics has always been that you have the option to see thumbnails of images when viewing a file directory. As you'll discover quickly, one of the toughest problems in dealing with image management is that the difference between one picture and a dozen others is often so subtle that the difference can only be adequately described visually. (See Figure 2-2.)

The Mac, however, even in OS X, doesn't carry this far enough. Thumbnails are still fairly small. Furthermore, without special third-party software, you can't read the XIF data (which tells you all the technical information automatically recorded when you take the picture) attached to photos taken with most digital cameras.

FIGURE 2-2
Browsing images in Windows XP

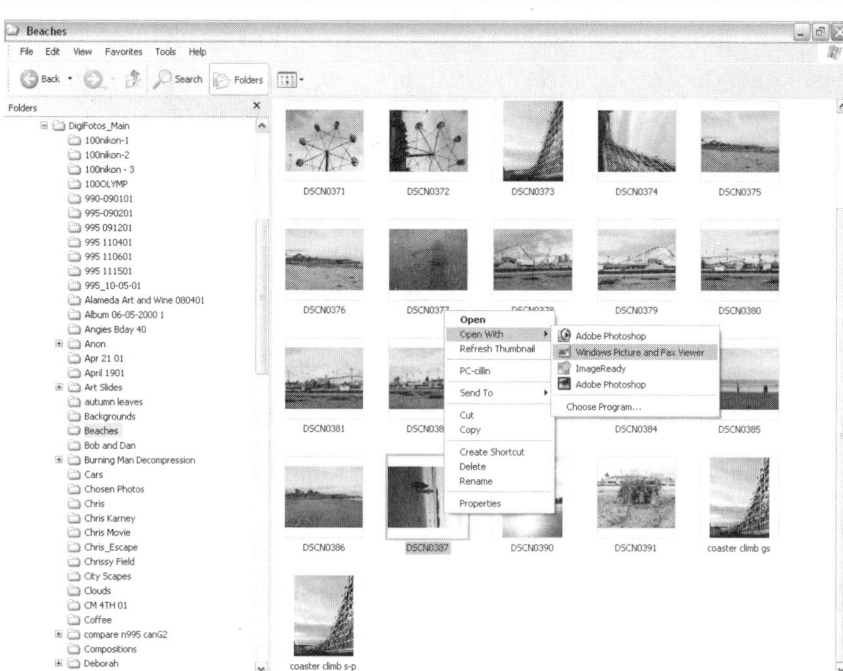

Finally, you can't rotate vertical pictures to the proper orientation without first placing them into Photoshop or some third-party software.

Of course, this doesn't mean you should throw out all the Macs in your shop and buy Windows PCs (though after seeing XP, you may be tempted). When you want to do these things, simply open the Photoshop 7 browser.

On the other hand, if you have Windows, upgrading to XP will mean a much more stable OS (than older versions of Windows), an interface and color scheme (silver) that is much more suited to viewing and working with images, and (best of all) built-in visual image management that competes directly with third-party programs.

XP automatically interfaces to scanners and cameras, so you no longer need specialized software from the hardware vendor in order to transfer files to a directory on your computer. If, for instance, you hook a USB-enabled camera to Windows XP, the camera will automatically appear in Windows Explorer as an external disk drive. Click the camera's icon, and thumbnails of the images will appear onscreen. If there are any photos of your feet, awkward and embarrassing expressions on your lover's face, or a finger in front of the lens, you can save time and disk space by CTRL-clicking them (to select multiple noncontiguous files), right-clicking one of the images, and then choosing Delete from the in-context menu.

Once you've got a thumbnails page with all the files automatically named and numbered, it's easy to organize files into the folder categories I previously suggested. In fact, if you open two Explorer windows, you can just drag and drop them into the appropriate folders.

You can't rotate thumbnails in Windows XP Explorer, but you can open any image in any program by choosing it from a menu. (Again, see Figure 2-2, which shows the in-context version of this menu.) If you don't want to take the time to rotate the image in Photoshop, you can choose Windows Picture And Fax Viewer, then click an icon to rotate the thumbnail. Windows Picture And Fax Viewer is built into Windows XP and has a number of other quick-edit features—but, alas, this book is only about Photoshop 7, so we won't be covering them here. The following illustration shows the Windows Picture And Fax Viewer page.

ARCHIVE YOUR PHOTO COLLECTIONS ON CDS

One of the most annoying characteristics of photo files is that they multiply like *big* rabbits on Viagra. So you need lots of room to store them. Thank heavens for thirty-cent CD-Rs and fifty-cent CD-RW discs. Do yourself a big favor: spend less than $100 and get a good, fast CD-RW drive installed on your computer. (If you have a computer that's less than 18 months old, you probably already have one.) If your only computer is a laptop, you can get an external CD-RW drive for just a bit more. Every time your My Photos directory approaches 500MB in size, copy all but the most frequently needed files to CD-RW disks. Then erase those files from the hard drive and start over. Every so often, copy the CD-RWs to more organized and consolidated folders on a hard drive, then burn CD-Rs of those folders for archival purposes. You can then erase your CD-RW disks and start collecting all over again.

MAKING CONTACT PROOF SHEETS

Another technique that will save you lots of time when trying to locate a specific image (especially if it's part of a collection of shots of the same subject, separated only by subtle differences) is

> **TIP** Contact sheets are a great way to let friends and clients choose which photos they want printed without having to access your computer simultaneously. They're easily carried and mailed, and you don't have to worry about platform compatibility. Also, there's a way to do a kind of "contact sheet" over the Web.

making proof (a.k.a. contact) sheets. This will show the contents of an entire image folder on a few sheets of paper. Here is a finished contact sheet:

Photoshop provides you with a way to specify that an entire directory folder be printed at a user-specifiable number of rows and columns of images per page. It then prints as many pages as are needed to display all the images in that folder. You can even check a box that will cause all the subdirectory images to be printed as well. There are also numerous other options that let you choose from such variables as the size of the page to be printed, the printing resolution, whether to order thumbnails from side-to-side or top-to-bottom, and whether to caption each image with its filename or not at all.

TIP If you want the largest possible thumbnail for the number of rows and columns you've designated, be sure that the Use Filename As Caption box is unchecked. (Click to toggle the check mark off and on.) If you use the filename, choose the smallest font size that will be readable. Sans-serif fonts, such as Helvetica and Arial, are usually more readable at smaller sizes.

To Make A CONTACT SHEET:

1 Make sure you have created a folder that contains all the images you want to place on the contact sheet. If you want to make a contact sheet that contains images from several folders, create a new folder, then place copies of the original files into that folder.

2 Choose File | Automate | Contact Sheet II. The Contact Sheet II dialog appears (see Figure 2-3).

3 To locate the directory from which you want to make a contact sheet, click Choose. A file navigation dialog will open. Double-click to choose the directory. The directory name and path will appear under the Choose button.

4 Enter the paper size (less any needed margins; see your printer's manual) for this contact sheet in the Document Width and Height fields. You can choose between inches, centimeters, and pixels as the units of page size measurement.

> **TIP** If you are making letter-size contact sheets, the default 8x10 dimension will usually give you the best result.

5 To decide between a black-and-white (well, grayscale, actually) or color proof, choose either RGB (for color) or Grayscale from the Mode menu. (Needless to say, choosing RGB won't turn your grayscale images into color.)

FIGURE 2-3
The Contact Sheet II dialog

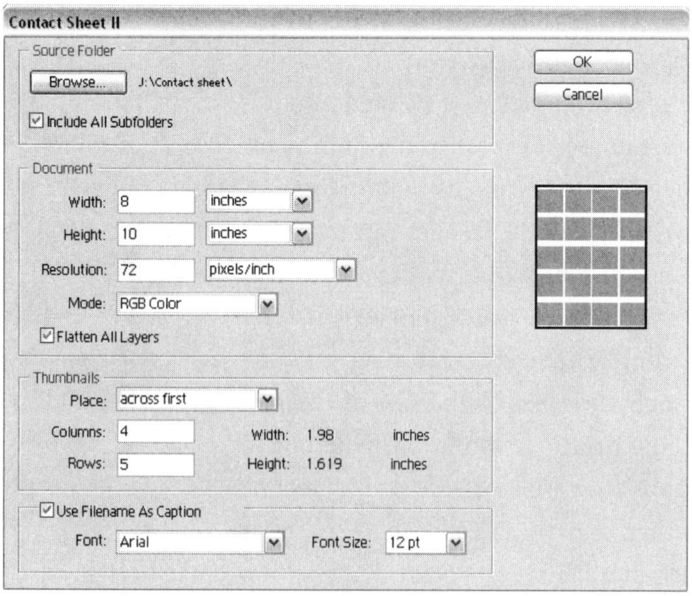

6 To decide the order of appearance of the images, choose Across First or Down First from the Place menu. Across First is the default. (After all, most of us read from left to right.)

7 To determine the size of the thumbnails, enter the number of thumbnails that must fit across the page in the Columns field, then enter the number of thumbnails that must fit down the page in the Rows field. You can see a preview diagram of how the thumbnails will look as you change these numbers. The area that the image will occupy is represented as a gray rectangle. Be sure to enter the correct number of rows and columns to make the gray area square. Otherwise, your images will be smaller than you predict, because they must be positioned within the gray area whether they are vertically or horizontally oriented.

8 The last thing you have to decide is whether to use the filename as a caption. Doing so is the surest way to make sure the image you choose is readily identified in a file directory. However, the resulting caption has to have room for a possible 32 characters, so it will take up a lot of your potential row/column space. To choose to use the filename as a caption, check the Use Filename As Caption box until the check mark appears.

9 Enter 4 or 6 (points) in the Font Size field.

10 To assemble the contact sheet(s), click OK.

11 Once you see that the contact sheet has been fully assembled, choose File Save As and follow the usual routine for saving a file.

BATCH CONVERTING IMAGES TO A COMMON FILE FORMAT OR SIZE

If you have collected the images for a project from a number of different sources, you'll find it much easier to work with them in the future if you convert them all to a single file format. This is especially true if those images are going to be used on a web site or in a multimedia presentation that requires a specific file format (usually JPEG). Photoshop has a command that will apply any *Action* (a series of commands executed with a single click or keystroke) to an entire folder of images. It's very easy to create an Action that resizes an image to fit a given height or width (you can't do both for a whole batch without distorting the images), then saves that image to a particular file format. In the example that follows, we've chosen to save the images to the JPEG file format as though we were saving them for use on a web site.

To Save THE IMAGES TO JPEG:

1 Create a new folder and copy all the files you want to convert into that folder. It is important that all the images that are affected by the Action you're about to create be duplicates of the originals; otherwise, you'll lose much of the data contained in the originals because the Action will convert the images to lower-resolution images that use "lossy" JPEG compression.

2 Choose Window | Actions. The Actions palette appears. From the Actions palette menu, choose New Action. The New Action dialog appears, as shown here:

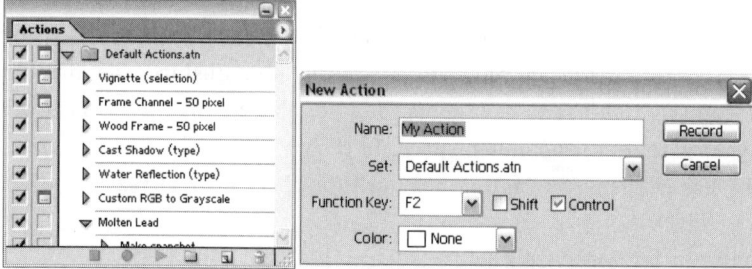

3 In the Name field, type a title (such as "Convert to JPEG") that will remind you of the purpose for the Action you're about to create.

4 In the Function Key field, pick the handiest keyboard function key number from the Function Key menu. You can also choose to check either the CMD/CTRL or OPT/ALT boxes, so you can assign up to 36 different function keys.

5 Click Record. Notice that the Record icon at the bottom of the Actions palette has turned red to indicate that whatever commands you execute are now being recorded.

6 Choose Image | Image Size. The Image Size dialog appears. Make sure that both the Constrain Proportions and Resample Image boxes are checked.

7 Since we want all our images to have a maximum height of 3 inches at a typical screen resolution for the Web, type 3 in the Height field.

8 Since 72 pixels per inch is considered the median resolution for web pages, type 72 in the Resolution field and click OK. The dialog disappears and the image appears much smaller.

9 When you resize an image, it's a good idea to sharpen it slightly to make up for edges that have been softened in the resampling process. Choose Filter | Sharpen | Unsharp Mask. The Unsharp Mask dialog appears.

10 Enter 50% in the Amount field, 1 pixel in the Radius field, and 0 levels in the Threshold field; then click OK.

11 Choose File | Save As (CMD/CTRL-SHIFT-S). The Save As dialog appears. From the Format menu, choose JPEG.

12 Make sure that the Use Lower Case Extension box is checked, since all web sites demand this extension. Make sure none of the other boxes are checked; then click Save. The JPEG Options dialog appears.

13 Choose Medium from the Quality menu. This gives you the best chance of having acceptable quality across a number of different images after JPEG compression.

14 Under Format Options, the Baseline ("Standard") box should be checked. Click OK.

15 Now you need to stop recording. Click the Stop Playing/Recording icon at the bottom of the Actions palette.

Now you should place all the images you want to resize and convert into the same folder. Be sure the folder *does not* contain any images you don't want to resize and convert (including the copy of the file you've used for setting up your Action).

To Run THE ACTION ON THE ENTIRE BATCH OF FILES IN YOUR TARGET FOLDER:

1 Choose File | Automate | Batch. The Batch dialog appears.

2 In the Play section, choose the name of the Actions set that the Action you just created is in (probably Default Actions.atn) from the Set menu, then choose the name you gave to this Action. (I called mine *Resize and Convert to JPEG*.)

3 In the Source section, choose Folder from the Source menu, then click Choose. The Browse For Folder dialog appears.

4 Browse the dialog for the folder that contains the images to be resized and have their file format changed. Leave all the other options in this dialog at their defaults, and

make sure all the boxes except Suppress Color Profile Warnings are unchecked; then click OK.

One by one, you will see each of the images in the folder open, resize, and then be saved until the process is complete. If you now open the folder, all the files that have a .JPG extension will be those destined for your web site. Since all the files in the folder were duplicates, you can delete any that have other file extensions.

WHAT'S NEXT?

In this chapter, we've learned some basics about how to save ourselves time when working with Photoshop. In the first part of the chapter, we learned to make Photoshop run as fast is it can, given the computer it has to run on. In the second part of the chapter, we learned to use Actions in order to perform a whole series of commands with one click of the button.

In the following chapter, you'll take the next logical step in evolving an image to its final form by doing things that change its resolution. In other words, you'll learn to crop, resize, and correct distortion in your images. Cropping trims information from the edges of images, while resizing increases or decreases the image's resolution. Correcting distortion involves creating distortion(s) that is equal to the original distortion(s), but in the opposite direction. The end result is that the image appears to have no distortion at all.

 ON THE VIRTUAL CLASSROOM CD-ROM In Lesson 1, "Personalizing Your Workflow," you learn to set up your working environment so that it doesn't clash with your ability to judge the color and contrast of the photos you're editing. You also learn to calibrate your monitor using Adobe's built-in Monitor Calibration Wizard.

3

Cropping, Sizing, and Correcting Distortion

Because photo files can use gobs of system resources (especially memory and disk space), you can greatly expedite your job (and save money) if you start the project by trimming away any unneeded portion(s) of the image. You may also want to correct perspective distortion (key stoning) if you have photographed straight-edged objects, such as buildings, from an angle. On the other hand, working with too little information can mean you lose some resolution and detail as you add more elements or make image-correcting adjustments. Try not to throw out more information than you can afford to lose if you think you may need to make a print of a given size at a later date. For instance, a digital camera image large enough to produce a photographic-quality 8-inch by 10-inch image should be roughly 2400 by 3000 pixels (roughly 5 megapixels), although you can generally get away with about half that amount in the original version.

DUPLICATE THE WORKING FILE

I covered this in Chapter 2, but it's important enough to repeat: Never do any Photoshop work on your original file. If you do, you'll never be able to improve on the image if you learn a better technique later (something that's bound to happen). Working from a duplicate is especially important if you want to correct perspective and lens distortion before you continue working on the photo. That's because if you do want to correct distortion, it should be the very first correction you make to the image. Otherwise, there's a good chance of not getting as accurate a correction as you'd like, because the other processes, will have already removed some of the information from the original file. Of course, it's not the end of the world if you don't correct distortion first; we only mention this because we're assuming this book is being read by people who have spent the $600 or so bucks for Photoshop because they want to get the best possible quality.

I've already given you the procedure, but just to drum it in, here's how you duplicate the original file (or any progressive version of the file).

To Duplicate THE ORIGINAL FILE:

1 Choose Image | Duplicate Image

2 A duplicate of the currently active image immediately appears. Note in the title bar that the duplicated file has the same name as the original, with the word "copy" added.

3 Close the original file without saving it. It is especially important to close JPEG files without saving, because they will be recompressed in the process, causing loss of data.

You are now ready to continue working on your file.

CORRECT PERSPECTIVE DISTORTION

You usually want to correct perspective distortion when you've been forced to tilt the camera in order to frame the subject as desired. When there are no straight lines (such as the horizon or the edges of buildings), the eye doesn't pay much attention to perspective distortion. In that case, there's probably no need to make the correction. On rare occasions, however, you'll want to make a perspective distortion correction because you wish to correct for an effect, or because you are compositing one image with another and need to match the perspective of the two images. Of course, if you don't need to correct for distortion, you can skip this procedure altogether. The photo on the left here shows an image badly in need of perspective distortion correction.

Notice that the horizontal straight lines seem to drift downward as they move away from the camera, while the vertical straight lines seem to slant toward the lens. You want both sets of lines to be parallel to the edges of the image.

To Correct FOR PERSPECTIVE DISTORTION:

1 Open your original image and duplicate it, as described in the preceding exercise.

2 Choose View | Layers. The Layers palette appears. So far, there is only one layer, called Background. Since you cannot perform transformations (in other words, image stretching) on a background layer, you'll want to change it to an ordinary layer.

3 Place the cursor over the Background Layer's Name bar and double-click. The New Layer dialog appears.

4 By default, Layer 0 appears in the name field. Rename this layer Perspective Correction so you can easily identify it later. Then click OK.

5 Drag a corner of the image window to stretch it so the image doesn't fill the entire window. Leave as much of a border as your screen will allow so you'll have room to stretch and rotate the image.

6 (Optional) If your lines are far from the frame's edge, it may help to place a temporary guideline in the image so you can make sure the line you're moving is exactly parallel to the edge of the image. To do this, choose View | Show Rulers. Rulers will appear at the top and left edges of the frame. Place your cursor on one of the rulers and drag in a perpendicular direction. A guideline will follow the cursor until you release. If you like, you can add both horizontal and vertical guidelines in this manner.

7 Choose Edit | Free Transform (CMD/CTRL-T). The Transform marquee appears, surrounding the currently active layer (which, in this instance, is the entire layer). Also, the Transform Options Bar appears.

8 You are going to make the perspective correction by dragging the corners of the marquee independent of one another. Press CMD/CTRL and drag the corner closest to the line that slants the most until that line is parallel with the edge of the frame. Release the mouse button when you are satisfied that the edge has been straightened.

9 Repeat step 8 on each corner until all the important straight lines are parallel to one another, and to the edges of the frame. Be sure when you do this that you are always dragging *away* from the edge of the frame.

10 When you are happy with how the image looks, click the Commit button on the Options Bar (or just press RETURN/ENTER). This will automatically crop the image and render it to the new proportions.

11 If you have used guidelines, you'll probably want to remove them. To do so, choose View | Clear Guidelines.

CORRECT WIDE-ANGLE LENS DISTORTION

Digital cameras, except for the very cheapest of them, are equipped with zoom lenses so the operator can seamlessly change the view from wide-angle to telephoto. Having this ability means that the photographer can do most of the cropping with the camera, thus preserving all the resolution that a particular camera offers. I'm speaking here of real or "optical" zoom lenses. Digital zooming doesn't do anything you couldn't do much better in Photoshop by using the Image Size command and bipolar interpolation. But enough ranting about that; back to zoom lenses. Sweet as they are, most digital camera zoom lenses are prone to barrel distortion when zoomed to their widest angle. What's barrel distortion? Imagine the following image started out as a straight-edged rectangle.

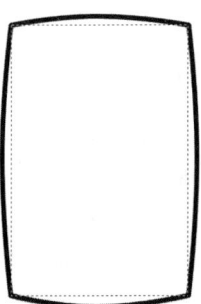

The arc of the edges occurs because of barrel distortion. Even if you have a distortion free zoom lens, you will, at some point, want to add an even wider-angle supplementary lens. Supplementary (a.k.a. screw-on) wide-angle lenses almost always exhibit barrel distortion.

If you're going to correct for image distortion, this may be the time to do it, since you probably will want to eliminate that distortion in whatever versions of your file you produce down the road.

Photoshop doesn't currently have a command for correcting lens distortion. If you want to try to make the correction, it will take some experimentation, and you'll have to settle for "good enough" in lieu of technical perfection. So, if you're patient and have a fair amount of RAM, here's a technique you can try:

Start by doing any necessary perspective correction. (See "Correct Perspective Distortion" earlier in the chapter.) Enlarge the canvas to the point where you can drag a full circle around the image. This means creating a square canvas that is the same height and width as the diagonal measurement of the image. Then you can experiment with using the Filter | Distort | Spherize command to correct pincushion distortion (where the sides of the rectangle curve inward rather than outward) or the Filter | Distort | Pinch command to correct barrel distortion. Illustrated here from left to right, an original (with no distortion), pincushion distortion, and barrel distortion.

Note that I said *experiment*. The settings for the degree of distortion corrected by these filters are not intended to correct for anything in particular. I work by zooming the image out far enough in the preview that I can see the edges. Then I move the slider that controls the degree of distortion until it looks as though the distortion has been corrected. Next, I write down the Spherize or Pinch settings shown onscreen, and click OK to go ahead and perform the distortion.

If the result is a bit over- or under-corrected, I immediately press CMD/CTRL-Z to Undo; then I reselect the same filter and type a number in the Amount field. (Don't use the slider unless you want to spend your life in the trial-and-error stage.) I write that number down for reference, click OK, and wait until I see the result.

If you don't like what you see, keep undoing and recalling the same filter and typing in an adjusted number until you've got the result nailed. Be sure to keep writing down your numbers. Use your favorite word processor or text editor to create a document for lens distortion correction, and write down the filter and percentage of distortion needed for each lens. Ever after, when you are correcting the distortion for the same lens at the same (or nearly the same) zoom level, you won't have to guess at the proper settings. On the other hand, if you have to do it that often, you might prefer to spend the 89 bucks it costs to follow my next suggestion for correcting lens distortion.

Okay, so that's the best way I know to correct for lens distortion without buying additional software. However, the only way to really correct barrel distortion accurately and easily is through the use of a third-party plug-in from Andromeda Software called Lens Doc. You can find a free trial version of Lens Doc on the Andromeda web site at www.andromeda.com. Since this book is about Photoshop, and not about all the third-party products you can use with it, there's no room to take you through an exercise. However, if you're serious about correcting for all sorts of lens distortion, this is the program to use. It will correct for both barrel and pincushion distortion.

If you own one of the more popular digital cameras, there are even built-in settings for zooms made at various focal lengths with a particular camera. All you do is find the right setting and click. The distortion is automatically (and miraculously) corrected. If you don't find your lens listed in the software, making pincushion, barrel, and (yes) even rotation and perspective corrections is still quick and easy. You just place three points along the vertical lines you want to correct. If there's a curve in any of those lines, the program knows to also correct the top and bottom for barrel or pincushion distortion. If the lines are straight, the program automatically corrects for perspective distortion. If the lines are slanted, the program first rotates the image, then corrects for whichever type of distortion is detected. The results are stunningly accurate, and the work takes a fraction of the time required by the method mentioned previously. It's very hard to find any smeared pixels or data loss as a result of all this rerendering. Again, LensDoc's suggested retail price is $89.

CROP 'TIL YOU DROP: ELIMINATING UNWANTED IMAGE AREA

Often, an unwanted object, such as a shoulder or tree branch, will creep into your photo. Perhaps you just couldn't zoom in on your subject tight enough. Thankfully, you can resize the image in Photoshop by simply trimming one or more of its edges—a process called *cropping*.

Once again, although there's no Photoshop rule that says you *should* do it, it's usually more efficient to crop your image before you start working with selections, layers, filters, and special effects. Cropping is dead easy. However, before you do it, there are some things to consider:

▶ Do you want the end result to be a particular size?

▶ Do you need to crop away pixels left around a border after scanning or taking a screen shot?

▶ Does the cropped result have to have a particular proportion?

▶ Do you need to rotate the cropped result, or make it a different file size?

CROPPING WITHOUT MAKING THE CANVAS SMALLER

There is a technique that lets you keep your canvas the same size after cropping. (This way, at a later time, you can show the entire canvas.)

To Keep YOUR CANVAS THE SAME SIZE:

1 Open the file you want to crop

2 Choose the Crop tool. The Crop tool's Options Bar will appear. Immediately click the Clear button to empty all the fields of data—otherwise, the image will be resized when it's cropped, and you won't be able to recover the precropped image.

3 In order for this technique to work, you must make a duplicate layer of your file. To do this, choose Window | Layer. The Layers palette appears.

4 If you've already created several layers that comprise the image, choose Image | Duplicate. A duplicate copy of the image appears. Flatten the image by choosing Flatten Image from the Layers Palette menu. This merges all the parts of the image onto one layer.

5 If the file has only a single layer, drag that layer to the New Layer icon at the bottom of the palette and it will be duplicated. On the Layers palette, click the new layer's Name bar to make sure it is selected.

6 Make sure the Crop tool is still chosen, and drag the cursor diagonally across the image until it is approximately the size and proportion you wish. A cropping marquee appears around the image, as shown here:

7 Drag the marquee handles until the crop is exactly as you want it.

8 To back up a little, as soon as you placed the cropping marquee, the contents of the Options Bar changed. Click the Hide radio button. A dot should appear inside the button to show that it is active.

9 Click the Commit Current Operation check box or press the RETURN/ENTER key. The image will appear to have been cropped, but all the information will still be there. If you had clicked the Delete radio button instead, the portion of the image outside the cropping marks would have been discarded.

10 You can now save the image. When you re-open it, you can regain the hidden portion of the image, if needed, by choosing Image | Reveal All.

It may be that at this point, you just want to crop the image to a framing you prefer, and you'll re-crop the image if it has to be made to fit a particular size or proportion. If that's the case, your job is simple. You can use either the Rectangular marquee, the Crop tool, or the Trim command.

CROPPING WITH THE RECTANGULAR MARQUEE

When you need to crop very close to the edge of the frame without having the edges of the marquee snap to the edges of the frame, the Rectangular marquee is the best choice—especially if you want to trim interactively by dragging a rectangle (as opposed to entering the exact number of pixels). It is also the only tool to use if you want to crop the image to a given proportion.

To Use THE RECTANGULAR MARQUEE AS A CROPPING TOOL:

1 Choose the Rectangular Marquee tool. The Rectangular Marquee Options Bar appears, as shown here:

2 (Optional) If you want to make a selection that is proportional (and, as in this instance, crop to the borders of that selection), choose Constrained Aspect Ratio from the Style menu on the Options Bar. Enter the number of units for width in the Width field and the number of units for height in the Height field. (These numbers don't have to be for any particular type of unit.)

3 (Optional) If you want to make the marquee a specific number of pixels in height and in width,

> **NOTE** If you want to move the marquee in exact increments after placing it, press the Arrow key that points in the direction you want to move it—one pixel per keypress. To move it ten pixels per keypress, press RETURN/ENTER-ARROW.

choose Fixed Size from the Style menu. Then type the number of pixels high by the number of pixels wide in the Height and Width fields. It is not possible to enter other types of units, such as inches and centimeters—you have to do that with the Crop tool.

4 Place your cursor in one corner of the area you want to keep after cropping, and drag diagonally until the marquee surrounds the area you want.

> **NOTE** Cropping isn't always the best way to eliminate unwanted objects at the edges of an image. See Chapter 4 for a discussion of the Clone tool and how to use it for this purpose. The advantage of using the Clone tool is that you don't change the size or shape of your photo.

5 To crop the image to the exact size of the marquee, choose Edit | Crop. The cropped image of the flower is shown in the following illustration:

CROPPING WITH THE TRIM COMMAND

The purpose of using the Trim command is to eliminate a solid-color border that is outside the picture. If the picture inside that border is rotated, you must first straighten the picture and then use the regular cropping tool to put it back into a rectangular frame before issuing the Trim command. Otherwise, the Trim command will only crop down to the smallest possible vertical rectangle. The following illustration shows an image to be cropped with the Trim command.

To Crop Away PIXELS LEFT AROUND AN IMAGE AFTER SCANNING OR TAKING A SCREEN SHOT:

1 If the image is on the background layer, double-click the Background Layer Name bar. The New Layer dialog appears. Click OK to convert the background layer to a conventional layer so you can rotate it.

2 Drag the corner of your work window to enlarge it beyond the boundaries of the image, so you'll have room to rotate.

3 Choose Edit | Free Transform command. The image will be surrounded by a Transform marquee with eight handles. Place the cursor near one of the corner handles (it will change to a curved line with arrowheads at either end to indicate that you are in

Rotate mode). Drag until the edges of the photo (not the edges of the colored or transparent border) are perfectly parallel to the edges of the window.

4 When you have finished rotating, press RETURN/ENTER to accept the rotation.

5 Choose the Crop tool and crop the image so it is rectangular, leaving in any part of the image that is the background trim.

6 Choose Edit | Trim. The Trim dialog appears.

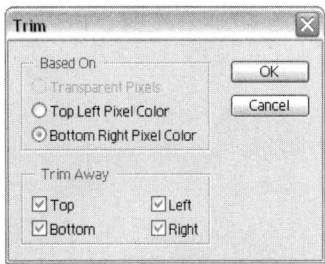

> NOTE Trimming is a great way to temporarily place a matte or border behind an image that's destined to be inserted into a presentation, layout, or web portfolio. Add a new layer, fill it with the color you want to use for the matte, then flatten the image, and save it. Any time thereafter, if you need to resize the image for a different target media and save it under a different name, preferably by adding its use to its original name (for example, my image web.jpg), save it in the target file format. If a time comes when you want to delete the border from the original, simply use the Trim command as described here.

7 If the border goes all around the image, choose either Top Left or Bottom Right Pixel Color. If the border is clear, no matter how many sides are bordered, choose Clear Pixels. If the border is only along one or two sides of the image, choose the corner that includes the side or sides you want to trim.

8 If you want to trim a four-sided border, make sure all the check boxes are checked. Otherwise, pick only the side or sides you want to trim.

9 Once you've clicked all the radio buttons and check boxes that are appropriate to what you want to do, click OK.

ROTATING AND CORRECTING PERSPECTIVE IN THE CROPPED RESULT

You can straighten images, such as the following, that have been shot with a tilted camera (or tilt images when you want to give them that wonky, tilted look) by using the Crop tool. Although perspective correction may not be quite as precise as with the Edit | Transform command, you don't have to do your cropping after the fact and then have the image be resampled to make it the right size. Of course, you'll lose some data in the resampling process, so you may want to reserve this method for images in which resolution and detail are of secondary importance. Once again, be sure to work from a duplicate so you can always return to the original if you reconsider which correction method to use.

To Simultaneously ROTATE AND CORRECT PERSPECTIVE:

1 Choose the Crop tool. Drag a rectangle of the approximate size that you want the final crop to be.

2 Place the cursor in the center of the cropping marquee and drag the marquee into position over the center of the area you want to crop.

3 Place the cursor just outside any corner of the marquee. The cursor will change to a rotation cursor.

4 Drag to rotate the marquee.

5 If necessary, drag from the center to reposition the marquee, and then drag any of the handles until the marquee is exactly the size you want it to be. The following illustration shows an image having its perspective fixed and being simultaneously cropped.

To Correct FOR PERSPECTIVE DISTORTION:

1 Click the Delete radio button on the Options Bar.

2 Click to check the Perspective box on the Options Bar (only visible after you've made the crop selection). Now you can drag the corner handles to any positions. Drag them so the lines in the image are parallel with the sides of the marquee.

3 Once you're satisfied with your rotation and perspective correction, press RETURN/ENTER or click the Commit button on the Options Bar. The finished image is shown here.

CHANGING THE FILE SIZE OF THE CROPPED RESULT

You can make Photoshop resample the image back to its original size or to the same size as any other image you're able to open in Photoshop. This feature is a magical timesaver when you have a whole batch of images to put into a web catalog (or into a print catalog, for that matter) and you want them all to be the same size and proportion. Without this capability, you'd have to enlarge all the images in order to match them in one dimension, then crop them with the Marquee tool set at a fixed size so you could select exactly which portions you wanted to keep after cropping.

To Sample IMAGES TO A PARTICULAR SIZE:

1 Open the image that's the size you want the rest of the images to be. If you wish to restore the current image to its original size and proportion after cropping, this is the only image you need to open; otherwise, leave this image open when you open other images to crop.

2 Choose the Crop tool. On the Options Bar, click the Front Image button.

3 If you want to crop another image to the same size, just open it (choose File | Open or drag it into Photoshop from any open folder). Otherwise, you can perform the next step on the original file.

4 Drag the Crop tool's cursor to form a marquee that encloses the area you want to keep. Notice that no matter how you drag, the proportion of the marquee will be the same as that of the original "Front" image. When you have the marquee positioned and sized the way you want (see Figure 3-1), click the Marquee tool, press RETURN/ENTER or click the Commit button on the Options Bar in order to render the cropped image.

5 Press RETURN/ENTER or click the Commit button. Photoshop resamples the cropped portion of the image to exactly the same size and proportion as the front image.

> **NOTE** As long as you keep the original "Front" image open, you can repeat this process using as many images as you like. You can even use it on images that are smaller than the Front image.

GETTING RID OF CAMERA NOISE

If you've ever taken digital camera shots using exposures longer than one second, or cranked up the camera's ISO ("film speed") rating, chances are you've seen lots of squiggly little lines and patterns in the darker or smoother-shaded portions of

FIGURE 3-1

The second image is exactly proportional to the original and will be resampled to the same size.

the image. It's an effect that looks a lot like what happens when you shoot high-speed film and then over-process it in a conventional darkroom.

Sometimes this can be a desirable effect—for instance, if you want the shot to look like it was taken under adverse conditions. Most of the time, though, you'll wish the graininess weren't there. If you want to minimize it, several Photoshop techniques can help. None of these is ideal for all situations, so you'll have to choose the one you think best for a particular image. In fact, there are times when a combination of these techniques will prove to be what you're looking for. For example, you can

- Blur one or both of the color channels when the image is in Lab mode
- Use the Median filter
- Use the Despeckle filter
- Use the new Remove Noise filter
- Retouch Small Areas with the Healing Brush
- Use Stuck Pixel Noise Reduction

The following is an example of a noisy image, which has been cropped and enlarged to better illustrate the problem.

REMOVE NOISE IN LAB COLOR MODE

Lab color mode differs from RGB mode in that the two channels that carry color information (channels a and b) are entirely separate from the channel that carries the information affecting sharpness (called the l channel, for Lightness). Fortunately, most of the noise exists in one or the other of the two color channels (most likely, the b channel). Because image noise (a grainy appearance to the image) can be caused by a variety of circumstances, you should experiment with blurring one, the other, or both color channels for any given image. Also, if there is graininess in the picture that is monochromatic (that is, the color is interrupted only by white space between the "grains"), this exercise will have no effect.

> NOTE If you frequently encounter noise problems, you might want to consider purchasing a Photoshop plug-in called Grain Surgery.

To Remove NOISE IN LAB COLOR MODE:

1 Choose Image | Mode | Lab color.

2 Select Window | Show Channels. The Channels palette comes to the front (or appears), as shown here.

3 Click the Channel bar to select the color channel you want to blur (either a or b, or eventually both). You will see a murky grayscale version of the image.

4 Choose Filter | Blur | Gaussian Blur. The Gaussian Blur dialog appears.

5 Enter 2 or 3 in the Radius field and click OK. The image in the channel will probably blur enough to make the noise blend.

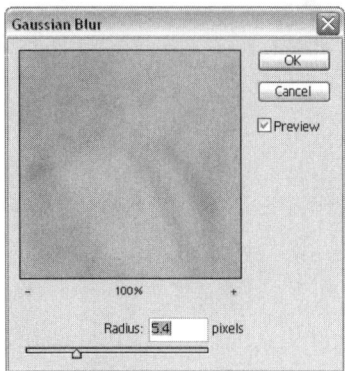

On the Channels palette, click to select the Lab Channel bar. You will see the full-color image. If the noise is still unacceptable, repeat steps 3 through 5 on the other Color channel, then look at the Lab channel again to check your result.

SIZING FOR VERSATILITY

To ensure that you can use your altered image in as many ways as possible, it's a good idea to set the resolution values to those you'll use (or start with) most frequently. The idea is to be sure you store your base image at the highest possible quality and resolution, given the alterations that you've already made to it. This way, you will always know the dimensions of your image at optimum, non-resized quality. Afterward, you will have a better idea of how much resizing is required when you need to reuse the image for different purposes and output devices—that is, before you do any or all of the other operations described in later chapters.

In case you don't understand why this section comes at this stage, I'll try to put it another way. At this point, you've just finished disposing of all the pixels you're likely to dispose of in the base version of the image. By "base version," I mean the version that could be the basis for different interpretations derived from the original for different audiences. You may want to turn one version into a painting through the use of special effects filters or paintbrushes. You might want to create another version using high-contrast and super-saturated colors to grab attention for an ad. You'll almost certainly want to reduce the same images for use in onscreen presentations or on the Web. The time to do this is now—not *before* you've thrown away all those pixels and made all those changes.

Your concern about image resolution may not be great at this stage, but that's only because you may be unaware (so far) of how many things depend on an image's resolution. For instance, optimum output resolution is different for different output devices and printing methods. For our immediate purposes, it's a good idea to store our images at the optimal resolution for our most frequently used high-quality output option. That's because, if you do so, when you open the image and look at the Image Size dialog you'll know immediately at what size the image looks best. Then, if you need a lower-quality image, it's easy to downsize the high-quality original without much loss in detail. On the other hand, you'll immediately know if you can enlarge the image to the needed size without making an unacceptable mess, because I'm going to tell you right now that you can't expect to do that using Photoshop alone if you have to resize the image more than 100 percent.

For instance, for Epson printers, optimum image resolution is 240 dots per inch. That's because, in higher-quality modes, the printer prints 720 dpi (dots per inch) horizontally. Vertical resolution may be as high as 2800 dpi, but the difference shows up more in the richness and smoothness of the image than in the amount of perceived detail, so most users discount the vertical resolution when calculating the amount of resolution needed for the original. Given this, if we figure that 720 dpi is the resolution that really matters, we divide that resolution by 3 to get the number of dots needed in the original. This is because 720 is the number of dots printed using all the colors in the printer. However, each dot printed by the printer consists of one dot for each primary color. Then the black and (if present) lighter-colored inks are added on top to bring that dot to the desired shade. Okay, okay, I know this is an oversimplification of inkjet printhead mechanics, but it works well for the purposes at hand. So, no matter which inkjet printer you're using, divide your horizontal resolution by 3 in order to get the optimal image resolution for that printer. The Image Size dialog is shown here.

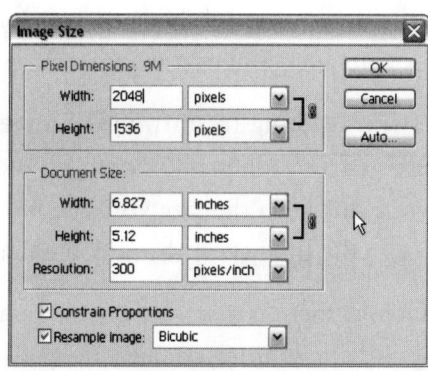

If you're more likely to want your images printed on a printing press, the optimum resolution for a 133 line screen is about 266 ppi (pixels per inch). Some high-quality publications use higher-frequency line screens, which tend to top out at around 150 lpi (lines per inch). The rule of thumb here is to set your image resolution at around 150 to 200 percent of your line screen frequency, which is expressed in lines per inch. A lot of folks simply set their primary archival image (the image you should have after you've followed all the recommendations in this chapter) resolution to 300 dpi.

To Set THE RESOLUTION FOR YOUR PRIMARY ARCHIVAL IMAGE:

▌ Choose Image | Image Size. The Image Size dialog opens.

2 Immediately uncheck the Resample Image check box. This ensures that any change you make in the Resolution field will automatically result in the correct dimensions for an optimum print appearing in the Height and Width fields in the Document Size area.

3 Type the choice you've made for optimal resolution in the Resolution field.

In the future, if you want to print at a different size, choose Image | Image Size. In the Image Size dialog, make sure the Constrain Proportions box is checked, then change either the Height or Width to the desired measurement, making sure the Resample Image box is still unchecked. Two things will happen: The resolution will change; and the dimension you didn't enter will be entered automatically. If you uncheck the Constrain Proportions box and enter both dimensions, the image is likely to be stretched in one dimension or another.

You're probably asking, why not resize the image to a higher resolution? First of all, if you do, you'll complicate what it takes to determine the size at which your image will print. You can do this in your Page Setup dialog, but you won't be printing at optimal resolution. Second, lying to your printer about how much information is actually in your image won't improve the print quality. In fact, it may slightly degrade it.

If you're going to start with a lower-quality image and then add brush strokes, elements from other photographs, and special effects, by all means resize (resample) your image to the size you intend *before* adding those enhancements. Then, at least, the quality of the added enhancements will be as high as possible.

Finally, there is a way to create a higher-than-optimal quality resolution image that maintains sharper, smoother edges than even Photoshop's excellent bipolar resampling can produce. That is, by purchasing a third-party product (such as Genuine Fractals PrintShop or S-Spline for enhancing the edges) that uses advanced techniques. Because these programs know how to produce images with smooth-looking, yet sharp edges, they can do a very good job of creating the illusion that the image is much more detailed than it actually is. You can learn more about programs like Genuine Fractals PrintShop and S-Spline by visiting their web sites at www.altamira-group.com (for Genuine Fractals) and www.ixalance.com/products (for S-Spline).

 ON THE VIRTUAL CLASSROOM CD-ROM In Lesson 2, "Cropping, Sizing, and Correcting Distortion," I show you how to crop an image using the crop tool—and how to correct perspective distortion in an image that's already been cropped.

Picture Perfect Retouching

This chapter demonstrates quick solutions to the most commonly needed categories of photo manipulation: the removal of things that don't flatter the person or scene. This includes such common problems as red eye (the demon eyes that result from the built-in flash in point-and-shoot cameras), scratches and dust that result from mishandled film, pimples and other skin problems in portraits, and parts of the image that detract from the strength of the composition. (Think trash on the lawn or an elbow sticking into the frame.) You will even learn to blur an overly busy background when your digital camera has kept everything in focus from three inches to infinity.

Using the Clone Tool

Up until Photoshop 7, the primary tool used in retouching has been a brush called the Clone tool...and it is still very important. I've started with this approach so that those who aren't all that familiar with it will better understand the Clone tool's close relationship to the brand new and very powerful Healing tool. The Clone tool can have all the shapes and characteristics of any other brush. For a map to all the functions of the Clone tool's Options Bar, see Figure 4-1. The function of each of the Options Bar's components is explained here.

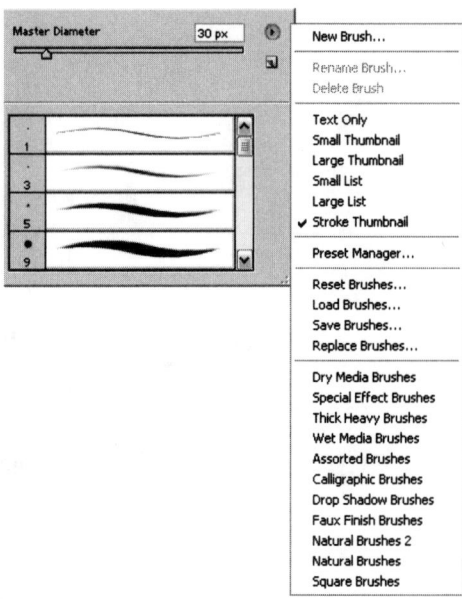

▶ **Reset Tool button** Click to choose between resetting all the Clone tool's options to their defaults and resetting all the Options Bars to their defaults.

▶ **Current Brush** This button shows the diameter of the current brush in pixels and illustrates whether the brush is hard-edged or feathered. Click the icon to reveal the Brush Options dialog (shown here), which lets you customize the size, feathering (edge hardness), spacing, angle, and roundness of the brush. Clicking the New Preset button lets you create a new preset brush by modifying the characteristics of the currently chosen brush. The Brush Name dialog appears. Enter a name for the new brush, then use the Brushes Palette to change the characteristics of that brush

▶ **Brushes Palette button** Click the button to bring up the Brushes palette. From here, you can choose any of the brushes by clicking its icon. If you double-click a

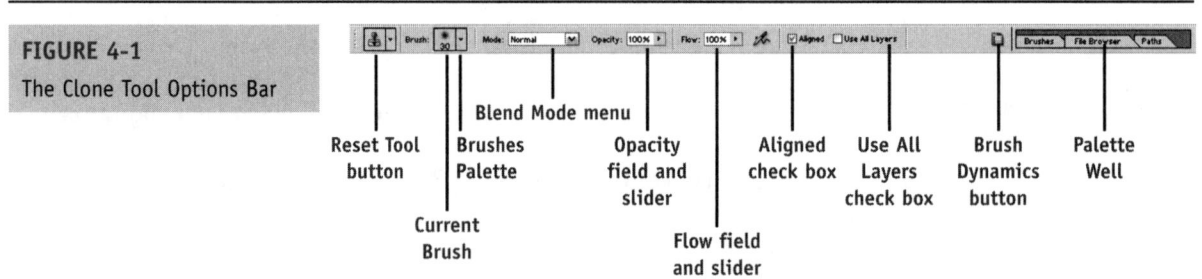

FIGURE 4-1
The Clone Tool Options Bar

Reset Tool button
Brushes Palette
Current Brush
Blend Mode menu
Opacity field and slider
Flow field and slider
Aligned check box
Use All Layers check box
Brush Dynamics button
Palette Well

brush icon, the Brush Name dialog appears so you can name the brush.

NOTE **You can also bring up the Brushes palette alongside your current cursor position by CTRL/-right-clicking while stroking.**

▶ **Blend Mode menu** These are essentially the same blend modes that apply to layers, and they react the same way when the color from the brush is overlaid on the image on the active layer. (The active layer is the one that is highlighted in the Layers palette.) For an explanation of how to use and preview Blend modes, see Chapter 5. The Blend Mode menu is shown here.

▶ **Opacity field and slider** The Opacity field and slider let you change the opacity (how much of the original you can see through the brush stroke) of the clone. You can type an exact percentage of opacity into the field or adjust opacity interactively by dragging the slider. If you're using a pressure-sensitive brush, you can have the brush pressure control the opacity (see the "Brush Dynamics button" entry that follows).

▶ **Aligned check box** This box lets you determine whether cloning is aligned or not. If cloning is aligned, the brush will always copy material that is at the same distance and angle from the original as from the brush. To copy an entire object to a specific place, no matter how many strokes it takes, *uncheck* the Aligned check box.

| Normal |
| Dissolve |
| Behind |
| |
| Darken |
| Multiply |
| Color Burn |
| Linear Burn |
| |
| Lighten |
| Screen |
| Color Dodge |
| Linear Dodge |
| |
| Overlay |
| Soft Light |
| Hard Light |
| Vivid Light |
| Linear Light |
| Pin Light |
| |
| Difference |
| Exclusion |
| |
| Hue |
| Saturation |
| Color |
| Luminosity |

▶ **Use All Layers check box** If you want to pick up any material that's visible (in other words, not hidden by a layer above), check this box. This is especially handy if you have created an extended area by selecting, cutting, and pasting large areas into a foreground or background and you want to blend those areas together by retouching with the Clone tool. Then you can clone from any of the areas you can see onto the borders between layers. (Be sure the Preserve Transparency check boxes for the layers in question are unchecked.)

NOTE **You can achieve the same effect by creating a new layer, then setting the Blend mode for the layer while leaving the brush in Normal mode. If you then paint (or clone) onto the new layer, you can change the transparency of the brush strokes, change the Blend mode, or erase the blend later.**

▶ **Brush Dynamics button** This button brings up a menu that controls how the brush will behave when used with a pressure-sensitive pen and tablet. For most brushes, there are three submenus on this menu, and each of these menus presents the same three choices. The submenus are Size, Opacity, and Color (not a choice for the Clone tool because the color is always that of the original image). The choices are Off, Fade, and Stylus. These settings let you change the opacity, size, and color of the stroke—even if you have to paint with a mouse. They also control which of the stroke's characteristics will be pressure-controlled if you are using a pressure-sensitive stylus instead of a mouse. If you choose Off, the stylus has no effect, and the stroke stays at the same intensity no matter how long the stroke is. If you choose Fade, you can also enter the number of brush diameters it will take for the stroke to blend from 100 percent to 0 percent of the size, opacity, or color. In other words, it will take a longer stroke for a large brush than for a smaller brush if each is fading over the same number of steps. The Brush Dynamics palette is shown here.

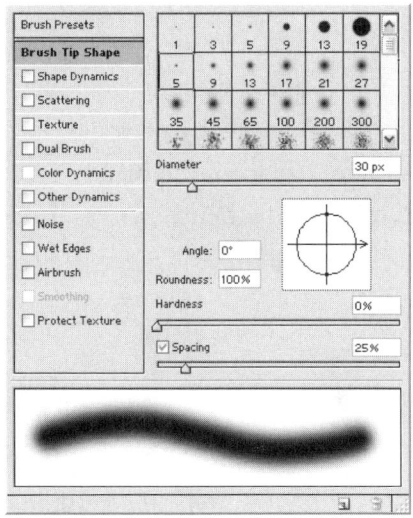

▶ **Palette Well** This rectangle gives you a way to keep palettes readily available without crowding the screen space you have available for working on your image. By default, the File Browser and Brushes palettes will be found in the Palette Well—provided your screen resolution is more than 800x600. You can also drag any open palette into the Palette Well and it will reappear there the next time you open Photoshop. Conversely, you can take any palette out of the Palette Well by dragging the palette into the workspace and then closing it by clicking the Close button.

RETOUCHING PORTRAITS WITH THE CLONE TOOL

The Clone tool is a good way to get rid of the most noticeable skin defects, such as deep wrinkles, pimples, wounds, and moles. The technique demonstrated here is also excellent for removing unwanted objects (such as debris) in other types of photos, such as landscapes. The new Healing Brush often does a better job on some of these problems. You'll have to try both for a while to decide when one is more appropriate for your situation. I find that it often works best to repair major damage first with the Clone tool, then fix any minor details or discolorations with the Healing Brush (more about that later).

When using the Clone tool for eliminating skin defects, there are a few "rules" you should remember:

▶ Make sure the Aligned box is checked.

▶ Keep relocating the anchor point so you don't clone repetitive patterns into the picture.

▶ Feather your brush heavily so no border appears at the edge of the clone stroke.

Some people rely solely on the clone tool for retouching skin in portraits. You can certainly use it for most of a job, but I prefer to use the "Retouching with Layers" technique described later for smoothing out small skin discolorations and age spots, a task which the Healing Brush is often even better suited for. Along those same lines, the Burn and Dodge tools are more suitable for eliminating bags under eyes and for brightening eyes. Similar techniques can be used to remove unwanted details from virtually any kind of image, or to get rid of dust and specks in images you are restoring.

The Clone tool is helpful for reshaping objects—for instance, straightening a nose. You use the same basic technique described here, but you start by making a selection around the area you want to be the new shape and then inverting the selection so the area is protected. You can then clone the surrounding background to cover the part of the object that you want to make smaller.

We will start with the portrait of Deborah Rombaut, a San Francisco model and actress, shown in Figure 4-2. Beautiful as Deborah is, this is not a terrific photo of her, so there is still some work to do to rid her picture of skin defects and discoloration that would be barely noticeable off camera.

FIGURE 4-2
An unretouched portrait
of Deborah

To Get Rid OF LARGER SKIN DEFECTS:

1 You should do all your retouching at 100 percent magnification of the image to ensure that your blending of retouching strokes looks entirely natural. You also want to be sure you didn't miss anything or create any visible "seams" between retouched areas and the original. The quickest way to zoom to 100 percent is to double-click the Zoom tool.

2 Before you get started cloning, it's a good idea to make sure the preferences have been set for your cursor to show the chosen brush size. This way, you get a good idea of how much area the brush will be copying as you use it. To do this, choose Edit | Preferences | Display and Cursors. When the Display and Cursors dialog appears, click to Activate the radio button labeled Brush Size. For the purposes of this exercise, you can leave the other settings as they are and click OK.

3 If your screen now shows only a portion of the image, Choose Window | Show Navigator. The Navigator palette appears. From here, you can move to any portion of the image without changing its size. Simply drag the red box in the preview window to the portion of the image you want to examine and edit.

4 Click to choose the Clone tool from the Toolbox. By default, it is usually the top icon, but it may be hidden by the Pattern Stamp tool. If that's the case, click and drag until a flyout menu appears, then drag to choose the Clone tool.

5 On the Options Bar, make sure that the Opacity is set to 100 percent and that the Blend mode is Normal. Also, be sure that the Aligned box is checked.

6 Place the cursor near the first mole, pimple, or freckle you want to eliminate. CTRL-right-click, and the Brushes palette appears.

7 Choose a brush that's approximately the size of the defect and that has fully-feathered edges.

8 Move the cursor to an area that is the same color, brightness, and texture as the skin surrounding the defect. This is the area you want to paint into the defect. Press OPT/ALT and simultaneously click to make this the anchor point.

9 Move the cursor over the defect and click. Presto—the defect disappears. You can probably remove several other small defects before you have to re-anchor the cursor. Notice that as you move the cursor, it is accompanied by a small cross. The cross indicates the target from which information will be copied into the brush area.

10 From time-to-time you will discover that you've cloned from an area that is too dark or too light, or that simply doesn't match the texture of the area surrounding the defect. In such cases, press CMD/CTRL-Z to undo that stroke. Then find another area to clone from, and set the anchor point there. See Figure 4-3 for the final look.

CLONING FROM A DIFFERENT LAYER OR A DIFFERENT PICTURE

If you simply can't find an area that matches the current picture, you may find one that exists in another frame from the same shoot. You may even want to

FIGURE 4-3
Deborah's portrait, repaired with the Clone tool

clone a texture or details into the background from another picture. I usually find that it's better to do such cloning onto a transparent layer immediately above the image I'm retouching. This makes it possible for me to erase anything I don't like without affecting the image itself. It also provides a way to adjust the results by changing the transparency or Blend mode of the clone layer.

In this instance, I'm going to add a texture pattern to the background of the image (see Figure 4-4) by cloning a leaf from another image. I could simply open the other image, make it active, then set my anchor point on the active image. From there, I could make the target image active and start cloning. However, I find it easier to copy the other image onto a layer of the image that I want to clone to. This way, I can scale the image I'm cloning from to any size before I start cloning the component. When I'm through cloning, I can delete the layer I've cloned from, thus saving file space. Another advantage is that I can change all sorts of characteristics of the layer without affecting the original image. This advantage is especially valuable when you need to change the exposure and color balance of the anchor image to match that of the target image.

You can use this technique to do such things as painting parts of trees into landscapes or clouds into skies, or using just about anything else to cover up something in the target image. When you use this method, there are two secrets to the success:

▶ Adjust the exposure, brightness range, and color balance of the anchor image to match the target image.

FIGURE 4-4
Deborah surrounded by the
cloned leaf texture

▶ Scale the anchor image layer so the size of the texture or object you are cloning "fits into" the target layer of the clone.

To Clone THE LEAVES INTO THE BACKGROUND OF DEBORAH'S PORTRAIT:

1 While the portrait of Deborah is open, open the image of the leaf. Make sure the leaf window's title bar is the one that's active (highlighted) by clicking that window.

2 To copy the image of the leaf to a new layer in the portrait of Deborah, choose Edit | Select All (or press CMD/CTRL-A). A marquee will appear around the entire image.

3 Choose Edit | Copy (or press CMD/CTRL-C) to copy the leaf image to the system clipboard. Then close the leaf image.

4 Make sure the portrait of Deborah is the active window, and choose Edit | Paste. The image of the leaf now appears as a new layer above the image of Deborah.

5 Scale the Leaf layer until the leaf is the size you want it to be on the background. (If you want the leaf to appear in several sizes, start with the largest size and clone as many copies as you want in that size, then scale the layer to a smaller size or a clone.)

6 As Deborah is probably in the Background layer, you now want to make that an ordinary layer so you can move the Leaf layer below her. Double-click the Background layer. The New Layer dialog appears. Type Deborah in the Name field and click OK. The Background layer is now named "Deborah" and is a regular layer.

7 On the Layers palette, drag the Leaf layer to a position in the stack below the image of Deborah. Now we can no longer see the leaf. The illustration here shows the Layers palette with the Leaf layer selected and the Portrait layer turned off.

8 Turn off the Deborah layer by clicking the Eyeball (Layer Visibility) icon.

9 Choose the Clone tool. Make sure the Aligned check box is unchecked. Set the other options according to your preferences.

10 Make sure the Leaf layer is active. If its Name bar on the Layers palette isn't high-lighted, click it. Place the cursor over the leaf you want to clone, and press OPT/ALT and simultaneously click to set the anchor point. Since the anchor point isn't aligned, you'll be able to paint copies of the leaf anywhere.

11 Click the Layer Visibility box on the Deborah layer until the Eyeball icon appears so you can see the layer again.

12 Create a new layer above the Deborah layer by choosing Layer | New Layer (SHIFT-CMD/CTRL-N) or New Layer from the Layer Palette menu or by clicking the New Layer icon at the bottom of the Layers palette. On the Layers palette, check to make sure the Lock Transparency box (the checkerboard icon) is unchecked.

13 With the new transparent layer active, position the cursor anywhere you want to paint a leaf, and then stroke as many times as necessary to paint a copy of the leaf on the Deborah layer. You can paint additional leaves wherever you like.

14 If there are leaves overlapping Deborah, use the Eraser tool to remove the overlapping portions.

15 On the Layers palette, enter the desired amount of transparency for the leaves by dragging the Opacity slider. The Opacity slider appears when you click the button at the right of the Opacity field. You can also experiment with Blend modes by pressing SHIFT while repeatedly pressing the + key to cycle through the Blend Mode menu choices. If you see one you like, stop pressing the keys.

16 When you've finished, drag the Leaf layer's Name bar to the Trashcan icon at the bottom of the Layers palette to delete it.

RETOUCHING WITH THE HEALING BRUSH

The Healing Brush acts so much like the Clone tool that you might think at first that they do exactly the same thing. Not so. When you choose the Healing Brush, Photoshop 7 asks you to set an anchor point, just as you do with the Clone tool. You then brush over the area that needs to be "healed." For a moment, it looks as though you've cloned from the anchor point, just as you do with the Clone tool, but then your brushwork starts miraculously blending with its surroundings until any color or shape you've brushed in starts fading into the surroundings. All you're left with is the texture from the area surrounding the anchor point, blending with the color and shading of the area surrounding the blemish. It looks like magic, and it is.

To Heal A PARTICULAR AREA OF YOUR IMAGE:

1 Load the original image of Deborah.

FIGURE 4-5
Deborah before the Healing Brush

2 Choose Image | Duplicate to make a copy of the original, and then close the original.

3 Double-click the Zoom tool so the picture is seen at 100 percent magnification. This makes it much easier to spot small defects.

4 Choose the Healing Brush. The Healing Brush Options Bar is shown here:

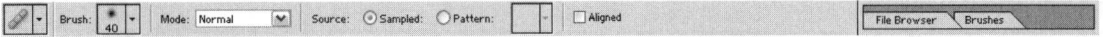

5 In the Options Bar, choose a brush size that is just large enough to cover a typical "pimplet." You can make the brush larger by pressing the [key, or smaller by pressing the] key.

6 Move the cursor to an area that typifies the skin texture and grain of the area you want to retouch. Press OPT/ALT and click to set the anchor point for the texture. The cursor becomes a cross hair.

7 Scrub (drag back and forth) the area you want to repair.

8 Wait...it takes the computer a little time to calculate the repair. Meanwhile, the area you just scrubbed looks discolored and strange...then...Vavoom! Perfect skin, perfect texture. (See Figure 4-6.)

RETOUCHING WITH LAYERS

There are many ways you can use layers to help retouch a photo, and you can do this more flexibly than if you retouch the image directly. That's because, as I men-

FIGURE 4-6
Deborah after the Healing Brush

tioned earlier, you can change the layer's Blend mode and opacity at any time after you've finished retouching, and the layer you've retouched will simply revert to its original state. You can also just delete the retouching layer and start over. In addition, you can easily match blurring and sharpening in a variety of small areas all at once. Powerful stuff, indeed.

AIRBRUSHING OUT TINY SKIN DEFECTS IN GLAMOUR PORTRAITS

This technique is very similar to the one described next for eliminating scratches and dust when you're restoring old, damaged photos. It is more appropriate than the Clone tool when you don't want the retouching to show any texture—just glamorized, pearlescent surfaces.

In fact, most of the techniques in this book are useful for working on image types other than the one described here. (The actual photo is shown in Figure 4-7.) However, the technique is most often used for glamour portraits.

This technique works by duplicating the layer to be repaired, blurring the original with the Gaussian Blur filter until the small defects disappear, using the Add Noise filter to match the

> **NOTE** Be sure you have cloned out all the larger and significantly darker or lighter defects before you start this process. Otherwise, you will have darker or lighter areas that don't blend. (See "Retouching Portraits with the Clone Tool" earlier in this chapter.)

FIGURE 4-7
Deborah before airbrushing

original grain in the blurred filter, and then erasing through the original image to reveal the smoothed and blurred layer beneath it.

To Airbrush Out DEFECTS WHILE ADDING A CERTAIN GLOW TO THE SKIN:

1 If the Layers palette isn't already visible, choose Windows | Show Layers.

2 Make sure the image you want to retouch isn't on the Background layer. If that's the case, you can skip this step. If it is on the Background layer, CTRL/right-click the layer's Name bar. The Layer Properties dialog appears.

3 Enter Original Image in the Name field. Click OK.

4 Drag the Original Image layer bar to the New Layer icon at the bottom of the Layers palette. A new layer will appear just above the original layer. CTRL/right-click its Name bar. The Layer Properties dialog appears. Enter Blur in the Name field and click OK.

5 Choose Filter | Blur | Gaussian Blur. The Gaussian Blur dialog appears. In the Radius field, enter just enough of a radius to make the discoloration of skin blemishes blend with the surrounding colors. In Deborah's case, the radius is 4. Click OK.

6 On the Layers palette, drag the Blur layer's Name bar below the Original Image layer's Name bar.

7 Click the Original Image layer's Name bar to make that layer active.

8 Double-click the Zoom tool to increase the image magnification to 100 percent (something you should always do when retouching so you can immediately spot less-than-perfect blending between original and retouched areas).

9 Choose the Eraser tool. On the Eraser tool Options Bar, choose Brush from the Mode menu and make sure 100 percent is entered in the Opacity field.

10 Click to open the Brush Preset picker button (the small down arrow to the right of the brush-shaped icon). The Brush Picker palette appears. Choose the size and style of the brush closest to the size of the defects you want to erase. If you want most of the skin to take on a somewhat surrealistic glow, choose a large brush. If you just want to smooth small details, choose a smaller brush.

11 Erase little blemishes, tiny wrinkles, and anything else that makes the skin look mottled or unattractive.

12 Since you are working at a 100 percent zoom, you will probably need to pan around the image often in order to work on the entire face. The easiest way to do this is to press the SPACEBAR as you are erasing. The cursor will immediately change to the Hand tool as long as the SPACEBAR is depressed. Then, just drag to pan around the image.

> **NOTE** If you want the background to be a little more out of focus, you can also erase it away. A more sophisticated technique is explained later, in "Creating Photorealistic Depth-of-Field Effects."

13 Once you have done some erasing, you will probably notice that the "grain" or texture of the portions that have been smoothed don't match that of the original. To fix this, click the Blur layer's Name bar to activate that layer, then choose Filter | Noise | Add Noise. The Add Noise dialog appears. Pictured here is the Add Noise dialog matching the original grain pattern.

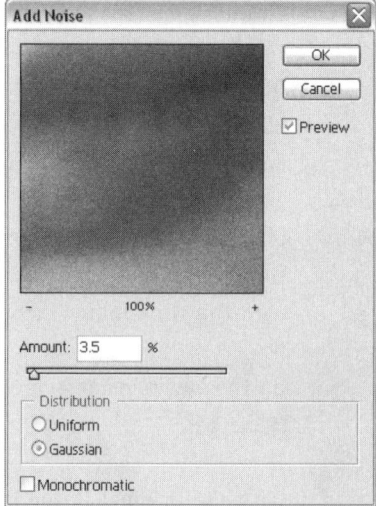

14 Make sure the Gaussian radio button is black by clicking it. In the Amount field, enter the same number as the number of pixels that you blurred on the layer. Examine the areas you've erased. If the texture inside them is now too coarse, enter one number lower. Be sure the Preview box is checked so you can immediately see when the texture matches. When it does, click OK.

15 Continue panning around the image and erasing blemishes until you're happy with the overall effect (see Figure 4-8). There will

FIGURE 4-8
Deborah after airbrush
retouching

still be some areas that are too light or dark, but I'll show you how to fix these in another exercise. Be sure to save the image at this stage so you can start at this point in the "Retouching from History" lesson that comes later in the chapter.)

ELIMINATING SCRATCHES AND DUST WITHOUT LOSING IMAGE SHARPNESS

This technique is also excellent for eliminating small irregularities in skin textures in glamour portraits. The advantage is that Photoshop's Dust & Scratches filter only blurs areas that contrast with the surrounding region (think of those little white dust specks that show up most in the darker areas of the picture), so there's not as much overall blurring. That's a good thing when you want to maintain overall sharpness to the greatest extent possible.

The Dust & Scratches filter does a pretty decent job of eliminating minor scratches and dust in one quick and easy operation.

To Eliminate SCRATCHES AND DUST:

1 Open the Dusty.jpg image (Figure 4-9) on the CD-ROM.

2 Duplicate the Background Layer.

3 Select the top layer.

FIGURE 4-9
The Dusty.jpg image before retouching

4 Choose Filter | Noise | Dust & Scratches. The Dust & Scratches dialog appears.

5 Make sure the Preview box is checked, and drag the Radius slider to the right. Stop just at the point where you can't eliminate any more defects by blurring the image further. Better yet, stop at the point where only a few of the largest defects are still visible. It's sometimes best to use the Clone tool retouching techniques, demonstrated earlier to remove any big flaws. This way, your overall picture will remain sharper. In the end, you'll find that the correct balance is a matter of experience and personal taste.

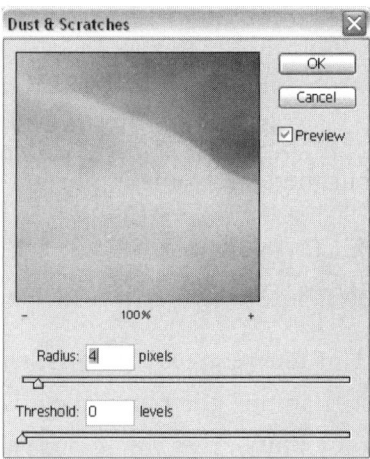

6 Drag the Threshold slider to the point where the image regains as much of its sharpness as possible without causing any of the image to be lost. You may have to experiment a bit with the two sliders in order to get the best compromise between image sharpness and lack of defects. When you arrive at that point, click OK. You've done as much as you can with this filter.

7 If there are still areas in the image that aren't as sharp as you'd like them to be, choose the Eraser tool. On the Options Bar, set the Eraser at 100% Opacity in Paintbrush mode. Choose the smallest brush size that will erase the details you want to eliminate.

8 Look for important areas that aren't quite sharp enough and erase just enough so the original image shows through (see Figure 4-10). You may pick up a few more defects, but you can clone them out after you've flattened the image.

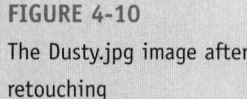

FIGURE 4-10
The Dusty.jpg image after retouching

RETOUCHING FROM HISTORY

Photoshop's History Brush tool allows you to paint from any state in the History palette. It's a lot like painting with the Clone tool from another layer or image, but there are some important differences:

▶ You can't scale or move the History state.

▶ You can take a snapshot of the image at any History state and then delete the state.

▶ You don't have to have an extra layer, so there's no worry about stacking order.

One especially good use I've found for painting from History is adding in small details after making a change in the layer that contains the original image. I can make whatever editing changes I like, take a snapshot of the layer at that state, and then revert the original to its original state by deleting the History palette states that represent the steps I took in altering the original. I can then add the changes I'd like to make to specific areas of the image by choosing the History Brush and painting them back in.

In the next example (Figure 4-11), I'm going to sharpen Deborah's irises and eyelashes, and a few strands of her hair. This will give an impression of a very sharp picture, even though we have used several softening techniques.

NOTE We could also do retouching by selecting those areas that we wanted to correct and then sharpening them. However, the History Brush method is faster and provides much more flexibility in how you apply the end result.

FIGURE 4-11

Deborah after airbrushing and before localized sharpening

To Sharpen YOUR IMAGE:

1 Open Sharpen.psd from the CD. (This exercise assumes you saved the image from the "Retouching with Layers" exercise earlier in this chapter.)

2 Click the original image layer's Name bar to activate it.

3 Drag the original image layer's Name bar to the New Layer icon at the bottom of the Layers palette to activate it.

4 Double-click the new layer's Name bar and rename the layer Sharpen.

5 Click the Eye icons in the other layers to turn them off so you can see the original layer.

6 Double-click the Zoom tool to enlarge the image to 100 percent. Press the SPACEBAR to pan and move the image until one of the eyes is at the center of the window.

7 Choose Filter | Sharpen | Unsharp Mask. The Unsharp Mask dialog opens, as shown here.

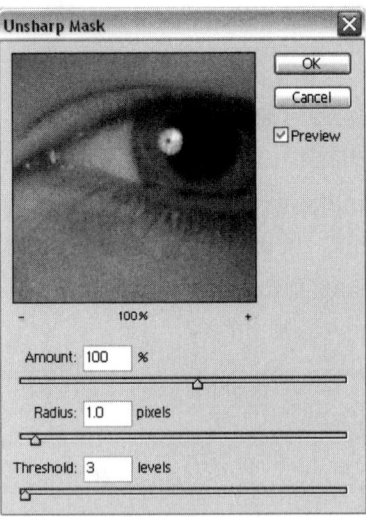

8 Check the Preview box so you can see the results of your adjustments. For a good start with most images, try 100% in the Amount field, and 1 in the Radius field. Leave the Threshold at level 0 or 1. Now you can zero in on the exact effect you want by dragging the sliders while you observe their effect. Drag the sliders until you see exactly the desired degree of sharpening. Since you are at 100%, you should be able to tell exactly when you have over-sharpened. (Curves will get jagged and a halo will appear when edges contrast strongly.) When you're satisfied, click OK to render the sharpening.

> TIP Like many other effects in Photoshop, sharpening with the Unsharp Mask dialog is largely a subjective matter.

9 Take a Snapshot of the image in its current state; make sure the layer you just sharpened is still active (highlighted on the Layers palette). Choose Window | Show History (or open the History palette by clicking its tab in the Palette Well, if it's there). From the History palette menu, choose New Shapshot. The New Snapshot dialog appears.

10 Type Sharpened Original in the Name field.

11 From the From menu, choose Current Layer and click OK. A new shapshot will appear near the top of the History palette.

12 To return the original image layer to its original (unsharpened) condition, on the Layers palette, drag the Sharpened layer to the Layers palette's Trashcan (Delete Layer) icon.

13 If there are multiple layers in your file, click each of the Eye icons for the other layers to turn them back on.

14 Click the name bar of the topmost layer to make it active, then click the New Layer icon to place an empty layer at the top of the layer stack.

15 When the new layer appears, rename it Sharpened Areas. Make sure that the Lock Transparency button is not highlighted by clicking it. (If transparency is locked, the rest of this exercise will not work.)

16 Choose the History Brush, then click the box to the left of the Sharpened Original snapshot to make a History Brush icon visible. This indicates that the History Brush will be painting from that state or snapshot.

17 Paint over the areas that you want to sharpen. I chose the eyelashes, eyebrows, and some of the highlights in Deborah's hair that were closest to the camera.

18 Save this image as it is and with its original name, without flattening it. (See Figure 4-12 for the sharpened result.)

FIGURE 4-12
Hair, eyes, brows, and lips have been regionally sharpened.

CHANGING THE EXPOSURE IN SPECIFIC AREAS OF THE IMAGE

The next step in retouching involves lightening and darkening certain areas of the image as a means of correcting or enhancing makeup, lighting, and exposure. The traditional tools for this purpose are the Burn and Dodge tools. They are represented in the Toolbox by icons that show the traditional darkroom tools: a cupped hand for the Burn tool and a piece of round dark cardboard attached to a wire coat hanger for the Dodge tool. In the darkroom, you would darken a portion of the subject by passing more of the enlarger's light through a small hole, often made by leaving just enough space between cupped hands. (This is similar to how the Burn tool works.) Also in the traditional darkroom, you would lighten a portion of the image by holding back part of the light while you were making the main exposure (an operation which the Dodge tool imitates). The process is much easier in Photoshop; because you do it after the fact, you know you've got the main exposure correct before you even start. The Burn and Dodge tools are really brushes, with essentially the same controls in their Options Bars and exactly the same brush palette.

I find the Burn and Dodge tools handy for quick and easy noncritical work, but there's a better method for more exacting work—especially if you might want to make changes later. In case you haven't guessed, it involves painting in either black or white on a separate layer whose Blend mode has been set to Soft Light. This Soft Light layer is placed at the top of the layers stack so that your work affects all the visible layers below it. You can then change the opacity of the layer to intensify or lessen the effect, erase any changes you don't like, or paint over them to modify them. You can even blur or sharpen them.

If you look at Deborah's portrait (in Figure 4-13) as it is at this stage, it looks pretty good. I would, however, like to remove the highlight from the shadow side of her nose. Burning and dodging with the Burn and Dodge tools will take care of that.

To Use THE BURN AND DODGE TOOLS:

1 Choose the Burn tool. In its Options Bar, lower the opacity to around 17%. Also, if you are working with a pressure-sensitive tablet (which I can't recommend enough for anyone working in Photoshop), click the Brush Dynamics icon (it resembles a brush with a down arrow on the left side of the Options Bar) to open the menu. From the Size and Pressure menus, choose Stylus. Open the Color menu and choose Off.

2 Now you're all set to burn and dodge. For each area you want to change, choose a brush that's highly feathered and that's large enough to cover most of the area in question for any given change. Start large and work down to small. (This way you're less likely to get streaking.)

3 Start with the highlight on the right size of Deborah's nose. Zoom to 100 percent and choose a brush size of about 30. Darken the shadow side of the nose.

4 I lessened the intensity of the highlight on the right side of her nose by reducing the Opacity to 5%, cutting the size of the brush in half (you can change brush sizes very

FIGURE 4-13
Deborah before burning and dodging

quickly by pressing the [key for a smaller brush and the] key for a larger brush), and then painting over the highlight until the strokes blended smoothly.

5 To take away the redness and the bags under the eyes, choose the Dodge tool. (See Figure 4-14 to view the improvement.)

RESHAPING THE SUBJECT

One problem that often crops up when the aim of your photograph is to idealize someone or something is that part of that someone or something looks too big or too small in relationship to the rest of the image.

You've already seen how you can use the Free Transform command to stretch, scale, and distort an entire object. But the Transform command doesn't help much when you want to shrink a waist or straighten a nose, because the rest of the face or body is changed as well.

RESHAPING WITH THE LIQUIFY COMMAND

In version 6.0, Photoshop came to the rescue by including a new plug-in called Liquify. The Liquify plug-in doesn't appear on the Filters menu (except in Photoshop Elements). Instead, it shows up on the Image menu. What is does is let you shmoosh pixels around as though the image were printed on stretchy plastic or gelatin. The image in Figure 4-15 originated as a landscape photograph, but it was turned into an abstract by means of the Liquify command.

FIGURE 4-14
Deborah after burning and dodging

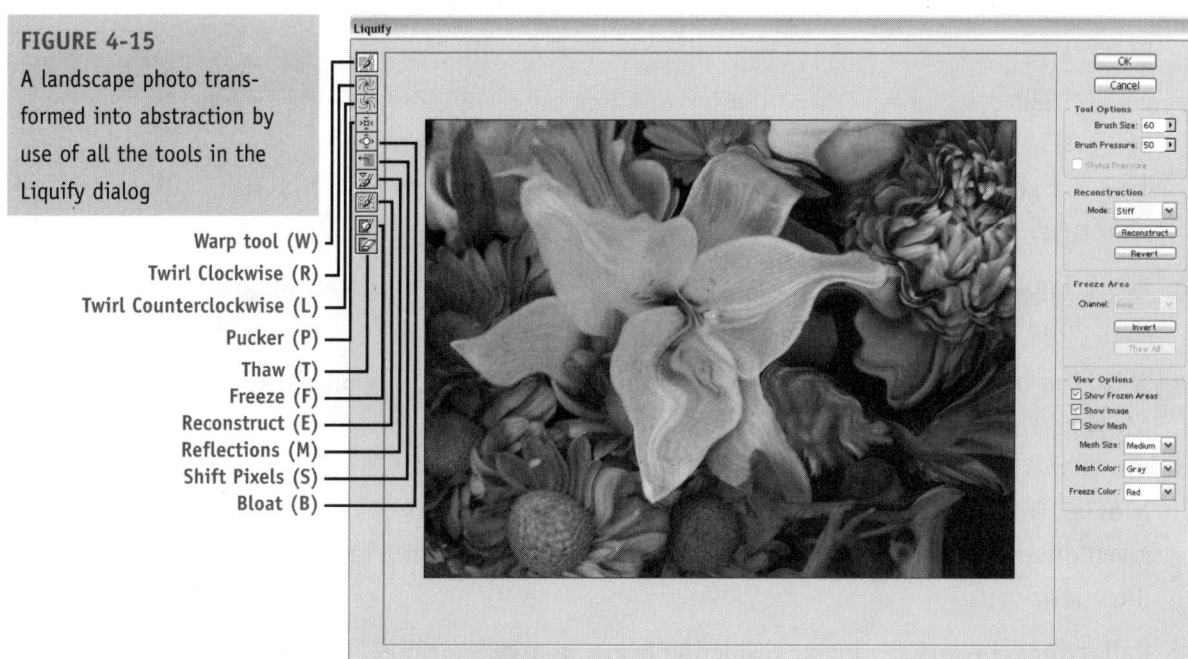

FIGURE 4-15

A landscape photo transformed into abstraction by use of all the tools in the Liquify dialog

Warp tool (W)
Twirl Clockwise (R)
Twirl Counterclockwise (L)
Pucker (P)
Thaw (T)
Freeze (F)
Reconstruct (E)
Reflections (M)
Shift Pixels (S)
Bloat (B)

The Liquify command brings up a dialog that fills the entire screen. The image appears inside a large preview window, and you can use a Zoom tool much like the one in the Toolbox to zoom in and out when you need to work on small details.

The Liquify dialog is shown in Figure 4-15. Notice that there are ten Liquify tools to the left of the workspace. Since the operations I'm going to show you for changing shapes as a retouching technique barely scratch the surface of what you can do with the Liquify command, I'll at least give you a tour of what each tool does and how to use it.

> **NOTE** You cannot zoom in using the Liquify window. If you want to work on only a small portion of the image and be able to see it up close, use the Lasso tool to select just the area that you want to shrink, stretch, or move. Since only pixels inside the selection can be liquified, be sure to feather the selection. This will cause the image to be gradually stretched away from the selection border.

▶ **Warp** Acts a lot like the Smudge tool, pulling pixels along behind the cursor as you drag.

▶ **Twirl Clockwise** Creates a whirlpool of pixels that becomes more noticeable the longer you hold down the mouse key or push on the pen. Use the twirl tool to make waves or whirlpools. Experiment with what happens when you drag, click and hold, or make a series of contiguous clicks along a line.

▶ **Twirl Counterclockwise** Behaves exactly like the Twirl Clockwise tool, but in reverse.

▶ **Pucker** Self-descriptive. Draws the surrounding area toward the center of the brush. That is, the image shrinks as it moves toward the center of the brush. This is a good tool to make an eye or a nostril smaller—or to make the fruit on a tree look larger.

▶ **Bloat** Looks like an air bubble has pushed the image outward under the brush. Very good for making cartoon eyes and Walter Keen-style photopaintings.

▶ **Shift Pixels** Pushes pixels 90 degrees to one side of the line in which you drag. Moving from top to bottom pushes pixels to the right. Moving from bottom to top pushes pixels to the left. Moving from left to right pushes pixels upwards. Moving from right to left pushes pixels downwards. To push pixels further in a given direction, use a larger brush or start the stroke over, moving in the same direction.

▶ **Reflections** Inverts the image inside the brush in a very strange, bubbly way. You can make amazing abstractions this way.

▶ **Reconstruct** Gradually returns the stroked area to its original state. This is the tool to use if you overdo it a bit with one of the other tools.

▶ **Freeze** Airbrushes an orange mask color that protects whatever portion of the image is so colored from being distorted by any of the Liquify tools.

▶ **Thaw** Unprotects areas that have been frozen (and unpaints the mask color).

As with all these tools, you'll get a smoother effect with a larger brush. For small changes, use a smaller brush.

To Use A SMALL BRUSH:

1 Open the file.

2 Duplicate the image and flatten it. Close the original.

3 Duplicate the background layer and rename it Reshape.

4 Activate the Reshape layer.

5 Choose Image | Liquify (SHIFT-CMD/CTRL-X). The Liquify dialog opens.

6 Set the brush size at about 60 pixels.

7 Choose the Pucker tool (P) and center it over Deborah's nose. Click and hold briefly and watch her nose narrow slightly.

8 Choose the Bloat tool. Press the] key until the brush circle is large enough to cover the eye on the right side of the picture. Press and hold to enlarge the eye slightly.

9 You can experiment with the other tools all you like, then press OPT/ALT and click the Cancel button to restore the image to its virgin state. Repeat the preceding steps to make the minor shape changes suggested and click OK.

RESHAPING WITH THE CLONE TOOL

If the picture contains something you want to trim, such as a thigh or waist that's too close to the camera, you can use the Pen tool to draw a path that is just the shape of the new silhouette that you want. Then you can turn that path into a selection that will protect the interior shape of the object you are thinning. Finally, you can use the Clone tool to paint the background over the old shape.

To Reshape WITH THE CLONE TOOL:

1 Open the image Deb Reshape.psd (Figure 4-16).

FIGURE 4-16
Deborah before a Photoshop nose job

2 Choose the Pen tool. Click where you want the path to start, and drag in the direction you want the curve to move in. When you want the curve to take a new direction, click again and drag in the new direction. When you want to make a corner, click (but don't drag) and then move the cursor to the next point and either click or click and drag, as appropriate to the shape you want to make.

3 Complete the path by clicking the same spot where you started the path. Now you want to convert the path to a selection. (See Figure 4-17.)

4 Choose Window | Show Paths (or click the Paths palette tab in the Palette Well). The Paths palette will come to the fore. At the bottom of the Paths palette is the Load Path As A Selection button. Click to turn the path into a selection.

5 Press CMD/CTRL-J to lift the selection to a new layer. The new layer will appear just above the original.

5 Choose the Move tool and drag the new layer to where its edge matches the new size of the item you are resizing. You can also transform the new layer to stretch or squeeze the area—or use the Liquify filter to change its shape in just about any way you like.

7 Click the Eyeball icon in the new layer's Name bar to temporarily turn off the new layer.

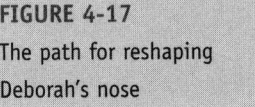

FIGURE 4-17
The path for reshaping
Deborah's nose

8 Choose the Clone tool. Clone information from the background onto the old shape so that only the background will be seen below the new layer when you turn it back on.

9 Click the Eyeball box in the new layer to turn it back on.

10 Choose the Eraser tool, choose Paintbrush from the Mode menu in the Options Bar, and enter 100 in the Opacity field. Choose a fairly large and highly feathered (soft-edged) brush from the Brushes palette. Erase away any hard edges or duplicated information so that the new layer blends better with the former background. (See Figure 4-18 for the dramatic new look.)

> **NOTE** You will normally need to experiment with the Clone and Blur tools in order to smooth skin tones and blend the edges of shapes so the end result looks natural.

There will be times when you'll just need to eliminate the part of a shape that's sticking out in the background. Ordinarily, I fix these problems with the Liquify command. However, there are times when you will need to reshape the area without distorting or changing the texture of the background. One approach would be to draw a path that exactly conforms to the new shape. Make the path so that it encloses the entire area you want to reshape, then convert the path to a selection and lift the selection to a new layer. Next, clone the background so it tucks under

FIGURE 4-18
The reshaped nose

the new shape layer, thus hiding the old shape. You will have lost some highlights and shading on rounded shapes (such as bodies and limbs). Use the Burn and Dodge tools to add the highlights and shading on the new shape layer. Be sure the Lock Transparency box is checked for the new shape layer before you start burning and dodging.

RETOUCHING BY COMPOSITING AND BLENDING

There are many uses for compositing and edge-blending techniques. (These uses and techniques are explained in depth in Chapter 10.) I just want to mention it here because one need not do hyper-complex compositing (as is often required for creating a whole new image from bits and pieces of other images) in order to make an image much more effective. You can often cover the ugly area of a photograph, or improve a boring composition, by adding an object that might have been there in the first place if only the photographer had taken the picture from a different angle or waited a week. I can remember turning a fairly dull shot of an apple tree into a blast of springtime by populating it with apples that I shot at a farmer's market. Or, maybe you just want to move two objects different distances apart. You might go back and reshoot the background at the same time of day without the people, and then just reposition the people in the scene in a way that is more ideal. All of this is very doable in Photoshop. (Just pop over to Chapter 10 to discover the myriad techniques that make it possible. You'll also want to carefully study Chapter 6, which discusses selections and shapes.)

CREATING PHOTOREALISTIC DEPTH-OF-FIELD EFFECTS

Sometimes, everything in an image (no matter how close to, or far from, the camera) is so sharply focused that there is no separation between the main subject and all the confusing detail that surrounds it. The best way to solve this problem is to shoot the subject in a studio against a fairly plain background. Problem is, there are just too many times when that's not a practical solution. I mean, what are you supposed to do if you're covering wild cats in South American jungles? Most photographers solve this kind of problem by shooting at a high shutter speed (which also defeats unwanted motion blur caused by shaky hands) and using a wide-aperture (small f-stop number) to narrow the distance from the lens over which the image will stay sharp.

There are a couple of occasions however, when the traditional "shallow depth-of-field" technique just doesn't work:

▶ The light is too bright to allow for decent exposure with the lens wide open.

▶ The photograph is taken with a digital camera which has a small light sensor requiring that the lens be so close to the sensor that everything is sharp from a couple of feet away to infinity.

No matter what the reason for too much depth of field, Photoshop can rescue the situation. At first glance, this may seem like an easy problem to solve: Just lift the subject from the background onto another layer, and then blur the original layer. It's a technique that works pretty well if:

▶ You're expert enough and careful enough to make an accurate and realistic separation around the subject—even though the subject may be wearing shorts, a long, fur jacket, and a Rasta hairdo. (You'll learn to take care of all that in Chapters 6 and 10, but you'll get some hints here.)

▶ Whatever is in the background is grouped pretty closely together so it seems natural that they're all equally blurry. Unfortunately, this last circumstance is a pretty unnatural one.

Here's a plan for creating much more realistic depth-of-field effects. (Refer to Figure 4-19.)

FIGURE 4-19
The original digital camera depth of field

To Create REALISTIC DEPTH-OF-FIELD EFFECTS:

1 Copy the Background layer and then use the Extract command to remove the subject from its surroundings. (If you're not already familiar with the Extract command, take a look at Chapter 10.)

2 Choose the Lasso tool. Draw a selection that encloses the most distant objects. If those objects aren't all grouped together, press the SHIFT key to make additional selections so that all the areas will be selected at once.

3 Now you are going to invert the selected areas so you can raise the rest of the image to a new layer. Invert the selection by pressing CMD/CTRL-I. Then press CMD/CTRL-J to raise the selection to a new layer.

4 If there are objects in the second layer that are noticeably closer to the camera, repeat steps 2 and 3.

5 You are going to blur the background to throw it out of focus. You need to keep your subjects from blurring outward into the background.

6 Duplicate the Background layer so you can start over if need be. Then turn off all but the duplicated Background layer. Choose the Clone tool and clone the background into your main subjects.

7 Leave your duplicate background selected, but turn on all the layers.

8 Now you're going to start with the farthest layer, blur it, and then work your way up through each succeeding layer, blurring each just a little bit less. Don't blur the top layer at all, since it's the one that contains your subjects. To defocus a layer, choose Filter | Blur | Gaussian Blur. The Gaussian Blur dialog appears.

9 In the Gaussian Blur dialog, make sure the Preview box is checked. Then drag the slider until you see the background go as far out of focus as you'd like. Remember, each time you blur a layer, move up a layer and repeat the process at a somewhat lower blur setting.

10 If the change in focus between layers seems too abrupt, you can soften the edge of each layer. Make a selection just inside the edge of the layer, then press CMD/CTRL-I to select the area outside the selection. Feather the selection slightly (OPT/ALT-CMD/CTRL-D), then use just enough Gaussian Blur to give you the edge falloff that looks natural to you.

▌▌ That's about it. Save your image in Photoshop format with its layers intact in case you change your mind later. Figure 4-20 shows you how natural this depth-of-field effect is.

REPLACING THE BACKGROUND

There will be times when you just want a solid, textured, or patterned background instead of the trees, cars, buildings, or whatever else might be in the background of the original photo.

To Change THE BACKGROUND:

1 Duplicate the background layer, and name the duplicate layer Subject.

2 Extract the subject in Figure 4-21 from the Subject layer using any of the techniques described in Chapter 6 or 10. The selection and/or extraction method you use will have to be the one that is most appropriate to the different types of edges on your subject.

3 Create or open an image with the new background that you want to place behind your subject. Ideally, this image should be the same or nearly the same size as the image you will be using it in.

FIGURE 4-20
A more narrowly focused depth of field keeps attention on the subject.

4 With the new background image active, press CMD/CTRL-A to Select All, then press
CMD/CTRL-C to copy the image to the Clipboard.

5 Click inside the image where you want to place the new background, and press CMD/CTRL-V
to paste it. It automatically becomes a new layer.

6 On the Layers palette, drag the layer containing the new background below the Subject
layer. If you have done a good job of extracting your subject, it should look pretty natural in front of the background.

7 You may want to use the Image | Adjust | Levels, Curves, Color Balance, or Hue/
Saturation dialog—or a combination of them—to fine-tune the background's appearance or to make its color balance more in tune with that of the subject. You should
feel free to experiment.

Depending on the lighting of your subject, you may want the subject to throw a
shadow on the background. If so, duplicate the Subject layer. Click the Subject
layer's Name bar to make sure it's active, then click to check the Lock Transparent
Pixels box.

To Turn THE SUBJECT'S SILHOUETTE BLACK:

1 Choose Edit | Fill. The Fill dialog appears. From the Use menu, choose Black. The Blending Mode setting should be Normal, and the Opacity 100%. Click OK. The subject will now be a black silhouette on an otherwise transparent layer.

2 Right-click the silhouette layer. The Layer Properties dialog appears. Enter Shadow in the Name field and click OK.

3 Now you want to move the shadow layer to the position that it would occupy if the shadow were cast on the background. Choose the Move tool and, making sure the Shadow layer is active, drag the Shadow layer into position.

4 Use the Gaussian Blur filter to blur the silhouette.

5 With the Shadow layer still active, adjust the Opacity slider until the Darkness value of the shadow is a little less than the Darkness value of the shadow side of the Subject layer. See Figure 4-22 to view the modified focus.

Be sure to save this image as **New Background.psd** in case we want to pick up later.

FIGURE 4-22
The finished portrait with the new background

ON THE VIRTUAL CLASSROOM CD-ROM In Lesson 3, "Retouching," you learn, in real time, how to employ the new Patch command to do airbrushing without having to rely on the multiple steps involved in blending layers. I also show you how to use the new Healing Brush so that you can see its action in live motion. *Approximate time: 4 minutes.*

5

Correcting Exposure and Tonal Range

Making the proper adjustments for exposure and color correction can do more than anything else to make your photos look as though they were shot by a pro. Although there's a single command in Photoshop that often does a near-perfect job of this, it doesn't work well on every image. "Perfect" exposure and color balance is what you get when the picture conveys exactly the mood and information you intend for the viewer to see and react to. This chapter teaches you to use the wealth of tools that Photoshop provides to help you make every part of the image appear just as you've envisioned it. Figure 5-1, for instance, shows the original of a photograph alongside its altered copy after some adjustments in Photoshop 7.

FIGURE 5-1
A photo before (left) and after repair (right) in Photoshop 7

BRINGING OUT THE
GREATEST DETAIL IN EVERY IMAGE

The easiest way to correct an under- or overexposed image is by executing one simple command, called Auto Levels. What Auto Levels does is move the lightest and darkest points of each color channel in the image very close to the end of that channel's brightness spectrum. This process moves the pixels that surround the midpoint to the center of the *histogram* (a diagram showing the percentage of pixels that resides at each point of brightness between 1 and 255). This adjustment usually has the effect of color-correcting the image by making the midpoints of each of the primary colors less likely to be off the center of the brightness range. So you get automatic color balancing…as long as there wasn't a preponderance of one primary color in the original scene. If there was, then the color-corrected result might look unnatural.

To Automatically CORRECT FOR EXPOSURE
(BRIGHTNESS RANGE AND COLOR BALANCE):

▶ Choose Image | Adjust | Auto Levels (CMD/CTRL-SHIFT-L).

Unfortunately, Auto Levels may not correct the image the way you want it to, because it has no way of second-guessing your subjective vision of how the brightness level of the midtones should be adjusted.

The Shortest Route to More Precise Personal Exposure Correction

In the next exercise, I'll show you how to almost perfectly achieve the brightness and color values you envision.

To Achieve your vision:

1 If you're still not pleased with the exposure or color balance, choose Image | Adjust | Variations. The Variations dialog appears (see Figure 5-2).

2 The Variations dialog shows you rows and columns of thumbnails of your image—each with a slightly different color balance. If all of these images seem overcorrected, drag the fine/course slider to increase or decrease the amount of correction shown in each thumbnail.

3 If the original picture is too dark or too light, choose a thumbnail labeled Lighter or Darker until the image in the middle is closer to the exposure you desire.

FIGURE 5-2
The Variations dialog

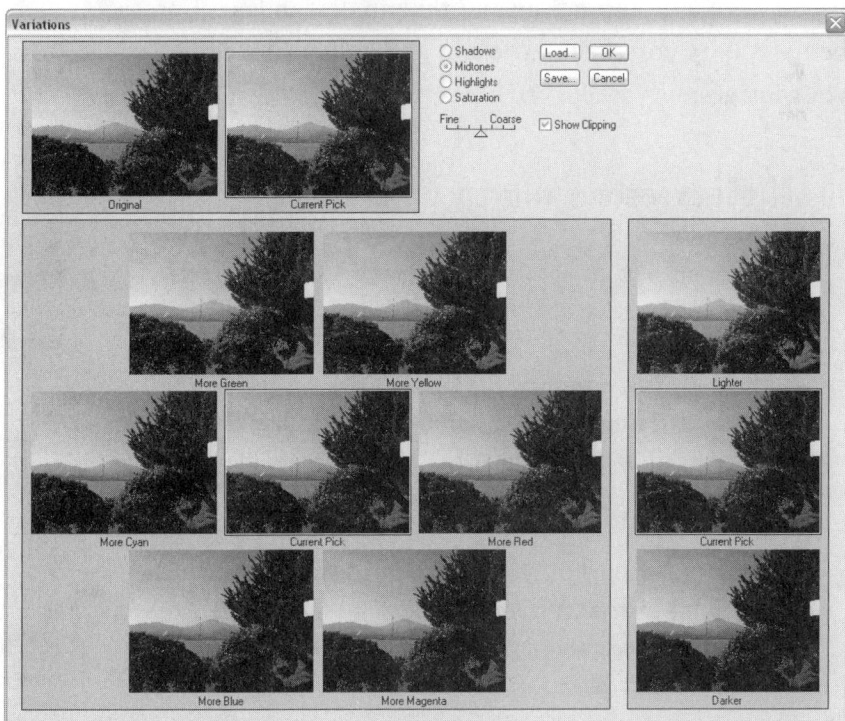

4 When you see a thumbnail closer to the color balance you're looking for, click it. The result will appear in the Current Pick thumbnail.

5 Now if you see another thumbnail that's even closer to the appearance you want, click it. The effect on the Current Pick thumbnail is cumulative.

6 Each time you click a thumbnail, its effect is added to the Current Pick. Keep clicking until the Current Pick looks as close as possible to the end result you want. You can also click radio buttons at the top of the dialog that will change the preview in the thumbnails to show the results of shifting values in shadows or highlights, or of adding color saturation. When you're finally satisfied, click OK.

> **NOTE** Any time you make changes in the Variations dialog, those settings remain the same the next time you use Variations. This makes it super-easy to adjust the exposure and color-correct a whole series of pictures taken in the same place, at the same time of day, of the same subject. Just choose Image | Adjust | Variations and click OK. When you want to start from scratch, however, you'll need to re-establish the default settings. Press OPT/ALT, and the Cancel button will become the Reset button.

A More Precise Method for Correcting Exposure and Color Balance

If you have a bit more time and the job demands real precision, here's a better way to corect the exposure and color balance of your images:

To Correct EXPOSURE AND COLOR BALANCE:

1 After opening an image, choose Image | Adjust | Levels. The Levels dialog appears, as shown here.

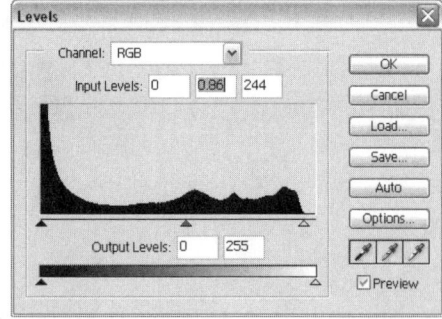

2 Press CMD/CTRL-L to show the Levels dialog for the Red channel (assuming you're working in RGB). Drag the Shadow slider (on the left) to the place where the histogram starts going uphill as shown here.

3 Drag the Highlight slider (on the right) toward the middle until the histogram starts going uphill (or, at least, showing some pixels above the bottom line). Don't touch the middle slider yet.

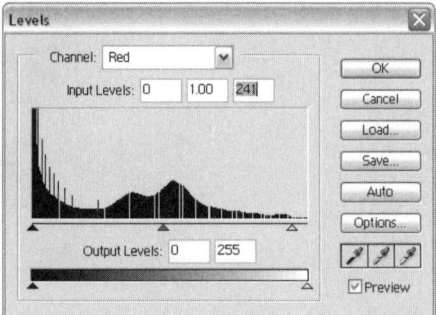

4 Press CMD/CTRL-2 to show the Levels dialog for the Green channel, and repeat steps 2 and 3. Don't move the middle slider.

5 Press CMD/CTRL-3 to show the Levels dialog for the Blue channel, and repeat steps 2 and 3. Don't move the middle slider.

6 Press CMD/CTRL-~ to show the Levels dialog for the RGB (composite) channel, and drag the middle slider until the midtones look the way you want them to.

7 If you feel that the image needs further color correction, choose the Levels dialog channel that needs the most correction. (For example, if the picture is too red, choose the Red channel.) It doesn't matter whether the image needs more or less of that color.

8 In the first color channel you choose, drag the midtone slider in the direction that brings you closest to the best result. Then do the same in each of the other two color channels. Click OK.

9 Choose Image | Duplicate. Save and close your original image. Keep the duplicate open. We're going to use it in the next exercise, picking up where we left off here.

You should now be very close to perfection—unless you have a really demanding image that requires adjustments in very specific areas of the brightness spectrum. That's where using the Curves command has offers significant advantages.

Using Curves to Isolate Image Control

At this point, everything we've been tinkering with works just fine...as far as it goes. But what if there's a little tint in the highlights or shadows that is the result of some stray light or a reflection? Or what if that little tie or ornament, or the texture in a tree bark, is just too dim or dull to pop out as we wish? In cases like these, we need to use the Curves command. The Curves command lets us change both the brightness and the contrast of any (or many) segments of the image's entire brightness range. The Curves command uses the Curves dialog, shown here, to control its settings.

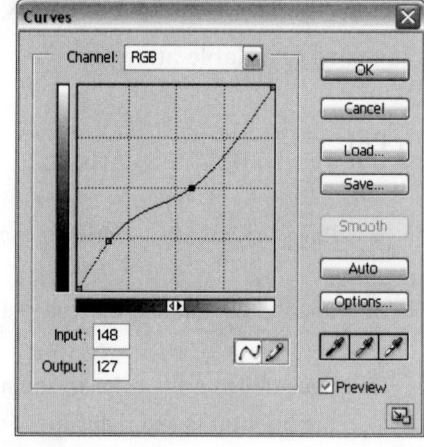

THROWING JUST THE RIGHT CURVES

The brightness values between 1 and 255 (as many levels of gray—or any other single color—as Photoshop can display) are represented as a line that slants between the lower-left and upper-right corners of the Curves dialog. To raise the brightness of any specific point on the brightness scale, simply click to place a point on the graph line, and drag it upwards to brighten that point or downwards to darken it. If you want the adjoining darker or lighter area to gradually reach the same point of brightness, just drag the whole line so it becomes a curve. Otherwise, place additional points along the line so you can hold the rest of the line in place, then drag the specific point at which you want to change the brightness of an isolated area.

> **TIP** An easier way to make adjustments in very specific areas of an image is to choose the Pencil tool's from the Curves dialog and simply draw the subcurve that you want to place at a specific area. Then click the Smooth button to smooth the transition between brightness levels.

SETTING WHITE BALANCE FOR A SERIES OF PHOTOS

The Curves and Levels dialogs also give you an excellent way to set the white balance perfectly in a single click—as long as there's a perfectly neutral area somewhere in the picture—such as a white shirt, a photographer's 50 percent gray card, a black tire. Unfortunately, you'd be surprised how hard it is to find a perfectly neutral color in most photos. However, if you're at an event where a whole series of photos are going to be taken at the same time and location (an indoor party or an on-location fashion shoot would be a couple of good examples), you can take at least one picture of a piece of pure white paper or of a photographer's 50 percent gray card (available at any photo store that caters to pros and serious amateurs).

To Set THE WHITE BALANCE:

1 Open Graycard.jpg—which is a photo that uses a neutral gray card.

2 Open either the Curves (CMD/CTRL-M) or Levels (CMD/CTRL-C) dialog.

3 Depending on the color of the neutral card, which you should hold at the place where the brightness and light direction are the most important—the most accurate—choice, choose the Eyedropper closest to it.

4 Click the card. The color balance will be exactly matched. If the key card is exactly 100 percent black or white, or 50 percent gray, you'll get technically perfect color balance and exposure in one click.

5 Make any other adjustments necessary to be certain the highlights and shadows achieve precisely the look and feel you're after for this series of photos.

6 Click the Save button in the dialog. A Save dialog appears.

7 Navigate to the folder where you want to save your Curves or Levels and open it.

8 Enter a name that describes the series and its lighting (for example, Jones Wedding Yard Mid-PM), then click Save. Photoshop will automatically add the .acv extension to the filename to identify it as an Adobe Curve.

9 Open the next picture in the same series, press CMD/CTRL-L to open the Levels dialog (or CTRL-M to open the Curves dialog, if you prefer), and click Load. Navigate to the Curve file you just saved and open it; then click OK. The same adjustments you made to the key picture will be applied to the new picture.

> **TIP** You may create a few Curves that are applicable as special "dramatic lighting" effects that you're interested in applying, just to see what happens. There are a few of these on this book's CD. Try them out. You'll either love 'em or hate 'em.

10 Repeat step 9 for all the other pictures in the series.

USING BLEND MODES TO CORRECT EXPOSURE

From time to time, you will so poorly expose an image that little or no detail appears in the shadow areas. This often happens in photographs of large spaces, such as room interiors or nature scenes. The camera meter happens to sense the brightest part of the image (probably because it's in the middle of the scene or because there's a window in the picture). Any time you take such a picture, there's a good chance you can save it by blending in a new solid white or black layer using the Screen, Overlay, or Soft Light blend mode.

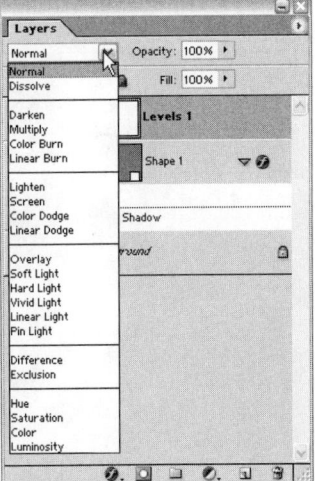

This book isn't encyclopedic enough to show you all the possibilities for using the three Blend modes, so we're going to concentrate on Soft Light because it is the most versatile of the three. When you do these experiments, also try tinkering with the transparency and color of the solid-color layers. If you really want to go crazy, try experimenting with multiple solid-color layers in different combinations of color, blend mode, and opacity.

The picture we are using has such strong highlights that the camera took them too heavily into consideration, and a great many of the shadows were just blocked up. (See Figure 5-3.)

Worse, in spite of the camera's compensation, some of the highlights were blocked up too. To make the situation even worse, there are so many small isolated areas blocked up that one could spend a week or two trying to get the burning and dodging to look smooth. But wait!

To Make BURNING AND DODGING LOOK SMOOTH:

1 Open the image in which you want to smooth the detail.

2 Open or activate the Layers palette. Choose Window | Show Layers.

3 If there's more than one layer, activate the top layer by clicking its Name bar on the Layers palette. The Name bar will be highlighted. This ensures that the new layer you're about to create will be on top. If you goof and it's not, then drag it to the top of the stack.

FIGURE 5-3
Before and after the Soft Light blend mode is used to brighten shadow detail

4 Create a new, empty layer. Click the New Layer button at the bottom of the Layers palette.

5 Fill the new layer with white: Choose Edit | Fill. The Fill dialog appears. From the Use menu, choose White. Leave all other settings at their defaults and click OK. Your workspace will turn solid white.

6 Change the Blend mode by choosing Soft Light from the Layers menu. Whoa! What an amazing difference. It probably looks pretty good at this point, but if you want the shadows a bit darker, drag the white layer's Opacity slider until they look just right. If they're still a bit dark, repeat steps 4 through 6, then lower the Opacity value of the top layer until you get it right.

7 If there are some highlights that need darkening, switch your foreground color to black, choose a fairly soft-edged paintbrush (to make it easier to blend the strokes into the surrounding areas), and paint onto the highlight areas. Just be sure you're painting onto one of the solid white areas and not onto the original.

USING ADJUSTMENT LAYERS

So far, we've pretty much concentrated on how to correct for exposure, color, and contrast on one layer. However, Photoshop has a special type of layer called an Adjustment layer that will let you use any of 11 dialogs to create the same effect on all the visible areas of each layer in the image (that is, the parts that aren't hidden by overlapping layers). The dialogs associated with Adjustment layers are identical to the dialogs associated with the main menu commands of the same name. The big difference is that you can change, throw out, add, or turn off layers without having to change the adjustments. Conversely, you can change adjustments without having to go through the agony of making the same type of adjustment match on (potentially) dozens of different layers—and you can change adjustments at any time you like, so long as you don't flatten all the image layers. (See Chapter 10.)

ISOLATING IMAGE CONTROL TO SPECIFIC AREAS

Once you have made your initial adjustments as desired, it's almost inevitable that you'll want to lighten, darken, sharpen, soften, or add contrast to specific details in the image.

CHANGING SMALL AREAS WITH THE TOOLBOX BRUSHES

There are brushes in the Toolbox that do various things to any small image area. All you have to do is be sure to size the brush (or tool, if that's what you'd rather call it) so it fits within most of the area you want to change, and feather the edge enough so the strokes blend when you scrub an area (drag back and forth) with that brush. You can make these changes on the Options bar for any of the brushes described here.

THE DODGE TOOL

The Dodge tool brightens the area that it passes over. Sometimes it decreases the contrast too much in the lightened area. You may be able to correct this with the Sharpen tool, but it's generally better to place a small selection around the area, feather it so that the adjustment blends, and then choose Image | Adjust | Brightness/Contrast on that area so you can apply the effect more evenly and control the brightness and contrast in one interactive step.

THE BURN TOOL

The Burn tool darkens the area it passes over. It can be an excellent way to de-emphasize an area without making the picture seem phony because the item is missing altogether.

THE SPONGE TOOL

Strictly speaking, the Sponge tool isn't an exposure control. It controls the intensity of color. It's a great way to make red lipstick look even more fiery, or blue eyes even more captivating. You can choose either Saturate or Desaturate from the Mode menu on the Sponge tool's Options Bar. The Sponge tool is also good for giving your Goth portraits even more of that "death after life" look.

> **TIP** When using brushes to adjust exposure, set their pressure or opacity (depending on the specific brush) at a low number. (I like it to be between 10 and 15 percent, but if the change you're making is really subtle, set it even lower.) Then you can use more strokes to "build" the effect.

CHANGING SMALL AREAS BY LIFTING THEM TO A SEPARATE LAYER

If you have a number of small areas to change, you may be able to change several at a time by working with layers.

To Change A NUMBER OF SMALL AREAS:

1 Select those areas that you want to either lighten or darken (not both at the same time) by choosing the Lasso tool (or any of the tools you'll find described in Chapter 6 for making precise selections). I find it fastest to select all the items that have to be brightened or darkened at one time by pressing the SHIFT key each time you make a selection.

2 Once you've selected all the items for either brightening or darkening, just press CMD/CTRL-J. All the areas will be lifted to the same new layer.

3 Choose Image | Adjust | Brightness/Contrast. The Brightness/Contrast dialog appears.

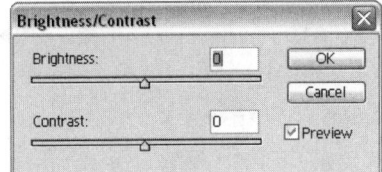

4 Check the Preview box so you can see the result of your adjustments in the image.

5 Drag the Brightness and Contrast sliders until the areas you want to affect the least look good to you.

6 Use the Lasso tool to select any items that need further adjustment, then repeat steps 2 through 5—except that instead of copying the items to a new layer, press CMD/CTRL-X to cut them from their parent layer, then press CMD/CTRL-V to place them by themselves on a new layer.

7 Keep repeating the process as many times as necessary to make all the needed adjustments. Usually, you will be able to adjust several items per layer.

The beauty of this technique is that you can always change your mind about how you've adjusted any one group of items by reselecting them, lifting them to a new layer, and then deleting the old layer.

COMBINING MULTIPLE EXPOSURES OR ADJUSTMENTS OF THE SAME IMAGE

So far, you've seen some lovely ways to improve your image. However, all these methods achieve at least some of their effects by moving pixels into other areas of the brightness range—so there is some loss of image details. There's one time when you can improve on this: When you have time to place or mount your camera on a spot where it won't move between shots, and then take a series of pictures of the same scene at slightly different exposures. (Those who are experienced photographers will recognize this as a technique called "bracketing.") Ideal candidates are scenics (especially in really "moody" lighting conditions), interiors, and product shots (especially if they require more lights than you actually own in order to place the highlights and shadows exactly where you want them).

Here's the principle: You make a series of exposures of the same inanimate subject, ideally at about half an f-stop or EV value apart. (This technique sucks for sports photography.) Usually, three to five shots in the series are sufficient. Then you place each shot on a different layer in the same file, carefully aligning each layer to make sure all the objects on it are in perfect alignment with the objects on all the other layers. Finally, erase the parts of any layers you don't want to keep (because a part has blocked either highlights or shadows, or because there's simply more detail, or a more desirable tone, or a more interesting highlight on another layer).

To Combine MULTIPLE EXPOSURES:

1 Open all the exposures.

2 Click the window that has the best overall exposure to make that the active window.

3 Choose Image | Duplicate. The Duplicate Image dialog appears.

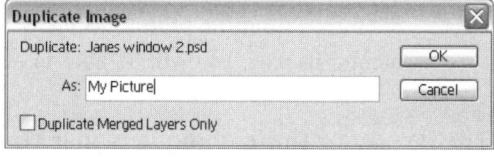

4 Name the new image, followed by EC for "exposure composite," and click OK.

5 Close the exposure you've just duplicated; then click to activate the image that has the next best detail that you want to keep.

6 Choose Edit | Select All (CMD/CTRL-A), then Edit | Copy (CMD/CTRL-C).

7 Activate the exposure composite window and choose Edit | Paste (CMD/CTRL-V). The image with the next highest amount of usable detail will appear on a layer directly atop the medium exposure. Rename the layer Details 2. Make sure it stays active.

8 Choose the Lasso tool. On the Options Bar, enter the number of pixels in the Feather field to smooth the lasso just enough so it can cross-dissolve smoothly into the surrounding area.

9 Select all the noncontiguous areas of the top layer containing details that you want to keep by pressing the SHIFT key to add new selections (see the following illustration):

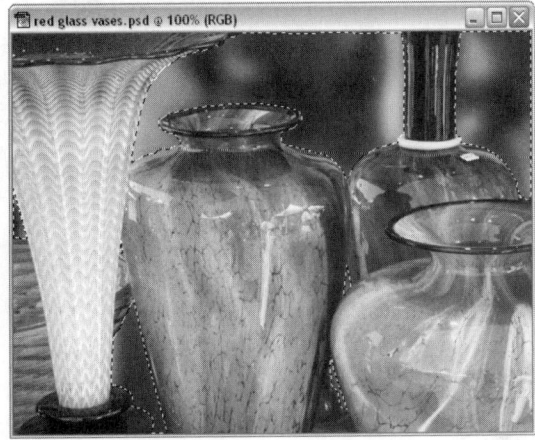

10 On the Layers palette, drag the Opacity slider to about 25 percent so you can see the original layer clearly. Now edit your selections so they include exactly those areas that contain the most detail. Then drag the Opacity slider back to 100%.

11 Invert the selection by choosing Select | Inverse (CMD/CTRL-SHIFT-I). Press BACKSPACE/DELETE to erase everything except the more detailed areas that you want to keep.

12 Repeating steps 5 though 11, progressing through the rest of the exposures and keeping only those areas that contribute more details to the image.

13 If, when you've finished, one or more layers seems a little too bright or dark, click that layer's Name Bar on the Layer's palette, then choose Image | Adjust | Brightness/Contrast. The Brightness/Contrast dialog opens; here you can drag the sliders to adjust the brightness of the channel. If only one or two areas on the layer don't match (not likely, but it happens), select them with the Lasso tool (see Chapter 6) to isolate them before making the Brightness/Contrast adjustments.

USING THE EQUALIZE COMMAND TO CREATE MORE DETAIL

There are times when certain areas of an image will seem totally washed out or lost in the deepest shadows. The fact is, as long as there's some part of the original (as opposed to the previously manipulated) image that's brighter or darker than those parts that seem lost, you can rescue some of your detail. The secret lies in the Equalize command. What this little marvel does is evenly distribute all the shades of color in the image to an equal level of brightness. To visualize this, look at the histograms of the original and equalized versions of the following image:

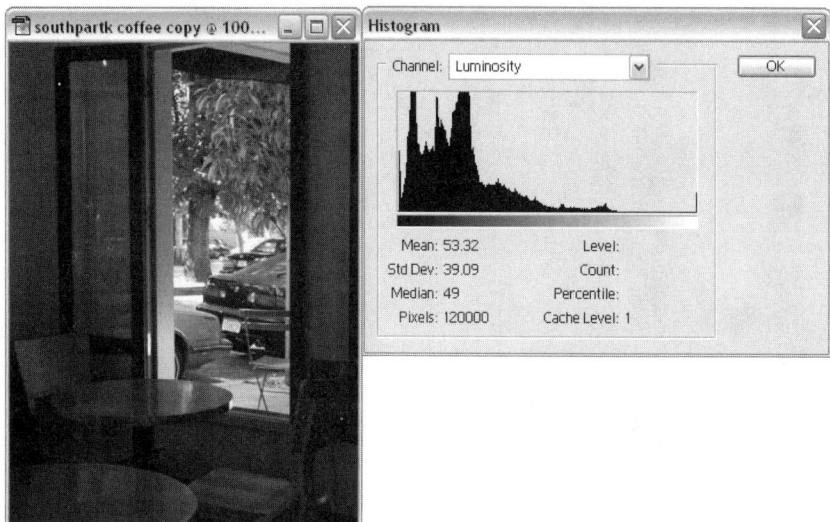

You can bring out detail in every part of an image by using the Equalize command, as you can see in the equalized version of the photo:

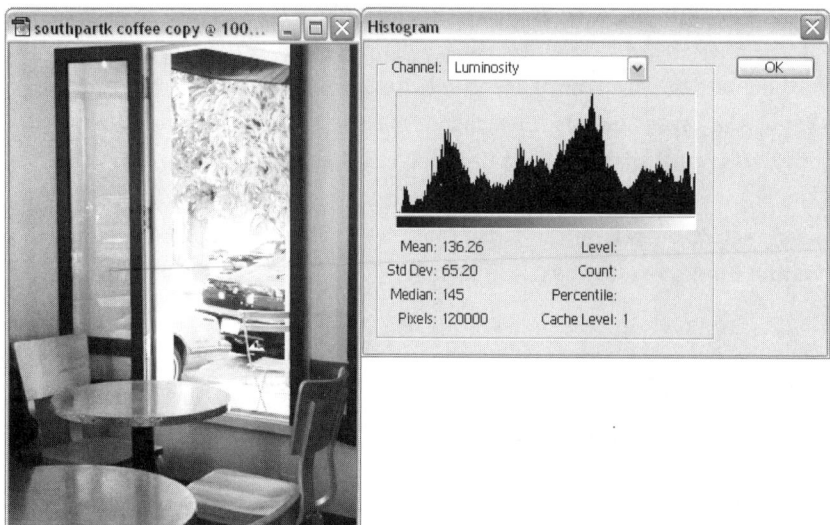

As you can see, the first image doesn't show us all the detail we'd like to see. The second brings out some additional detail—particularly in shadows and highlights—but it just doesn't look natural. By using a little trickery, however, we can bring the right amount of detail into all areas of the image. Here's how to go about it:

To Bring DETAIL INTO ALL AREAS OF AN IMAGE:

1. Open the image that you want to change. Be sure there's a Snapshot of the image in the History palette (which there will be if you've instructed Preferences to create a Snapshot as soon as a file is opened). By the way, be sure you don't close this file before you've completed the job; otherwise, you'll lose the Snapshots.

2. Choose Window | Show Layers to ensure that the Layers palette is where you can get to it. Drag the Background layer to the New Layer icon at the bottom of the Layers palette to duplicate it.

3. CTRL/right-click the new layer's Name bar and choose Layer Properties from the in-context menu. The Layer Properties dialog appears. Enter Equalized in the Name field and click OK.

4. Choose Image | Adjust | Equalize. Wham! You see a new version of the image, in which every tone is distinct from every other tone.

> NOTE If using the Soft Light mode on a white-filled layer produces an effect that's too exaggerated, lower the transparency of the layer by dragging the Opacity slider to the left until the image reflects the result you would like.

5. Choose Window | Show History. You should see a thumbnail of the image at the very top of the History State bars. To the left of the thumbnail is a History Brush icon. It indicates that this is the state that the History Brush will paint from if you click that square. To take a Snapshot of the equalized layer, choose Take New Snapshot from the History palette menu. A new Snapshot is automatically created.

6. If there are small areas where you want to add some detail, choose the History Brush tool.

7. If the History palette isn't already visible, choose Window | Show History. Click the box to the left of the equalized Snapshot so the History Brush icon appears there.

This indicates that what you paint with the History Brush will come from that Snapshot.

8 Using the History Brush, paint onto the areas where you want to see more detail. If you want the detail to only darken or only lighten what's already there, just change the Blend mode for the brush on the Options Bar. Screen mode will likely be your best choice for lightening, and Multiply mode your best choice for darkening. You can use the Options Bar to change the opacity of the brush from one area to another. Take a look at Figure 5-4 to see the final result.

SHOWING THE SAME PHOTO IN DIFFERENT COLORS

One situation that often arises is that you want to show the same item in several different colors...or maybe you just want to change the color of an item because the new color seems better suited to the mode of the photograph. You can make either change in just a few moments by using an image adjustment command called Replace Color.

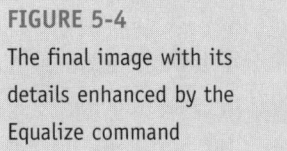

FIGURE 5-4
The final image with its details enhanced by the Equalize command

To Replace A COLOR:

1 Open the photograph you want to modify.

2 You want to make as many copies of the image you can in which the object in question is a different color than in the original. Choose Image | Duplicate. The Duplicate Image dialog appears. Add the name of the new color to the existing file's Name field. Repeat this step as many times as necessary.

For each file in which you will change the color of the object, repeat the following steps:

To Change THE COLOR OF AN OBJECT:

1 Choose Image | Adjust | Replace Color. The Replace Color dialog appears.

2 Make sure that Selection is the chosen radio button in the Selection area.

3 Move the cursor to the place on the image that represents the largest and most typical area of the color that you want to change. Notice that the cursor has changed to an Eyedropper. Click the colored area.

4 In the Replace Color dialog, notice that the white area in the Selection preview has expanded.

5 Drag the Fuzziness slider to include all of the area that you want to recolor, but don't let it start selecting areas that you don't want to recolor. If this should happen, back down a bit.

6 If there are still areas you want to recolor, choose the Add To Sample Eyedropper (there's a + sign in its icon) and click on those areas. You will see the shape of

> **NOTE** Replace Color really only works well for items in an image that have clear color separation from the background (or foreground). If the object of interest is close in color to its background (a simple example would be a white cup on a white tablecloth), then the best course of action for recoloring the cup would be to mask it using Quickmask mode and then use the Hue, Saturation, and Lightness sliders (in the Replace Color dialog) to adjust the color of the cup.

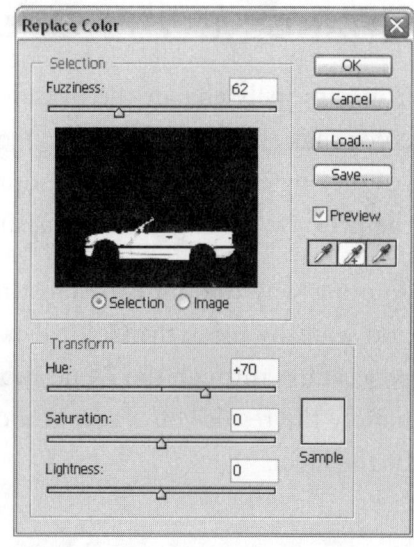

each selection change, and you may have to further modify it by adjusting the Fuzziness slider.

7 If there are areas selected that you don't want to recolor, choose the Subtract From Sample Eyedropper (the icon with the – next to it). Click the areas you don't want to recolor.

8 Once you feel you've got a selection pretty well nailed, drag the Hue slider until you see the approximate color that you want your selected item changed to.

9 Now you'll know if your selection is just right, because you'll be able to see whether the color change is limited only to the areas you wanted to change. If necessary, use the Eyedroppers and the Fuzziness slider to fine-tune your selection.

10 Use the Hue, Saturation, and Lightness sliders to make the new color just what you want it to be. When all's right with the world (or at least with your picture), click OK.

CHANGING THE OVERALL MOOD OF A PHOTO

You can easily change the overall mood of a photograph by tinting it with the color that evokes that mood. One way to do this is to simply change the color balance by choosing Image | Adjust | Hue/Saturation. Drag the slider bars until the preview looks good to you, and click OK.

Another way to do it is by creating a new layer, filling it with the exact color you want by using the Color Picker (see Chapter 8 regarding its use), and then proceeding through the Blend modes by pressing SHIFT-+ until you see approximately the result you want. You can fine-tune the result by changing the opacity of the layer.

WORKING IN BLACK AND WHITE

Most folks these days take their pictures on color film or with a digital camera. Some digital cameras have a black-and-white mode, but there's a good chance that something you want in black and white (or, more accurately, grayscale) will have been shot in color. If that shot is history, it's, well, history. The chances that you can re-create what was in the shot are slim but don't lose heart. Photoshop gives you a bevy of ways, each with a slightly different appearance, to turn a color image into a brilliant black-and-white one. The most commonly used methods are

▶ Changing the color mode to grayscale

▶ Desaturating the image with the Desaturate command

▶ Desaturating the image with the Hue/Saturation slider

▶ Splitting the color channels and saving the one you like best as a new file

▶ Using the Channel Mixer command

▶ Making a toned print

CHANGING THE COLOR MODE TO GRAYSCALE

When you choose Image | Mode | Grayscale, your image will automatically convert to grayscale. If you want to subsequently color the image, you will have to select a different color mode (ideally, RGB). Changing the color mode to RGB discards all color information. The problem with this method is that you have no control over which color channels contribute the most information. This is the quickest method for turning color into black and white, but since it gives you the least control over the final result and discards all color information, you might try one of the other methods first. Then, if you get it to a stage where you're going to send the image out for publication and want to make sure it is published in black and white, and you desire the smallest possible file size without loss of image data, use this command.

DESATURATING THE IMAGE

The quickest and simplest way to change a color image to grayscale is to simply choose Image | Adjust | Desaturate. Zap! It's suddenly grayscale, but you're still in whatever color mode you were in when you started, so you can still use colors in the image. However, just as with the Grayscale command, you can't control how individual colors are interpreted (for instance, if you want the sky darker relative to the rest of the picture).

DESATURATING THE IMAGE
WITH THE HUE/SATURATION SLIDER

Maybe what you want isn't really a black-and-white image, but one with an old-fashioned or antiqued look—or perhaps, you want to hand-color the image without having to color every single detail.

To Use THE HUE/SATURATION COMMAND:

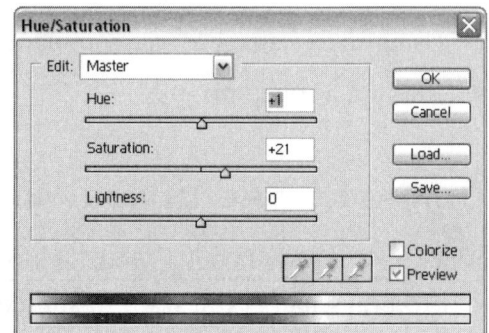

1 Choose Image | Adjust | Hue/Saturation. The Hue/Saturation dialog appears.

2 Drag the Saturation slider to the left until there is as little color in the image as you'd like. (Keep in mind that if you drag it all the way to the left, there won't be any color in the image at all, and you won't be able to change the Hue value.)

3 (Optional.) If you want to change the apparent exposure, you can also lighten or darken the image with the Lightness slider.

SPLITTING THE COLOR CHANNELS

Splitting the color channels and saving the best variation is my favorite way of converting an image to black and white—and making it look like it was shot by a photographer who knew what he was doing. Such a photographer would take advantage of the color sensitivities of various black-and-white emulsions and use color filters to emphasize various areas of color.

To Split THE COLOR CHANNELS:

1 Choose Window | Show Channels or drag the Channels Palette tab from the Palette Well.

2 From the Channels Palette menu, choose Split Channels. Each channel will automatically become a separate grayscale image (though the Color mode will still be RGB; see Figure 5-5). A separate window appears for each of the split channels, every one now an independent file that can be edited using any of the Photoshop commands and tools.

FIGURE 5-5
A separate image window
for each split channel

3 Examine the channels side-by-side, close those you don't want to keep, and choose File | Save As. The Save As dialog appears.

4 Navigate to the folder where you want to keep the black-and-white file. In the Name field, enter the name you want to use for this version (I just add "grayscale" to the original), and click OK.

> **TIP** If you really want to get serious about creating the effects of color filters on black-and-white versions of your color images, look into Nik Color Efex (www.tech-nik.com).

USING THE CHANNEL MIXER COMMAND

You have even more power at your disposal when it comes to deciding how much of the original color information you want to use in your grayscale interpretation of the subject. You can mix data from any or all of the color channels into a single grayscale file.

To Use THE CHANNEL MIXER:

1 Open the image you want to convert to grayscale.

2 Choose Image | Adjust | Channel Mixer. The Channel Mixer dialog appears.

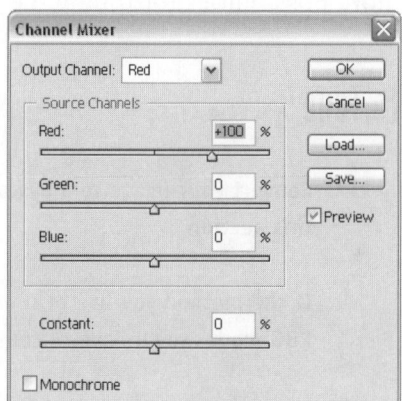

3 Check the Monochrome box.

4 Drag the slider for each of the color channels until you get the range of tones you want. The sliders enable you to increase or decrease the contribution that each primary color makes to the tones in the image.

5 In the process of mixing the color channels, you may lighten or darken the image too much. If so, correct it by dragging the Constant slider.

6 When you are happy with what you have, click OK.

7 Choose File | Save As to preserve your original color file by saving this new version under another name.

> NOTE If you have a whole photo session that you want to apply the same treatment to, click the Save button in the Channel Mixer dialog. You then save the settings with a .cha extension. Afterward, create an Action that automatically opens the Channel Mixer and loads the settings you've saved, applying them to the image.

MAKING A TONED PRINT

There are a couple of ways you can make an image resemble an old-fashioned sepia-toned print. (Actually, the tone can be any color you like.)

▶ Add a solid-color layer to your image, and then use the Color blend mode to tone the whole image in that color.

▶ Place the image in Duotone color mode and choose the color of each of the inks to be used in the print.

We've done enough with Layers and Blend modes in this chapter that the first method should be self-explanatory. Working in Duotone mode offers you many more possibilities for toning the image.

To Tone AN IMAGE:

1 Convert your image to grayscale using any of the methods described earlier in this section.

2 If the method you use to convert the tonal values to grays leaves the image still in RBG mode, you'll have to convert it to grayscale before you can convert it to Duotone.

Choose Image | Mode | Grayscale. The conversion to grayscale is automatic, with no adjustments required.

3 Convert the image to duotone (or monotone, or tritone, or any combination of up to four colors) by choosing Image | Mode | Duotone. The Duotone Options dialog appears.

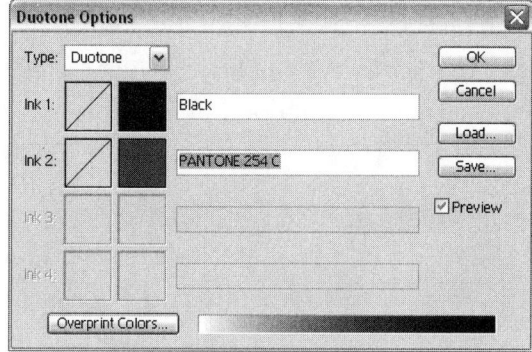

4 Choose the number of colors you want to use for toning from the Type menu. Monotone is usually best for hand-coloring the toned image. If you're going to use the image for publication or exhibit, you'll get richer tones and deeper blacks by using duotone.

5 Choose Duotone from the Type menu.

6 Click the Color Picker box for Ink 1. (It's black by default.) A Pantone color picker shows up so you can choose a color other than black. Most of the time, you'll want to leave it as-is.

7 Click the Color Picker box for Ink 2. A Pantone color picker shows up again. This time, choose another color. As soon as you do, you'll see the result in your image. Experiment to your heart's content with both colors. You might also try adding colors by changing the Type to Tritone or Quadtone and then picking colors for Inks 3 and 4. When you see what you want in your image, click OK.

HAND-COLORING AN IMAGE

Hand-colored images not only look beautiful and modern, but can also appear very old-fashioned and traditional. The effect you achieve will depend on the type of toned image you use for the base, and the coloring method you employ.

To hand-color an image, first use one of the methods described earlier to change it to grayscale. Next, you may want to tone it so that most of the color in the image represents either the desired mood or the color most prevalent in the original image. (That's why most hand-colored portraits start out being sepia-toned—sepia is the color closest to a flesh tone.)

Next, you can hand-color either by painting directly onto the image with either the Airbrush or Brush tool, with the Blend mode set to Color in the Options Bar, or by using the same tool and painting onto a new transparent layer whose Blend mode has been set to Color. Of course, the advantage of painting onto a layer is that you can then make individual image adjustments on the colored layer. Furthermore, if you don't like your results, you can simply delete the layer.

 ON THE VIRTUAL CLASSROOM CD-ROM In Lesson 4, "Correcting Exposure and Tonal Range," you get a demonstration of using the Levels command's Eyedroppers to quickly correct color balance, and maximizing the amount of visible information in a picture by making exposure corrections with the individual color channels in the Levels command. *Approximate time: 6 minutes*.

Controlling Selections and Drawing Shapes

Here we show you how to do "impossible" things such as isolating each strand of blowing hair or separating the opaque from the transparent areas in a glass of iced tea. You can also use Photoshop to mathematically draw geometrically perfect shapes, then turn them into smooth-edged selections. Shapes can even be used as a way to guide Photoshop's brush tools along a precise predefined path—no worries about bumpy edges due to the shakes.

UNDERSTANDING THE DIFFERENCE BETWEEN MASKS AND SELECTIONS

Selections are made with the selection tools (Marquees, Lassos, and the Magic Wand) which designate the border of a selected area by using an animated dashed line.

Since the dashed line is reminiscent of both the blinking lights around an old-fashioned theater marquee and a line of marching ants, the selection border has come to be known as "the marching ants marquee." Whatever is inside a marching ants marquee—no matter how it was made—is editable. Whatever is outside the marquee is protected from editing. You can see the difference between a mask and a selection in Figure 6-1.

Various changes can be made to selections once enclosed in a marquee. A few are included in the following:

▶ Selections can be feathered

▶ Selections can be anti-aliased

▶ Selections can be saved as masks

▶ Selections can be moved and re-shaped

▶ Selections can be edited

SELECTIONS CAN BE FEATHERED

Selections don't have to have hard-edged borders. This gives you control over how edits you make within a selection blend with the area outside the selection. The degree of protection offered can be graduated from 100 to –0 percent over a border width of a specified number of pixels. By default, that graduation is spread evenly on both sides of the selection border. As a result, a feathered

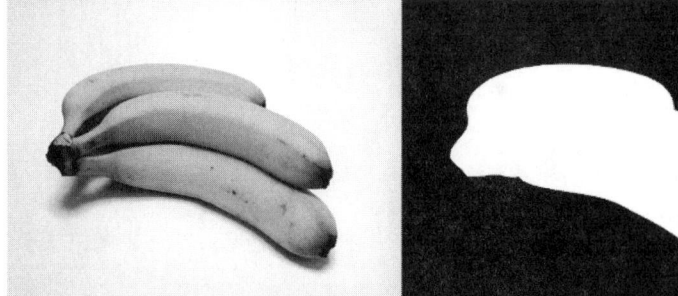

FIGURE 6-1
A selection (left) and a mask of the same selection

selection looks like this upper starburst if you delete what's outside the selection.

If the selection is neither feathered nor anti-aliased, it looks like the lower starburst.

You can either feather a selection before you create it or after. To feather it before it's created, simply type the number of pixels you want the feathering to occur over into the Feather field in the Options Bar of the tool you are going to use to make the selection. Thereafter, when you use that tool to create a selection, the feathering automatically happens at that width unless you purposely change the number in the Feather field before drawing a new selection.

You can change the feathering of any active selection at any time: Choose Select | Feather (OPT/ALT-CMD/CTRL-D). When the Feather Selection dialog appears, enter the pixel radius over which the feathering will occur. This is particularly valuable when you have saved a selection but want to change the feathering when you subsequently Load the selection to be reused.

SELECTIONS CAN BE ANTI-ALIASED

In the Options Bars of all the selection tools is an Anti-aliased check box. Clicking in the box toggles anti-aliasing on and off. For those not familiar with the term, *anti-aliasing* creates the illusion that edges are smooth by shading the brightness of edge pixels so that the "jaggy" or "stairstep" effect is less obvious. It's easier to show the effect than to describe it. In the following illustration, an 800-percent enlargement shows a regular selection edge on the right and the anti-aliased edge of the same selection on the left.

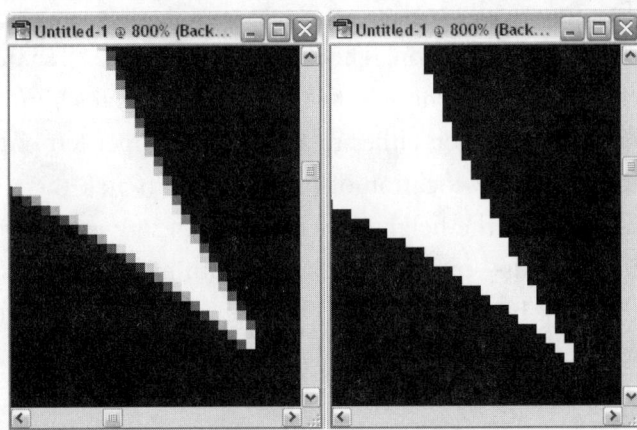

You will generally want to use anti-aliasing unless the aliasing causes the selection to include pixels of a color shade that look unnatural if the edit (such as a color-correction) has miscolored the bordering pixels, thus creating a halo.

SELECTIONS CAN BE SAVED AS MASKS

The difference between a selection and a mask is that a selection is strictly temporary. As soon as you save it, it becomes a mask. A mask is an Alpha channel (any channel other than a spot color channel above and beyond the channels required by the primary colors for the current color mode). When you save a selection, it is recorded as a grayscale image in an Alpha channel. In the illustration here, you see a selected starburst that has been saved as an Alpha channel.

SELECTIONS CAN BE MOVED AND RESHAPED

You can move and reshape selection marquees without changing the contents of the selection. To move the selection, choose any selection tool, place the cursor directly on the dashed line of the marquee, and drag. (The cursor will change to a white arrow with a box attached to one corner.)

Do not drag inside the marquee unless you intend to move the contents of the selection rather than the selection itself. You can also move a selection when you are in the Transform Selection command (see the following illustration) without using the Move tool. This way, there is no danger of unintentionally moving the contents rather than the selection.

You can also change the height, width, slant, or rotational angle, or move any of the corners of the selection. Lumped together, all of these operations are called *transformations*.

To numerically transform a selection (rather than its contents), choose Select | Transform Selection. The Transform Options Bar immediately appears. You can then transform the selection by entering exact numbers for the location of the upper-left corner, either relative to the upper-left corner of the image or relative to the current location of the selection. (Click the relative selection button.) You can change the height or width by entering a percentage of change in either of those fields—or you can change both measurements proportionately by clicking the Link button and then entering a percentage in either the Height or Width field. You can also change the slant numerically by entering an angle in the angle field.

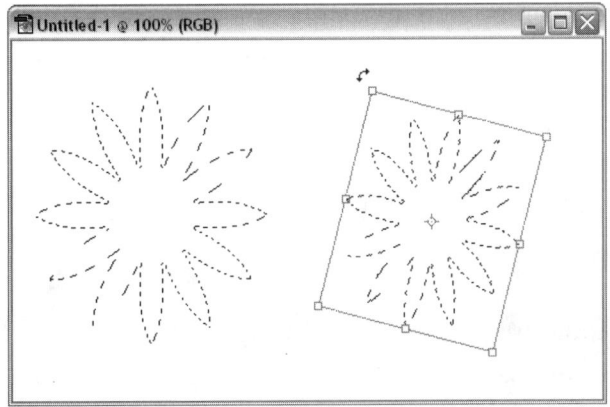

SELECTIONS CAN BE EDITED

Any time you have to make a very complicated selection manually, you'll save time if you make a rough selection first, then add to and subtract from the selection while tightly zoomed in so you can make sure you've drawn the selection exactly where it needs to be. Keep saving the selection as you move along so you can pick up where you left off if you accidentally drop the selection. Remember, all it takes to drop a selection is to inadvertently click outside the selection while your selection tool is in New Selection mode.

Selection modes (New, Add, Subtract, and Intersect) are controlled by the four buttons at the far left of the selection tool's Options Bar. The tool will stay in the chosen mode until you select a different mode.

You can also temporarily choose to add or subtract from a selection by pressing a modifier key while making a selection.

▶ Press SHIFT to add to a selection

▶ Press OPT/ALT to subtract from a selection

The selection tool will have a small plus (+) sign next to it denoting when an area will be added to an existing selection, and a small (–) sign next to it when a chosen section will be subtracted from it.

I could put you through a tedious step-by-step procedure of how to carefully refine the shape of a Lasso selection, but it's far more effective to see the procedure as a movie on the Virtual Classroom CD.

SELECTION TOOLS AND OTHER SELECTION BASICS

Strictly speaking, the selection tools are the Marquees (Rectangular, Elliptical, Single Row, Single Column), Lassos (Lasso, Polygon Lasso, Magnetic Lasso), and the Magic Wand. In addition, several other ways are used to isolate portions of images, so many in fact that I find it helpful to think of them as part of the arsenal of actual selection tools. Here's a list of the selection tools and commands, and what each is most useful for:

▶ **Rectangular Marquee (m)** Makes a freehand rectangular selection, as long as Normal has been chosen from the Options Bar Style menu. If you want to restrict the rectangle to a square shape, you can either press SHIFT before you start to draw the rectangle or choose Constrained Aspect Ratio from the Style menu in the Options Bar and then type **1** into both the Width and Height fields. You can type any two numbers in the Height and Width fields as a ratio. If you choose Fixed Size from the Options Bar Style menu, you need to enter the desired size in the Width and Height fields in pixels.

▶ **Elliptical Marquee (m)** Makes an oval freehand selection. Pressing SHIFT before dragging restricts the oval to a circle. All other options in the Options Bar are the same as for the Rectangular Marquee (described earlier).

▶ **Single Row Marquee (m)** This is really a single dashed line that travels horizontally across the entire canvas at whatever point you click. Of course, this alone won't select anything, but you can choose Edit | Trace to draw a straight line across the image.

NOTE Rectangular and elliptical (circular) selections can also be made from the center outwardly by pressing the OPT/ALT key before making the selection.

▶ **Single Column Marquee (m)** A vertical version of the Single Row Marquee

▶ **Lasso Tool (l)** Lets you draw a freehand selection to silhouette any shape you like…even if there's some reason you don't want to strictly follow the form of an object. For instance, you may want to change the brightness of a free form area. It is also very useful for selecting shapes that are too low in contrast to be automatically selected by one of the other selection tools.

▶ **Polygonal Lasso (l)** Lets you select an area bordered by straight lines in any shape. You simply click to indicate where to start the shape and then continue to click any other point to which you want to extend a straight line selection. The standard freehand selection tool can also select polygonally by pressing the OPT/ALT key before making the selection.

▶ **Magnetic Lasso (l)** The Magnetic Lasso is so called because it automatically attaches itself to the nearest row of contrasting pixels. To limit the distance from either side of the cursor within which the Lasso will look for an edge, enter a number of pixels in the Options Bar's Width field. This distance is called the Pen Width. You can determine the pen width by changing the pressure of your pressure-sensitive pen if you check the Stylus Pressure box. To determine which pixels will be considered different enough for the Magnetic Lasso to consider them as an edge, enter a percentage in the Edge Contrast field. As you drag the cursor along the edge, the Magnetic Lasso will lay down anchor points that prevent the marquee from wandering. You can choose the distance between these anchor points by entering a number of pixels in the Frequency field.

▶ **Magic Wand (w)** The Magic Wand automatically makes a selection within a range of brightness of all the pixels surrounding the point you clicked. You set the brightness range for the selection by entering a number between 1 and 255 in the Tolerance field. You have a choice between selecting all the pixels that aren't bordered by pixels outside the chosen range or selecting all the pixels within that range no matter where they occur in the image. To select all the pixels within the chosen range no matter what their location, click to uncheck the Contiguous box. By the same token, if you click to uncheck the Use All Layers box, the selection will include only those pixels that reside on the currently active layer.

▶ **Color Range** This command, found on the Select menu, is used to select any areas in the image that fall within your chosen range of a particular color(s) (as opposed to brightness). It is often the best way to separate the sky from a horizon line. You can also use it instead of the Replace Color command to change the color of an object when you don't want to change all the objects of the same color. This is useful because there is no way to edit which areas of color are selected by the Replace Color command, whereas you can always edit any selection. You will find instructions for using the Color Range command in the "Using the Select Menu" section later in this chapter.

▶ **Pen (p)** The Pen tool draws shapes using vector-controlled paths. This makes much smoother and more geometrical lines than most of us are able to make with the selection tools. Photoshop lets you change any of its paths into a selection by choosing Window | Show Paths and then clicking the Load Path As Selection button at the bottom of the Paths palette. If you use any of the Pen tools to create a selection, be sure to click the Create New Work Path button in the Options Bar for whatever Pen tool you're using.

▶ **Freeform Pen (p)** The Freeform Pen forms a path from whatever freehand shape you draw. There are two modes for this tool, which you choose between in the Options Bar: Freeform and Magnetic. If you choose Freeform, drawing a path will be just like using the Lasso tool, except that you can edit the path after you've drawn it. If you're using a mouse

NOTE If you're using one of the new optical mouses, you don't need a mouse pad. I suggest you use a smooth surfaced table that doesn't have a mirrored, glass, or highly polished top. This can cause stray reflections of the laser beam and results in poor tracking.

instead of a pressure-sensitive tablet, this is an especially important advantage because it's much harder to keep a mouse steady. You edit a path by dragging control points, and the smoothness of the path is determined partly by the number of control points you specify to be automatically entered within a specific number of pixels. You enter that number in the Curve Fit field in the Options Bar.

▶ **Shape tools (u)** Shape tools are used to create new layers in a specific shape, create a preshaped work path, or to draw a rasterized shape on the current layer that is automatically filled with the current foreground color. The only one of these options you can turn into a selection is the work path. The shape tools automatically draw paths that have been predrawn and saved (Custom Shapes) or that are one of several specific geometric shapes: Rectangle, Rounded Rectangle, Ellipse, Polygon (you can enter the number of sides in the Options Bar), or Line. You can draw any of the predefined shapes to any size or proportion simply by choosing them from the Shapes fly-out menu and then dragging diagonally from the upper-left corner to determine their size and height-to-width ratio. Each of the Shapes tools also has an Options dialog accessible from its Options Bar. You make it appear by clicking the down-arrow button immediately to the right of the Tool buttons. The Options dialogs let you enter the exact size of the shape, let you draw the shape by dragging from the center (except for the Line shape tool and the Polygon shape tool), let you determine whether the shape is constrained by checking the appropriate box(es), and so forth. The exact options are different for each shape and will be obvious when looking at the specific Options dialog.

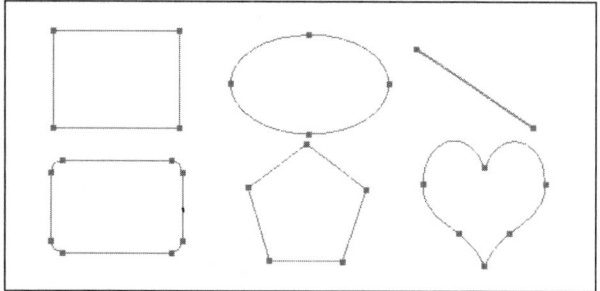

▶ **Extract Command** (OPT/ALT-CMD/CTRL-X) This is another Photoshop command that isn't, strictly speaking, a selection tool. Its purpose is to make very sophisticated knockouts. A *knockout* is an old prepress term for isolating an area or object in a photograph from its background—usually so that it can be placed against another background or in another photograph. An example can be seen here. The Extract command is fully explained in Chapter 10. It's mentioned here so you know there's a way to lift areas with very complex edges onto their own isolated layers. You can then do anything you like to that layer without affecting the rest of the image.

> **NOTE** The keys in parentheses next to the bulleted tool name are those you press in order to choose the associated tool. The Rectangular and Elliptical Marquees share the M key. In order to switch between them press SHIFT while pressing the M key. To switch between the three Lasso tools, press SHIFT-L. Each press of either of these combinations will toggle to another of the keys in that group.

TRANSPARENCY IN SELECTIONS

Although selections are represented as marching ant marquees with a definite border, they are actually representations of grayscale images which, if saved, become channels. Any area that you want to be less affected by whatever command or tool you apply within the selection is affected to the degree that the selection is transparent or opaque.

You have already seen a hint of this in what happens at the edges of a feathered selection. If you fill that feathered selection with a color, that color fades to white as the selection outside the feathering radius is reached, as shown here in the middle illustration.

If you save this selection and then look at the channel in which it was saved, it looks like what you see in the bottom illustration.

As you can see, it's exactly the inverse of what happened when we filled the selection with black. Had we filled the selection with a photograph, its edge would have been vignetted—that is, it would have faded out to white at the edges (like an old-fashioned portrait).

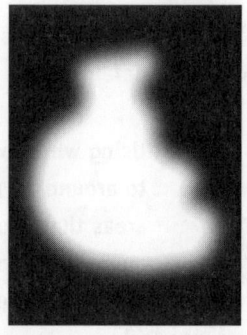

Now, suppose you made a selection with a Lasso tool, but inside that selection were areas you didn't want fully opaque when you moved the selection's contents to a new layer. Or you want to apply a color fill or a texture filter and have the result be less apparent in some areas than in others. All you have to do is put some gray into those unmasked (white) areas of the saved selection (mask) that you want to be partially opaque. The darker the shade of gray in any given area of the mask, the less effect you will see when that mask is applied as a selection by clicking the Load channel As Selection button at the bottom of the Channels palette.

To Paint GRAY INTO A MASK:

1 Edit the image in the Alpha channel

2 Edit the selection in Quick Mask mode.

To Edit THE IMAGE IN THE ALPHA CHANNEL:

1 Make your selection

2 Choose Selection | Save Selection. The Save Selection dialog appears.

3 Enter a name for the selection and click OK.

4 Choose Window | Show Channels. The Channels palette will appear. You will see the shape you just selected in the thumbnail of one of the channels that is not a primary color channel.

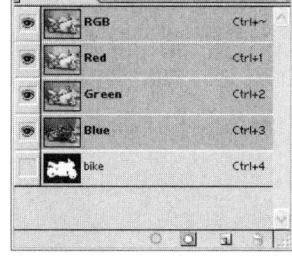

5 Click the selection's Channel Name bar to select it. The black and white image of the selection will appear in your workspace window.

6 Press D to ensure that the foreground and background colors have been set to their default white and black.

7 Using whichever brush seems appropriate to the task at hand, lower the pressure to around 10 percent, and paint with white in the black areas or black in the white areas that you want to protect. Each stroke will make the affected area 10 percent more or less opaque, so you can easily build opacity up or down by adding strokes of black or white.

USING QUICK MASK MODE

If you just want to make a quick change or have some reason to not want to save the selection before editing it, you can paint opacity in or out in Quick Mask mode. By the way, if you're wondering why you might not want to save the mask? Saving the mask makes the file 25 to 30 percent larger.

To Add Or Subtract OPACITY FROM A SELECTION BY WORKING IN QUICK MASK MODE:

1 Make your selection.

2 Click the Quick Mask button. Areas that are masked by the selection will appear covered by a layer of red at 50-percent opacity. (At this point, any tool you use will either add to the orange mask or take away from it.)

3 Press D to ensure that the foreground and background colors have been set to their default white and black.

4 Using whichever brush seems appropriate to the task at hand, lower the pressure to around 10 percent, and paint with white in the black areas or black in the white areas you want to protect. Each stroke will make the affected area 10 percent more or less opaque, so you can easily increase or decrease the opacity by adding strokes of black or white.

You don't have to work with a red mask in Quick Mask mode. It's better to make sure you use a color that matches as few of the image's colors as possible, so that you can tell when you're painting into the mask. Double-click either the Quick Mask icon or the Quick Mask Name bar in the Channels pallete. The Quick Mask Options dialog will appear.

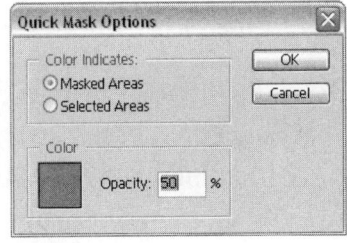

Clicking the Color Swatch brings up the Color Picker and from there you can select any color. You can also change the density of the color by entering a number between 1 and 100 in the Opacity field. Finally, you can invert the colored area, changing it from being the protected area to being the unprotected area, by clicking to turn on the Masked Areas or Selected Areas radio button.

USING THE SELECT MENU

The Select Menu is used to control a currently active selection. If nothing is selected, every command in this menu is grayed out, meaning they're inactive and unavailable. Each of the headlines in this section names a Select menu command (in order of appearance).

ALL

All (CMD/CTRL-A) selects the entire image. If you are zoomed out far enough to see the complete image in your workspace, you will see a marching ants marquee bordering it. Use this command when you want to unprotect the entire image. You can then protect specific areas by pressing OPT/ALT while dragging a selection tool over the target area. If you want to protect several small areas, continue to press OPT/ALT, but also press the SHIFT key to add each additional area after the first. You can then protect the entire image by pressing CMD/CTRL-SHIFT-I to invert the selection.

DESELECT

To make sure that no selection (especially any that might be outside the window or that might have been hidden by the Hide command) is in effect before you issue a command that you want to affect the entire image, choose the Deselect command (CMD/CTRL-D).

RESELECT

The Reselect command (CMD/CTRL-SHIFT-D) is like an Undo command for selections. It's especially handy if you accidentally click while a selection is active, causing it to be dropped.

> **NOTE** I have talked about using brushes to add and subtract opacity in a selection/mask. You can also texture or blur the mask with filters, or use the selection tools to define an area that you will fill with a solid shade of gray for a specific and evenly-distributed level of opacity.

> **NOTE** Every select command on this menu will work while you use Quick Mask mode, save one: Select | Color Range. However, once you've made a Color Range selection, Quick Mask mode offers, by far, the best way to include the little spots of color inside the selection that were outside the color range. Quick Mask mode also lets you "tune" the edges of these selections to blend with the variety of edges typical for such a selection by feathering the edges of the Paintbrush tool.

INVERSE

Mentioned earlier, the Inverse command (CMD/CTRL-SHIFT-I) is used if you want to reverse which areas are protected (masked) and with those that are unprotected.

COLOR RANGE

The Color Range command is used to select a range of colors (not brightness levels, as is the case with the Magic Wand tool) throughout the selected area of the image (or currently active layer). Though termed a command, it is actually a kind of selection tool. It is on the menu instead of in the Tool box because it requires that you use a dialog in order to properly control the borders of the selection.

To Work THE COLOR RANGE DIALOG:

1 Choose Select | Color Range. The Color Range dialog appears.

2 Choose Sampled Colors from the Select menu.

3 Drag the Fuzziness slider to about 50 (or just type 50 into the Fuzziness field).

4 Click the Selection radio button under the Preview window to turn it on.

5 Choose None from the Selection Preview menu. This choice should be named Marquee, because you actually do get a marquee preview of your selection. Once you've started selecting colors, you may want to experiment with the other choices on this menu. Different choices will work best with different types of subject matter, colors, and image contrast.

6 Now it's time to start actually making your selection. You will see three Eyedropper buttons under the Save button. The Eyedropper button (the one that doesn't have a plus or minus sign alongside it) is already chosen by default. When you move your cursor over the image area, it is represented by an eyedropper icon.

7 Click the most prominent area of the color you want to select—either in the image or in the Preview window in the dialog. In the Preview window, the chosen color will turn white.

8 If all the colors you want to select are not yet selected, you can do one of two things: either drag the Fuzziness slider to the right until you see enough of the area you want to select selected, or...

9 Choose the Add To Sample Eyedropper and click the image wherever there are colors you want to add. If you overdo it, you'll have to choose the Subtract From Sample Eyedropper to subtract colors. At the same time, you can use the Fuzziness slider to fine-tune the selection.

10 When you have selected what you want, click OK.

Since you are selecting a color range (probably because you want to change, intensify, or modify the brightness of that color), your selection edges are going to wrap around other colors. You may have also selected some color in portions of the image where you do not want to change the color. If that is the case, choose the Lasso tool, press OPT/ALT and encircle the areas you want to eliminate from the selection.

FEATHER

When you want a selection to blend with its surroundings, you feather the selection. Feathering a selection actually means graduating the edge from 0- to 100-percent opacity over a given radius of pixels. Using the Feather command (OPT/ALT - CMD/CTRL - D), there are two ways to feather a selection: before you make the selection, enter the number of pixels to be feathered in the Feather field of the Feather tool's Options Bar; or after you make the selection, choose Select | Feather.

ADDING BORDERS

To select an area or border that is a given number of pixels on either side of the area originally selected is quite simple.

To Add A BORDER:

1 Choose Select | Modify | Border. The Border Selection dialog appears.

2 Enter the width of the desired border in pixels into the Width field, then click OK.

The marquee for the border selection will appear. Note that it will be an equidistant number of pixels on either side of the original selection.

SMOOTHING

If you're a bit shaky as you move your mouse and you want your selection to be less jagged, use the Smooth command. However, be careful if you're selecting an item with highly irregular edges—especially if you're going to color or knock out the selection. It is likely, if you smooth the selection (which rounds corners to the radius you specify), that the selection will no longer exactly match the edges.

To Smooth THE PATH OF A SELECTION:

1 Choose Select | Modify | Smooth. The Smooth Selection dialog appears.

2 Enter the pixel radius by which you would like to round any sharp corners in your selection. Click OK.

> **NOTE** Smoothing your path is an easy way to round the corners of a rectangular selection.

EXPANDING

The Expand command let's you enlarge your selection by a given number of pixels. You simply enter the number of pixels by which you want to move the selection outward from its current location.

CONTRACTING

The Contract command is, as you might imagine, the reverse of the Expand command. You enter the number of pixels by which you want to move the selection inward from its current location.

THE GROW COMMAND

At first hearing, the Grow command sounds as if it does exactly the same thing as the Expand command, but this is not so. What the command actually does is enlarge the selection by the number of contiguous pixels that match the brightness levels you've chosen as the range for the Magic Wand.

THE SIMILAR COMMAND

The Similar command expands the selection by the same criteria as the Grow command, but selects all the pixels, contiguous or not, in the image that fall within the brightness range of the selection—plus the additional levels of brightness range currently entered in the Magic Wand's Options Bar Tolerance field.

TRANSFORM SELECTION

This command lets you interactively transform (the catch-all word for rotating, resizing, stretching, or distorting something in Photoshop) a selection marquee without disturbing the image itself. It's especially handy as a way to resize geometric (rectangles, ovals, and shapes) selections for use in another area of the image, to create a different size frame around a picture, or to make a different button shape for use on a web page or in an interactive multimedia presentation.

To transform a selection, choose Select | Transform Selection. *Do not* use the CMD/CTRL-T shortcut because you will transform the contents of the selection rather than the selection marquee. Speaking of which, the Options Bar and the methods of reshaping are exactly the same as for a regular image transformation.

LOAD SELECTION

This command lets you retrieve any selection you've previously saved with the currently active image file.

To Load A SELECTION:

1 Choose Select | Load Selection. The Load Selection dialog appears.

2 From the Channel menu, choose the name of the selection you previously saved.

3 If you want the retrieved selection to be the inverse of the original selection, click to check the Invert check box.

4 You can click the appropriate radio button if you want the retrieved selection to be added to, subtracted from, or intersected with any selection that might currently be on screen.

5 When you're ready to have the Previously Saved Selection marquee appear on your image, click OK. It will appear in exactly the same location it occupied when saved. If you want to move it, drag from inside the marquee.

SAVE SELECTION

Any time you need to make a complex selection, you should keep saving it as you build it. Then, if you accidentally drop the selection, you can always retrieve the last version you saved instead of having to start all over again.

To Save A SELECTION:

1 Choose Select | Save Selection. The Save Selection dialog appears.

2 In the Name field, enter a name you will recognize when you want to retrieve the selection—or, if you're overwriting a previously saved selection, choose the name of that selection from the Channels menu.

3 You can also add to, subtract from, or intersect another channel by choosing its name from the Channel menu and clicking the appropriate radio button.

DRAWING A SELECTION WITH THE PEN TOOL

If you need to select an object that has a smooth edge—especially if that object is machine-made—it is much easier to make smooth, "machine-made" looking selections by using vector path drawing tools (resolution independent Bezier curves, used primarily in illustration programs) to create the shape that defines that object's silhouette. Then, with one click, you can change the shape into a selection. As a matter of fact, I know a lot of people who select very complex edges with the aid of the Pen tool. They quickly draw a path that's close to the edges they want to define, convert it to a selection, then use either the Lasso or the Magnetic Lasso to add to or subtract from that selection wherever needed in order to refine the edges to accommodate rough surfaces, textures, wrinkles in clothing, and other natural irregularities. The advantage is that it gives you a starting point and makes it easy to stay oriented when you zoom in tight to make your refinements.

It takes some practice to learn to draw a path accurately on the first attempt. Once you get used to doing this, you'll probably wonder how you ever did without it.

To Draw A PATH AND TURN IT INTO A SELECTION:

1 Choose the Pen tool. In the Options Bar, choose the Path pen (the middle icon in the group of three on the left side of the bar).

2 Place the cursor carefully on the edge of the object you want to select. Click to anchor the first point in the path (for example, a curve), and drag to indicate the direction in which the curve will be moving.

3 Place the cursor where you want to anchor the second point. Click if you want the line to go directly to that point—or—drag if you want to shape the line as it approaches the new point. Repeat this process as long as the curve keeps moving in the same general direction.

4 If you want to change direction, place the cursor directly over the last point you anchored and drag to indicate the new direction. This will make a corner point of the last anchor point. If you want a slight rounding of the curve as it heads off in the new direction, place the new direction point a short distance from the last anchor point before dragging in the new direction.

> **NOTE** You may want to make several paths in order to completely select your object if it has "holes," such as windows, space between a pocketed arm and a body, or the branches of a tree. Just draw a path for each of these holes. As long as all the paths are part of the same work path, you can convert them all at once into a selection.

5 Continue alternating between steps 3 and 4 until you come back around to the first anchor point and click to close the path.

EDIT THE CURVE

When you have drawn all the paths it takes to completely silhouette the object you want to select, you may need to edit the path so the curve fits the edges as closely as possible…though you want the path to flow just inside or just outside small "bumps and lumps." You don't need to use any of the Pen tools or the Path selection tools to do your editing, providing the path you are editing is active (in other words, selected). To select a currently inactive path, choose the Direct Selection tool (white arrow) and click on the path. The path's control points appear.

▶ To delete a point, place the Pen tool over an existing point and click.

▶ To insert a new point in the path, place the Pen tool over a place on the path where there is no point and click.

▶ To change the shape of the curve, place the Pen tool over a point and press OPT/ALT. The Pen tool will change to the Convert Point tool.

▶ To convert a curved point to a corner point, click an anchor point with the Convert Point tool.

▶ To convert a corner point to a curve point, place the Convert Point tool over the corner point and drag to indicate the direction of the curve.

▶ To change the shape and direction of a curve, press CMD/CTRL to convert the Pen tool to a Selection tool. Click to select the point, then press OPT/ALT and drag either handle to a new location.

CONVERT THE PATH TO A SELECTION

Once you have the path drawn to your satisfaction, you can convert it to a marquee selection and then use the Lasso and Magnetic Lasso tools to make the selection absolutely faithful to the irregularities in the object's edges.

To Convert THE PATH TO A SELECTION:

1 Choose Window | Show Paths.

2 If there is more than one work path in the Paths palette, click the Name bar of the path you want to change into a selection.

3 From the Paths palette menu, choose Save Path. The Save Path dialog appears.

4 In the Name field, enter the name of the path you want to save, then click OK. Later, if you need to remake the selection or to edit the path for a different purpose, you won't have to redraw it.

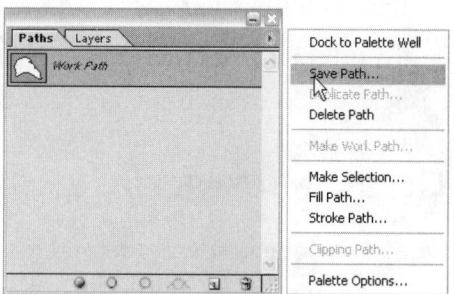

5 Make sure none of the individual paths in the currently selected work path is selected by changing to a Path Selection tool and clicking outside of any path.

6 Click the Load Path As Selection button at the bottom of the Paths palette. The path immediately becomes a selection. Now you can use the selection tools and their Options bar settings to edit the selection.

> **NOTE** Saving a path always takes far less disk space than saving a selection, because the selection is a bitmapped image rather than a mathematical formula.

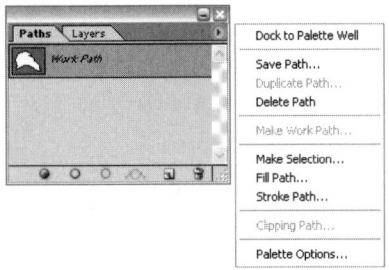

EDIT THE SELECTION

You can use any selection tool, in conjunction with either of the modifier keys (CMD/CTRL and OPT/ALT), to add to or subtract from the current selection. The most useful tools are the Lasso and Magnetic Lasso tools. To edit the selection, zoom in to 100 percent (double-click the Zoom tool) so you can see exactly where the path goes. As you edit, save the selection often so you don't have to start editing all over again. Later, if you don't anticipate needing the selection again, you can delete it to save disk space.

▶ To edit the selection, you will be either adding to or subtracting from the existing selection:

▶ To add to the selection, either press SHIFT or click the Add To Selection button in the Options Bar.

▶ To subtract from the selection, either press OPT/ALT or click the Subtract From Selection button in the Options Bar.

COOL MAGNETIC LASSO TRICKS

One of the quickest ways to make a selection is with the Magnetic Lasso tool—so called because it automatically adheres to the edges of shapes that contrast sufficiently with their surroundings. The problems lie in two areas:

▶ You may want to set an edge where there's not enough contrast between adjoining pixels for Photoshop to see the edge you had in mind.

▶ You can't easily make the marquee follow the path you want to use to close the selection when you don't want it to follow an edge.

The remedies for both of the preceding problems are detailed in the section that follows.

SETTING THE BEST EDGE CONTRAST FOR THE SELECTED IMAGE

If you hope to make the Magnetic Lasso as cool a tool as it promises to be, you'll have to learn to anticipate the best Options Bar setting to use for the specific image you're working with. Otherwise, you'll frequently find the selection wandering off-track.

Just to get an idea of how a picture can influence the way you should set the Edge Contrast field in the Options Bar, I've changed the edge contrast on two versions of the same image and left the Edge Contrast setting at 10 percent in both instances.

> **NOTE** When the selection does wander off-track, immediately press OPT/ALT - DELETE/BACKSPACE (repeatedly, if need be) and move your cursor backwards along the marquee path until you're back on track, er... back on the edge.

To Draw A MARQUEE WITH THE MAGNETIC LASSO:

▌ Choose the Magnetic Lasso tool. Set the Edge Contrast to a setting where you think you'll be able to follow the longest marquee path.

2 Set the Width to a number of pixels on either side of the selection path within which the edge contrast won't vary more than the percentage you've allowed in the Edge Contrast setting. You will then draw an accurate path just as long as you're within half that number of pixels from either side of the intended marquee.

3 In the Options Bar's Frequency field, enter a number of pixels that dictates how often the program will automatically enter an anchor point for the selection. Anchor points keep the selection from wandering when you reach a part of the picture where the edges being selected suddenly change in appearance or contrast. Also, the anchor points become control points if you convert this selection to a path.

> **NOTE** If you are using a pressure stylus, checking the Pen Pressure box will allow you to narrow the Width with more pressure on the pen tip. If you don't have a pressure-sensitive pen, you can still vary the width as you lay down the path by using the square bracket keys to vary width just as you would use them to vary brush size—press [to narrow the width and] to enlarge it.

4 Click the edge where you want to start your path. It should be the longest and most obvious edge. Move the mouse (no need to drag by pressing the button unless you want to set a definite anchor point) to select your edge. If the selection starts to wander more or less uncontrollably, you may want to change the Options Bar settings, or you may want to choose another selection tool.

> **NOTE** Extremely bumpy edges are one of the best applications for the Magnetic Lasso because they are so hard to select manually. However, you should be sure that the bumpy edges are within the Contrast and Width settings you've specified in the Options Bar.

5 Close the path. If a straight line between your opening and closing points can be drawn without causing the selection to overlap itself, just double-click the last point on the path. If not, click to place an anchor point, move the cursor away from the path line and place another anchor point. Repeat the clicking and moving to guide your path to a proper shape before closing it.

6 Save this selection so you can recover it if you accidentally drop it. To save the path, choose Select | Save Selection. The Save Selection dialog appears. In the Name field, enter a suitable name for this selection and click OK.

To Finish THE MAGNETIC LASSO PATH AFTER CHANGING THE OPTIONS BAR SETTINGS:

1 Change the Width, Edge Contrast, and Frequency settings in the Options Bar as appropriate for your new edge. Or...If the rest of the edge isn't well-defined enough to be easily selected by the Magnetic Lasso, you'll be better off using one of the other tools. In that case, just choose the tool you'd prefer to use.

2 In the Options Bar, click to choose the Add To Selection button.

3 Make sure your addition marquee path overlaps the original. When you close the path, it will be added to the original path.

4 Save the current selection. Choose Select | Save Selection. The Save Selection dialog appears. From the Channel menu, choose the name you gave to the original selection. Then choose the Replace Channel radio button (unless it's already selected) and click OK.

MAGNETIC LASSO EDGE CONTRAST SETTINGS

In fact, there is only one setting in the Magnetic Lasso Options Bar actually called Edge Contrast, but there are three settings that define the limits that the Magnetic Lasso will use to automatically find the edge it wants to select. They are Width, Edge Contrast, and Frequency.

WIDTH

Width is the slack space on either side of the marquee within which you can move the cursor and still expect the Magic Lasso to find the intended edge. If you set the width at 10, then the cursor can be within five pixels of either side of the edge. Move it more than five pixels away from either side and the Magnetic Lasso feels free to go find any other edge that meets the specification of the Edge Contrast setting.

EDGE CONTRAST

This entry is a percentage of the contrast (brightness values) between the foreground object and its surroundings. If the foreground object is in stark contrast to the background, you can raise the Edge Contrast setting. If you can hardly tell that there is a difference, then lower the value. There will come a point where the edge differences are either so subtle or so fuzzy you'd be better off to use the regular lasso and simply hand-sketch the edge.

FREQUENCY

This is the setting you use to tell Photoshop how often it should lay down an anchor point. If the edged is highly jagged or wavy, it's a good idea to raise the frequency. That way, if the marquee starts wandering aimlessly, you'll have a shorter distance to back up (press DELETE/BACKSPACE) before you get to an anchor point that was accurately placed. You should also raise the frequency if the difference between the edge and foreground are barely apparent.

SELECTING HAIR AND OTHER SEEMING IMPOSSIBILITIES

The technique for selecting hair is equally applicable to any highly complex edge, such as tall blades of grass against a contrasting background, or the gaps between leaves of a distant tree. Strictly speaking, this technique isn't a selection, it's something called a knockout. Knockouts are made by removing everything from the object's layer you want to keep except the object itself. So, if you want to use the knockout as a selection, you must first duplicate the layer it resides on. Then, when you manipulate the rest of the image (as long as you're not doing so with an adjustment layer), the knockout will remain intact because it resides on a separate layer.

To Duplicate A LAYER:

1   Choose Window | Show Layers (or drag the Layers palette tab from the Palette Well).

2   Drag the Layer Name bar of the layer you want to duplicate to the New Layer icon at the bottom of the Layers palette—or choose Layer | New | Layer Via Copy (CMD/CTRL-J)

Up until Photoshop 5.5, there was really no way to make such a selection without using a third-party application or plug-in such as Ultimatte (now Corel) Knockout (which is still more powerful for very complex edges and for partially transparent areas of the selection). Photoshop 5.5 introduced the Background Eraser tool and Photoshop 6.0 introduced the Extract command. Both of these tools have a lot in common, but the Extract tool is somewhat more powerful—especially given the refinements added in Photoshop 7.0.

Using the Magic Eraser to knock out subjects with complex edges is a quick way to knock out relatively smooth-edges (or at least well-defined ones) that have been shot against an evenly-lit, single-color, textureless background. The Magic Eraser behaves just like the Magic Wand, except that instead of making a selection, it simply erases what would have been a selection.

> **NOTE** This can also be a good technique for substituting a flat blue sky with a more interesting sky. Just be sure the substitute sky was shot when the sun was in the same position as it was in the sky you're replacing. Also, be sure to take a Snapshot before you knock out the sky so that, if need be, you can use the History Brush to paint back in any subtle details along the horizon.

To Use THE MAGIC ERASER TO KNOCK OUT A BACKGROUND:

1 Choose the Magic Eraser.

2 In the Options Bar, enter the number of shades (out of 256) that you want to delete in the Tolerance field. You want the range to be as broad as possible without removing excess foreground.

3 Also in the Options Bar, be sure that Anti-alias is checked and that Use All Layers is unchecked.

4 Uncheck Contiguous if you want to erase gaps between tree branches or closed in areas of other objects through which you can see the background. Just be sure you're not going to erase part of the foreground. If that will be the case, check Contiguous and make additional clicks in those areas independently.

To Place A NEW BACKGROUND INTO THE IMAGE:

1 Open the new background's file, choose Edit | Select All (CMD/CTRL-A), then CMD/CTRL-C to copy the entire image to the clipboard.

2 Click in the knocked-out image's window to activate it and press OPT/ALT-CMD/CTRL-V. The new background image will appear on its own layer.

3 Choose Window | Show Layers. The Layers palette appears.

4 Drag the Layer Name bar of the new background's layer immediately below the knocked-out layer.

To Use THE BACKGROUND ERASER TO KNOCK OUT AN OBJECT WITH A COMPLEX EDGE:

1 Duplicate the layer the object resides on (as instructed previously). If this is a virgin image, the object will be on the Background layer, so you should first convert it to an ordinary layer. To do so, double-click the Background Layer Name bar. When the Layer Properties dialog appears, enter a name other than Background and click OK.

2 Turn off the layer that was formerly the background layer (as well as any other layers except the one you duplicated) so you can see what you are doing.

3 Choose the Background Eraser from the Toolbox. Set the Background Eraser Options Bar as shown in the illustration. These settings are a good start, but don't be afraid to experiment with these settings in order to fine-tune the results.

4 Get close enough to the objects you're erasing so that the size of your brush extends into areas where the existing background shows through, as shown here.

5 If some areas have been erased too much, use the History Brush to paint them back in. It's a big help to have a pressure-sensitive tablet, such as a Wacom, for this because you can vary the size of the brush with pressure.

6 When you have cleaned up and cleared space around all the edges, choose the Lasso tool and make a selection through the cleared area.

7 Press SHIFT-CMD/CTRL-I to invert the selection and then press DELETE/BACKSPACE to completely isolate the object on a transparent background.

You can now place a different background on a separate layer or you can adjust the knockout layer and the other layers independently.

The Extract command is similar to the Background Eraser, but presents an independent and more versatile interface for making knockouts. If you look at this interface, shown in Figure 6-2, it looks a lot more complicated than it turns out to be for most operations. It will be easier to grasp if I first explain the principle of how it works and then give you a few tips before I have you do the step-by-step exercise.

Essentially, all you have to do is use the Edge Highlighter tool to outline the silhouette of the object you want to knock out, then use the Fill Bucket to fill the interior of the selection so that Photoshop knows what colors should definitely be kept. In addition to keeping everything covered by the fill color (yes, you can choose your own fill color) Photoshop keeps all the colors that are immediately next to the Edge Highlighter color—even if they're scattered throughout the Edge Highlighter border. That's how it does such a remarkable job of keeping parts of the object that stick out into space and overlap one another.

Now, if you've shot your subject against a plain background—especially one that's been evenly lighted in a studio. On the other extreme is a background that has color and texture similar to what's on the edge of the subject. In between is any kind of detail that uses some of the same color and intensity as objects you want to keep. If your photo falls into the last two categories, you can either use the Edge touchup or the Cleanup tools to tweak the edge into what you want it to be. If that's not enough, you can also use the Background Eraser and History Brush to fine-tune the selection of edge details.

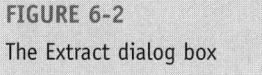
FIGURE 6-2
The Extract dialog box

To Knock Out THE EVER-POPULAR "GIRL WITH FLYING HAIR" SHOT:

1 Open the shot you want to knock out.

2 Click the Layer Name bar of the layer you want to knock the subject out of and press CMD/CTRL-J to duplicate the layer.

3 Choose the top layer. This is the one from which the subject will be knocked out.

4 Choose Image | Extract. The Extract dialog will occupy almost your entire screen. You cannot change the size of this interface.

5 Double-click the Zoom tool to zoom in to 100 percent so you can see all the fine hairs and other details that protrude into the background.

6 Choose the Hand tool or press the SPACEBAR to temporarily use the Hand tool and pan to those places where the edge is almost perfectly smooth. Check the Smart Highlighting box.

7 Choose the Edge Highlighter (marker). If you are using a mouse, you can enlarge and reduce the brush size by pressing [to reduce and] to enlarge. Make your brush about the size of a rubber eraser-head and trace along the smooth edges.

8 Continue panning around the image until you have highlighted all the smooth edges (in this case, that's mostly the girl's shoulders).

9 Uncheck the Smart Highlighting box. Trace along the edges that have complex details. Use a brush large enough to cover all the protrusions.

10 When you have highlighted all the edge details (see Figure 6-3), choose the Hand tool and pan around the image to examine the edges carefully. Make sure no tiny gaps exist in the highlighting.

11 If there are areas where the highlighting goes too far into the foreground, choose the Eraser and slim down the edges. When you're sure the edge is just as you want it...

12 Choose the Fill tool (G), then move the cursor inside the foreground object and click. The foreground will turn blue (or whatever you've chosen as your foreground color).

13 Click the Preview button. It takes a while for the preview to generate. When it's finished...

FIGURE 6-3

Covering protrusions with the highlighter

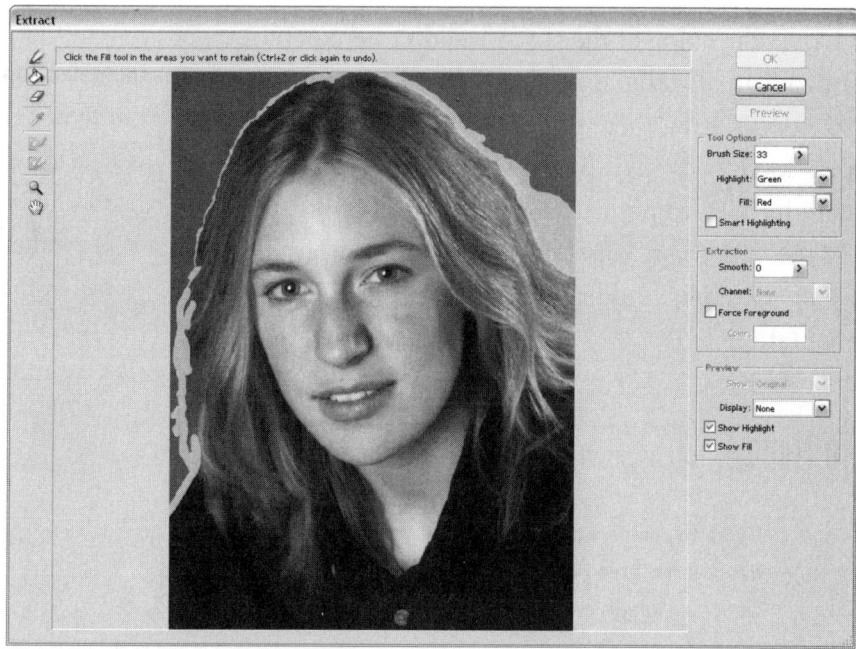

14 Double-click the Zoom tool, then pan around the edges. If there are mistakes, clean them up with the Cleanup and Edge touchup tools.

15 You can also continue to Highlight, Fill, and Preview. Each time, the selection will be completely regenerated according to how you most recently painted the edge highlight. When you're happy with what you've got, click OK.

If you selected the subject from a digital photo shot against a natural background, you'll probably want to use the Gaussian Blur filter on the underlying layer so you get some selective focus. Be sure to clone the background into the subject so you don't get a halo from the subject after instigating the blur.

SELECTIONS BASED ON A RANGE OF COLOR TONES

One way to make quick selections of highly complex and disconnected edges is to use the Select Color Range command. If there's enough of a difference between the areas you want to select and those you want unselected, you can make very complex selections very quickly. For instance, suppose you have a photo of a bare tree silhouetted against the sky and you want to change the color of the sky. Shouldn't be much of a problem, as long as the highlighted edges of the tree don't bring them to nearly the same brightness level as the sky. If that's the case, then you may have to combine this method with another. At the very least, you'll have to make your adjustments carefully and be willing to do some experimentation.

> **NOTE** One of the real beauties of making selections by color range is that you can then reinterpret the colors within that range in zillions of different ways, just by filling the selection in different colors while applying different blend modes in the Fill Options dialog.

To Make A SELECTION BASED ON A COLOR RANGE:

1 Open an image where the object you want to select has a large area of a predominant color that you want to change or reinterpret.

2 Choose Select | Color Range. The Color Range dialog appears and the cursor takes the form of an eyedropper icon.

3 Click in the area that represents the largest area of the color you want to select. A selection marquee will appear around some or all of the area you want to select. Chances are, it will need to be adjusted to include all of the color you want selected.

4 Your desired selection probably includes shades (blends) of the color you want to select. In that case, you'll want to expand your selection to include them. In that case, you should employ one, the other, or both of the next two steps:

5 To expand or contract the shades and tonalities included in your selected area (and enlarge the selection), drag the Fuzziness slider until colors you're sure you don't want selected are outside the selected area.

> **NOTE** You can select more than one color, but it's usually more accurate to stick to one range of a particular color at a time. If you want to pick areas of obviously distinct colors (such as a blue area and a yellow area), you're likely to have an easier time if you pick them as separate selections.

6 To add or subtract specific areas of color in the selection, choose an Eyedropper in the dialog that has either a plus or minus sign alongside the eyedropper icon. You can then click additional colors or shades to add to or subtract them from the selection.

7 Continue adding to or subtracting from the selection until it is exactly the shape you want, then click OK. The dialog will disappear and your selection marquee will remain. You can now use any of the other selection tools to edit the selection, just make sure you save the first selection so you can come back to it easily.

DIFFERENT FEATHERING FOR DIFFERENT EDGES OF A SELECTION

There will be times when you want to have a different amount of feathering for different segments of the selection marquee. For instance, imagine you want to employ a selective focus technique and some edges are closer to the camera than others. In that case, some edges would be more out-of-focus than others, so you'd want the Gaussian Blur filter to be applied over a greater distance for the more out-of-focus edges and over a smaller distance for those closer edges with less focus falloff.

To Edit THE SELECTION'S CHANNEL BY BLURRING THE EDGES OF THE MASK:

1 Select the edge that needs a different degree of feathering than the original. The selection can be made with any of the selection tools or any combination of them.

2 Once the selection has been made, choose Selection | Save Selection. The Save Selection dialog appears.

3 In the Name field, type the name you'd like to give this selection (I used "selection," just to make it obvious which channel we were working on) and click OK. You just created a new Channel in your image (document).

4 Now all you have to do is edit the Channel image as if it were any other Photoshop document. To do this, choose Window | Show Channels.

5 Click the Name bar (Selection) of the selection's channel, then click OK. The image in the workspace turns into a black and white silhouette. The white area represents the space that has been selected, the black area represents the space that has been masked.

6 Select the edge you want to blur more (the Lasso tool usually provides the easiest way to do this, but you can use any selection tool). Leave enough of a margin on either side of the edge you're selecting to include all of the blurring (see Figure 6-4).

7 Choose Filter | Blur | Gaussian Blur. The Gaussian Blur dialog appears.

8 Be sure the Preview box is checked, then drag the Radius slider until you see the degree of blurring you want to achieve. Click OK.

9 Repeat steps 6 through 8 until you have made all the edge variations you need.

10 Click the RGB channel Name bar in the Channels palette. You will now see the image in its normal mode.

11 At any time you want to use the selection with the complex feathered edges, choose Select | Load Selection. The Load Selection dialog will appear.

> **NOTE** Another way to invert a selection is to simply invert the image in the channel just as you would invert (change to a negative) any other Photoshop image. To do this, choose Edit | Invert (CMD/CTRL-I).

FIGURE 6-4
Selecting portions of the saved selection for different degrees of feathering

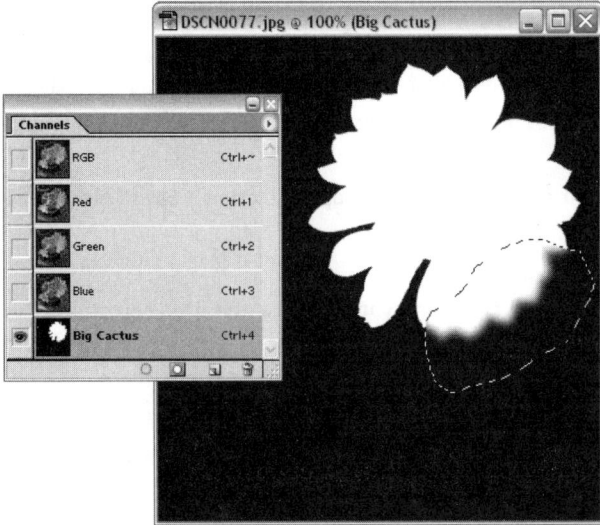

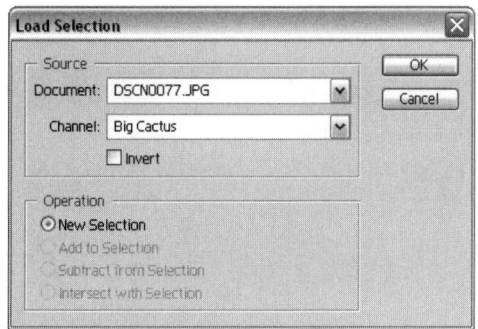

12 From the Channels menu, choose the name of the selection you saved and click OK. The selection will appear over your image. You may now proceed to apply whatever effect you wanted to apply gradually across varying widths throughout the selection.

NOTE You can also use the Blur tool to interactively blur the edges of a selection to different degrees.

ON THE VIRTUAL CLASSROOM CD-ROM In Lesson 5, "Making Selections," there are two demonstrations relating to this chapter. One shows you how to use the Magnetic Lasso. Another demonstration shows how to use the Background Eraser as a quick way alternative to the Extract command. *Approximate time: 5 minutes.*

Using Work Paths

What Photoshop calls work paths are known as
the Bezier paths, control points, and vector shapes that comprise images constructed in drawing programs such as Adobe
Illustrator, Macromedia Freehand, CorelDraw, and Deneba Canvas.
In other words, they are geometric formulas that define how
an output device of any kind (a monitor, printer, or plotter,
for example) should draw that shape at the best resolution
that the user specifies for that device.

USING WORK PATHS

Work paths are the best way to create smooth-edged, precisely geometric shapes that can be immediately turned into selections. Conversely, you can transform any selection into a work path that can then be smoothed, refined, and edited using Bezier control points and handles. In the illustration that follows, you see a selection (on the right) made freehand by a friend with little drawing experience, and a path (on the left) that outlines the same selection. It's obvious how much cleaner the path is.

MAKING SMOOTH-EDGED SELECTIONS WITH PATHS

One of the reasons work paths are such a popular way to select smooth-edged objects is that they are so easy to edit they can be fine-tuned with great precision. Figure 7-1 shows a path that has been precisely edited to become a selection, but that has not yet been converted, so you can still see its control points and handles. The accompanying callouts show what you move in order to be able to control the shape and direction of the lines and curves that form the path.

Of course, making a selection with a path isn't nearly as intuitive as simply tracing an outline freehand using the Lasso tool. However, practice the following exercise a few times and you'll quickly see how much easier it is to select highly geometric shapes (for example, smooth-edged fruits such as apples, or machine-made objects of almost any kind).

FIGURE 7-1

A path that will be converted to a selection

To Select A SHAPE:

1 Choose the Pen tool (or press P).

2 Click the Paths button on the Options Bar.

3 Place the cursor precisely on an edge, then drag for a short distance along the edge in the direction you want the line to follow. (The illustration here shows lines along a curved object.) A *control point* (which anchors the path) appears at the beginning of the line, and the end of the *control handle* (which controls the shape and curvature of the path) appears at the point where you stop dragging.

4 Move the cursor to a point on the path where the shape makes a more dramatic change. This could be a corner, an increase in curvature, or a change in direction.

5 If it's a corner (any sharp change in direction), click to anchor the point, press OPT/ALT to change to the Corner Point tool, and click the same point again, dragging it in the direction of the outgoing curve. (The new curve handle will be independent of the incoming curve handle.) Or...

6 If it's going to lead to a change in direction, click to end the previous line, then click and drag somewhat further along the path to make a curve in a new direction. Or...

7 If it's going to increase in curvature, drag to indicate the direction of the curve that follows the point by dragging the control handle further along the path.

8 There are two ways to close a path so that it becomes a shape. You can double-click when you place the last anchor point. This will draw a straight line between the last point and the first point. You can also place the last point immediately atop the first point.

MAKING A SHAPE BY DRAWING PATHS

Shapes, in Photoshop jargon, are vector paths much like those you may have used in an illustration or drawing program. The picture information in an object drawn with a path is constructed according to a geometric formula. Because such formulae are only numbers and operators, shapes (such as circles, squares, polygons, and even the silhouettes of familiar real-world objects—such as flowers or hammers) require very little disk space. Also, because they are composed of numbers, shapes can readily be scaled to suit the highest resolution of whatever device is displaying or printing them. This saves a great deal of time when you have to create shapes that are commonly used as elements in various illustrations, such as company logos or the icons and buttons used for interactive navigation.

Another reason shapes are important in Photoshop is that they can be made to be perfectly and mechanically smooth, and then can be readily turned into selections.

Photoshop draws two basic kinds of shapes: *predefined* and *freehand*. Predefined shapes can be found in the Toolbox on the Shape tool's fly-out menu, while others can be drawn freehand by you, the Photoshop user (with the aid of the Pen tools), and saved to the shape library.

Predefined shapes, known in Photoshop simply as Shapes, include:

▶ Rectangle

▶ Rounded Rectangle

▶ Ellipse

▶ Polygon

▶ Line

▶ Custom Shape (a Freehand shape that has been saved to a Custom Shape library)

You can access any of these Shapes from either the Shapes fly-out menu in the Toolbox or, once you've chosen any one of them, from the Shapes Options Bar. There are three ways you can manifest any Shape or Path. In the order in which these methods appear on the Options Bar, you can

▶ Have it appear on its own layer as a clipping path.

▶ Have it appear as a work path (or as part of a work path) on the currently-active layer.

▶ Have it instantly render itself as a bit-mapped shape once you have drawn the shape or closed the path.

USING CLIPPING PATH LAYERS

A clipping path layer uses the path as a mask, cropping whatever is below (or above) to the shape of the mask. If no image is designated, the content of the clipping path is simply a color. Any path or shape can be used as a clipping path layer. This is the way you export partly transparent Photoshop images to desktop publishing programs (such as QuarkXpress, Adobe InDesign, and PageMaker) and drawing programs (such as Adobe Illustrator, CorelDraw, and FreeHand). Areas outside of the clipping path are automatically seen as transparent by the drawing program.

To Save AN IMAGE WITH CLIPPING PATHS:

1 Draw the desired shape on the image using either the Path tools or the Shape tools. (Keep in mind that areas outside the paths will be transparent.)

2 Choose Window | Paths to show the Paths palette (or click it in the Palette well if its tab is there), then from the Paths palette menu, choose Save Path. The Save Path dialog opens, as shown here.

3 In the Name field, enter a name for the path.

4 From the Paths palette menu, choose Clipping Path, and the Clipping Path dialog appears.

5 From the Path menu, choose the title you gave to the saved path. Optionally, you can enter a number of pixels that will be turned into a flat line, thus simplifying the path. Click OK.

6 Choose File | Save As. The Save As dialog box appears.

7 From the Format menu, choose EPS.

You can now open your vector program and import the EPS file you've just saved. It will show a transparent area outside the path.

DRAWING A FREEFORM CUSTOM SHAPE

A custom shape is one that can be chosen from the menu in the Custom Shapes Options bar. Photoshop 7.0 comes with 249 predrawn shapes. You can add as many more as you like by collecting shapes from drawing programs and from third-party clip-art programs.

Most importantly, you can use the Pen tools to draw just about any imaginable shape. One trick many people use is to trace an object from a photograph to make a smooth selection, and then to save that silhouette as a custom shape or export it to an illustration program so as to make use of the more sophisticated tools in that program.

We've already seen how to use the Pen tools to draw a shape that includes Bezier curves. You can also create a shape by drawing it freeform. In fact, there are two kinds of tools with which this can be done: the Selection tools and the Freeform or Magnetic Pen tools.

To Create A PATH WITH THE SELECTION TOOLS:

1 Make your selection with whatever tool seems appropriate to properly and quickly create a silhouette of the object in the photograph. When the selection is complete...

2 Open the Paths palette. Choose Window | Paths, then click the Make Work Path From Selection button. The selection will immediately become a vector work path.

If it's a clean enough shape, and there's enough contrast between the object and the background, there is an easy way to draw a complex path.

To Create A PATH WITH THE FREEHAND PEN TOOL:

1 Choose the Freeform Pen tool. Use it exactly the same way as the Magnetic Lasso.

2 If you need to switch to the Freeform Pen, just double-click to stop the line, then uncheck the magnetic box in the Freeform Pen Options Bar. Click the last point on the existing path and continue on.

3 The shape is now a closed path. To turn your path into a shape, click the first point in the path.

> **NOTE** If you're going to use a magnetic tool to make a selection, you'll find the Magnetic Pen much more controllable than the Magnetic Lasso because you can use the path control points to edit the shape with extreme accuracy.

RENDERING PATHS AS BITMAPS

Any vector path can be instantly converted to a bit-mapped shape that then becomes part of the photograph or painting. You can also create a new, transparent layer before rendering the path. Then, when its rendered, it will reside on a separate layer until you merge that layer (or "flatten" the image) with the others.

Once you've rendered a path, you can then use the Photoshop editing and special effects tools to make the shape look more painterly or photographic. When the vector shape is rendered to a bitmap, you can even merge a photograph with it.

To Render ANY VECTOR SHAPE TO A BITMAP:

1 Draw a shape using any of the Shape tools.

2 (Optional) If you want to render the shape to a transparent layer, choose Window | Layers to show the Layers palette, and click the New Layer icon at the bottom of the Layers palette. A new layer will appear just above the currently selected layer.

3 Open the Paths palette. Choose Window | Paths or (if it's there) click the Paths Palette tab in the Palette well.

4 Select the path you want to render by clicking its Name bar on the Paths palette.

5 Click the Set Foreground Color tool, and use the Color Picker to choose your fill color.

6 Click the Fill Path With Foreground Color icon at the bottom of the Paths palette. You will automatically get a rendered shape.

NOTE If you choose the Fill Pixels button on the Options bar before you draw the shape, the shape will be rendered as soon as it closed (or, in this case, as soon as you draw it).

NOTE If a shape has been constructed (the first icon on the Pen tool's Options Bar) instead of created as a path, then you must create an explicit path by double-clicking the shape vector mask (on the Paths palette) and naming the path. It is this path name that will be available in step 3.

7 (Optional) If you want to place a border or an outline around the rendered shape, select the transparent area of the layer with the Magic Wand tool, and press CMD/CTRL-SHIFT-I to invert the selection.

8 Choose Edit | Stroke. The Stroke dialog box appears, as shown here.

9 In the Stroke field, enter the number of pixels wide that you'd like to make the stroke.

10 Choose a color for the stroke by clicking the Color field to open the Color Picker. Click OK when you've chosen the appropriate color.

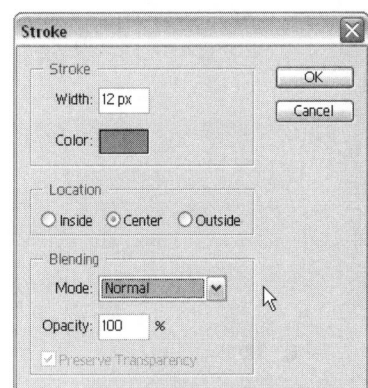

11 You can place the bitmapped stroke outside the marquee, inside it, or with the marquee centered inside it. Just choose the appropriate radio button in the Location frame.

12 You can also choose a Blending Mode from the Mode menu and enter an opacity (intensity of the blend) by entering a number between 1 and 100 in the Opacity field. If you don't want the blend to affect transparent areas of the layer, check the Preserve Transparency box. Click OK.

SAVING A SHAPE TO A VECTOR FILE FORMAT

Once you've drawn a shape, you can use it over and over again by saving it as an EPS (Encapsulated Postscript) or AI (Adobe Illustrator) file. You can then open it as a vector shape in any vector program that accepts EPS files...or you can open it in Photoshop, where it will be automatically rasterized (bitmapped). Then, if you want the rasterized version of the shape in your current Photoshop file, drag it from the opened file into your working Photoshop file.

To Save TO AN EPS OR ILLUSTRATOR FILE:

1 Select the shape you want to save. If you want to save it to a file by itself, choose the Path Selection (black arrow) tool to select the shape.

2 Choose Edit | Cut (or press CMD/CTRL-X)

3 If necessary, Choose Window | Layers to make the Layers palette visible. Otherwise, just click the Layers palette to make it active and bring it to the top. Click the New Layer icon at the bottom of the palette to create a new layer. The new layer will become the active layer.

4 Choose Edit | Paste (or press CMD/CTRL-V). The shape will be pasted in place onto a new layer.

5 One at a time, select each of the layers that doesn't contain the shape, and click the Trashcan (Delete Layer) icon at the bottom of the tools palette.

6 Choose File | Save As. The Save As dialog appears.

7 From the Format menu, choose Photoshop EPS.

8 Enter a name for your shape file in the Name field and click OK. Alternatively, you can select the specific shape, copy it, and paste it into a NEW document. This document can be saved in the Photoshop EPS format. The advantage of this method is that it preserves the original file from which the shape was extracted.

You can now open your file in a vector program as a vector shape, or in Photoshop, where it will be automatically rasterized. If you want to maintain it as a shape when you reopen it, open it in Adobe Illustrator and drag it into Photoshop.

RESHAPING A SHAPE

You can readily change the shape of things (or at least the shape of shapes). So if there's a shape you've already drawn, and the shape you need later is similar, all you have to do is modify the existing shape. The same is true of all the shapes in the Shapes dialog. There are two ways to modify a shape: You can transform it, or you can edit it with the Pen tools.

TRANSFORMING A SHAPE

Transforming a shape is essentially the same as transforming a layer or selection. The commands are the same, except that they're renamed to let you know you're transforming a path.

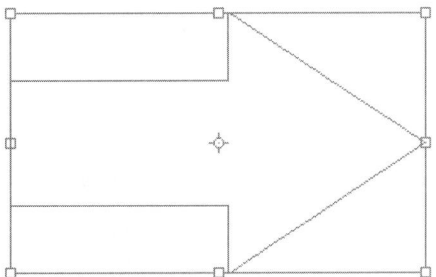

To Transform a shape:

1 Choose Window | Paths. The Paths palette will come to the fore.

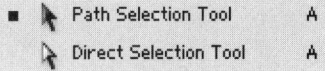

2 Click the Name bar of the layer containing the path you want to transform. Alternatively, you can choose the Path Selection tool and click the path itself.

3 The quick and easy way to make simple transformations is to press CMD/CTRL-T. A bounding box will appear around the path, and the Transform Options Bar will appear.

> **NOTE** You can also choose Edit | Transform Path to bring up the menu shown in Figure 7-2. Any of the choices on that menu makes a precise transformation, or brings up a dialog box that will let you make a precise transformation by entering numeric information.

4 Now you can either enter numerical numbers for transformations in the options bar, or drag the handles of the bounding box to make free transformations. Dragging the center handle stretches the side of the shape that the handle is on. Dragging a corner handle shrinks or enlarges the shape proportionately. Dragging just outside of a handle rotates the shape. Pressing CMD/CTRL and dragging a corner handle in any distorts the shape in that direction:

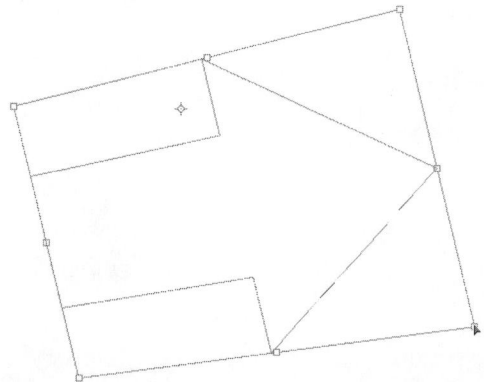

FIGURE 7-2
Choosing a transformation
from the Edit menu

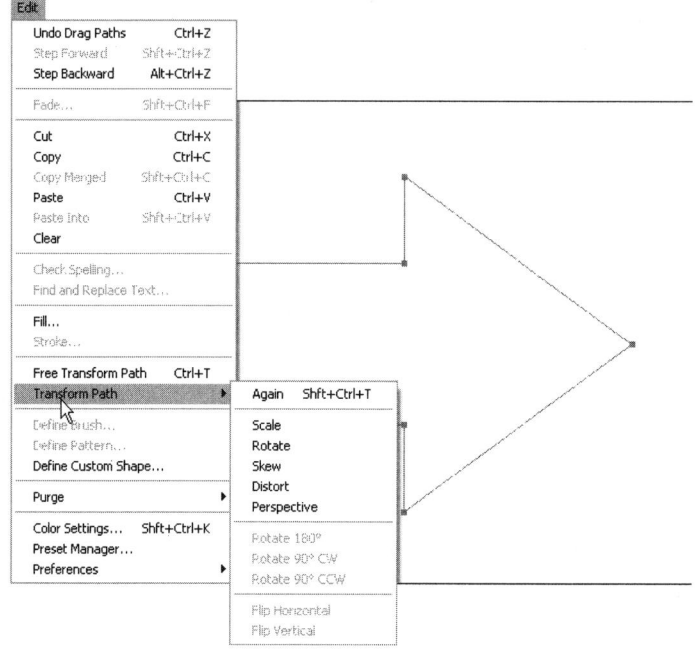

ON THE VIRTUAL CLASSROOM CD-ROM In Lesson 6, "Paths and
Shapes," you get a live demonstration of how to draw and edit paths using
the Pen tool. You also learn how to modify Shapes—including custom shapes.
Approximate time: 5 minutes.

Creating Original Art and Photopainting

Photoshop has been traditionally known as an image-editing program, not a paint program, even though you can do painting to a limited degree in earlier versions of Photoshop. Version 7 makes the extent of brush options so versatile that the ability to move more deeply into the painting realm has increased manyfold. This chapter will focus on two techniques that can be used to make photos look like traditional paintings. For you as a Photoshop user, this should open up a whole new area of creativity, lowering your dependence on third-party plug-ins for digital painting tasks.

The first technique involves painting from scratch. This means you simply pick up the mouse or stylus and begin painting on a blank document the same way a conventional painter might. Along the way, various steps and techniques will be explored that make the process easier and more foolproof. In addition, some of the new brush features in Photoshop 7 that make this kind of painting possible will be discussed.

The second technique is more akin to illustration and animation, where you can Capture a line drawing from a photo and then paint transparent color referenced from the photo over the lines to get a dramatic watercolor wash-and-ink drawing look. This simple procedure uses a process called photopainting—a new hybrid style that combines both photography and digital painting techniques.

DRAWING FROM SCRATCH

In this exercise, you'll paint some flowers. If you don't like flowers, feel free to use whatever subject inspires you. The techniques used here, which utilize the new brush options in Photoshop 7, can be applied to any subject.

Throughout, it will be assumed you're using a pressure-sensitive pen and tablet (painting with a mouse is only for masochists!). If you haven't yet purchased a pressure-sensitive digitizing tablet, Wacom makes a very affordable series called the Graphire (for about $100) that gives you all the pressure-sensitive options you need. Its pen enables you to create painter-like strokes, and makes positioning of the brush tip absolute—in other words, the brush tip occupies the precise screen position you're aiming for.

To Begin PAINTING:

1 Open a new document 1200x1500 pixels in size.

2 In the Layers palette, drag the base layer to the New Layer icon twice so you end up with three layers. The base layer will be your background, the second layer will be the layer you paint on, and the third layer is for your preliminary sketch.

3 Label the two created layers Paint Layer and Sketch Layer, respectively. If you feel insecure about drawing completely from scratch, you can place a photo reference on a fourth layer, placed below the Sketch Layer, and then reduce the Sketch Layer Opacity

to 50 percent so you can trace the photo. It is also possible to do a sketch on paper and scan it in.

As you can see in the following illustration, an outline of the flowers has been drawn in gray on the Sketch layer using a brush five pixels wide. Make sure there is no fill in any of the layers except the Background layer. The Sketch layer should just have line work on a transparent field. The Background layer should be filled with white for the time being so it gives you a good visual ground to paint over. You can sketch and erase as much as you want until you get the forms and composition where you want it.

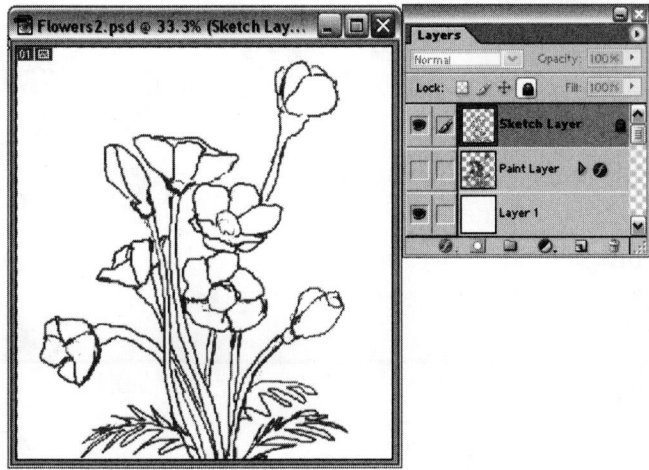

Now let's move on to the Paint layer. The first thing you will need to do is choose a paintbrush. That used to be a very simple task in previous versions of Photoshop, but in version 7 the brush selection process is much more complex. If you want brushes to simulate natural media, it is necessary to implement several various brush options, as you will see.

To Choose A PAINTBRUSH:

1 Choose the Paintbrush icon from the Tools palette.

2 Choose the Paintbrush Preset Picker from the Brush Options Bar. The Preset Picker palette appears.

3 Choose the menu arrow in the upper-right of the Preset Picker to reveal the Preset menu.

4 Choose Natural Brushes 2. This is a new library of brushes that have a more natural configuration than the simple round brushes you're used to. Quite a few brush libraries are available. The dialog box lets you replace or append the current library. For instance, if you want to continue using brushes in the current library in addition to the new ones, select Append. Otherwise, choose Replace.

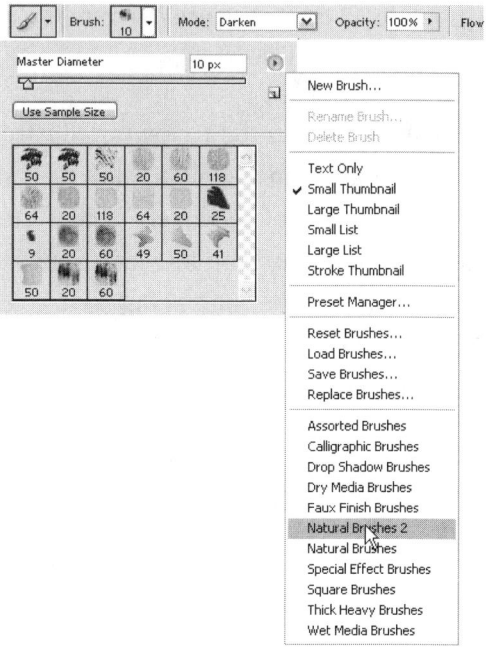

Choosing the right brush is a matter of taste, personal style, and the requirements of the painting job ahead of you. It's best to choose a size proportional to the areas of detail you are painting in—for instance, small details require a small brush, larger details a larger brush, and so on. Experiment with different styles to see which best fits you. Before you start painting, however, a few parameters need to be set. This is done by using the Brushes palette to add some powerful features.

To Add FEATURES:

1 Choose Windows | Brushes to open the Brushes palette. (If the palette is already in the Palette Dock, you can open it from there by clicking the Brush tab.) The Brushes palette opens.

2 Highlight one of the drawing tools to activate the parameters in the Brushes palette.

> NOTE Not all parameters in the Brushes palette are available for every tool. Those that aren't applicable will be grayed out.

Shape Dynamics, Texture, Color Dynamics, and Other Dynamics are all features that you will be changing the options for in this exercise. Feel free to experiment with other parameters later.

The Brushes palette is your control center for all the parameters each brush can take on. The first parameter to adjust is the Brush Dynamics. Before going further though, it might be best to discuss the term *jitter*. Jitter refers to a mathematical algorithm that changes a parameter from a fixed value to an oscillating random value within a fixed range defined by user input. The best way to understand the jitter effect of the various parameters is to watch what happens to the brush preview as you change the parameters.

Set the Shape Dynamics of the brush by adjusting the sliders and observing how the brush changes in the lower preview window. The Minimum Size slider will set the low end of the range of sizes that the pressure-sensitive pen will give you. Try out the settings on a test image (or in a part of the image you can easily erase) to see if the brush has the look you are after. Or just use the setting in the illustration here.

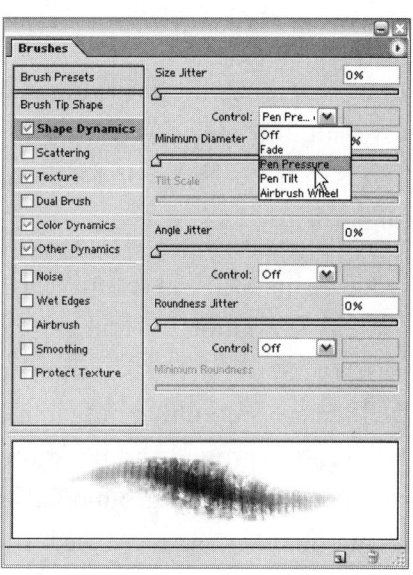

Next, let's give the brush some texture. Dynamic texturing is totally new to Photoshop 7, but not new to paint programs. The Texture dynamic simulates three-dimensional surfaces, such as watercolor paper or canvas, which cause the color to be applied unevenly. This is quite different than applying a texture afterwards. Dynamic textures actually affect the way color is laid down by the brush, giving the appearance of natural media on various surfaces that can add character to your painting. You can choose a type of texture from the Brush Presets menu, which is accessed by clicking the arrow next to the texture picture. The sliders allow you to set the depth, scale, and jitter of the texture to give it a stronger, subtler, or less uniform appearance. Adjust the texture by viewing the preview, or use the settings shown here.

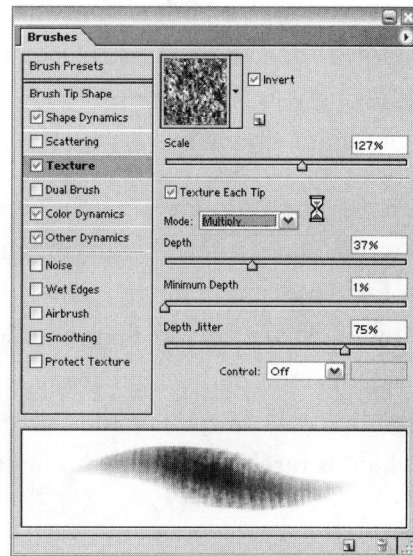

Next are the Color Dynamics. This allows you to use the foreground and background colors as a jitter range. But it's not just the jitter range that can be used to shift colors between the foreground and background. If Color Dynamics is selected and Pen Pressure has been chosen as the mode, then foreground/background colors can be dynamically mixed—even if jitter is set to zero.

The top slider determines the percentage of mixing between the two colors. Jitter produces fluctuations in the brush stroke colors, making the strokes look more natural. You can also jitter the color by hue, saturation, brightness, and purity to make your brush strokes even more complex. It's worth experimenting with the settings to get a feel for it. After all, there are few pertinent rules regarding do's and don'ts in the design world—though a class in art history might help.

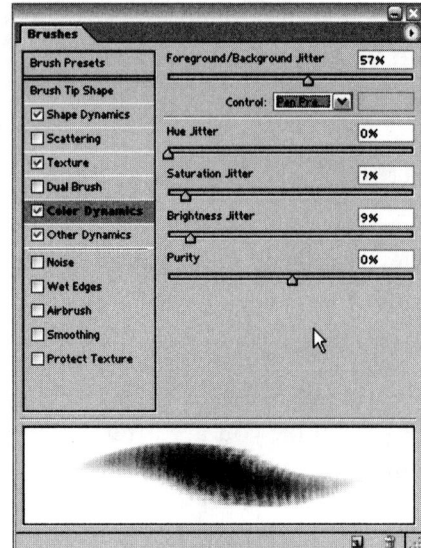

Once again, you can use pen pressure instead of jitter to cause the variations. If Foreground/Background Jitter is set to zero and the mode is set to Pen Pressure, then the artist can achieve smoothly graduated color variation and mixing between foreground and background depending on the pressure used. If the Foreground/Background Jitter is greater than zero, then the degree of smooth blending is reduced depending on the amount of jitter. A value of 100 gives a very spotty foreground/background color effect.

Other Dynamics allows you to set jitter controls for opacity and flow. Set both to function with Pen Pressure. This links the opacity of the stroke to the pressure of the pen, allowing you to feather out your brush strokes or build your color slowly by varying the pressure.

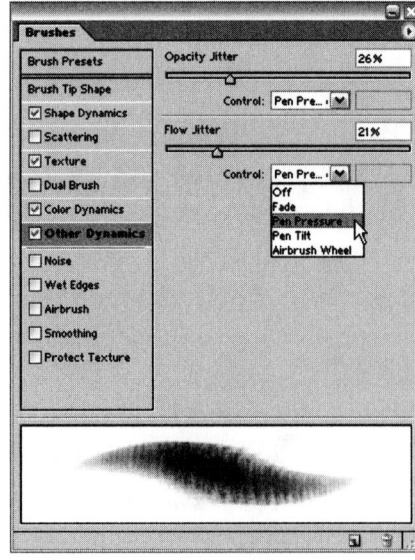

Choose the Paint layer. Choose the colors of your flowers. You will need a few foreground and background sets of color representing the range for your color jitter for the flowers, stems, and background. Keep the colors in the set close together in hue and shade so the effect is subtle. As a result, it will resemble paint taken from a real palette, which is rarely completely homogeneous.

Using the sketch as a guide, vary the pen pressure to adjust the thickness and opacity of the brush stokes. This may take some practice to master, since it may feel strange at first. Periodically, you may want to vary the colors slightly as well, in order to boost visual interest and create a more painted look. Paint midtones first, then add shadows, and finally highlights.

Vary the size of the brush as necessary to capture all the detail in the image. When you are through, it should have the appearance of the following illustration. Be aware that if you change brush styles, you will need to set the parameters for each in the Brushes palette. Varying the size of a preset brush can be done without affecting its dynamics. Since this is a true painting, the final look, of course, will depend on your style and composition. Feel free to use the following illustration as a guide, but keep in mind that no two artists paint exactly the same.

Select the Background layer. The final step is to choose a larger brush with a darker color set and brush in the background. Vary the Color Dynamic jitter to add more visual interest to the background. You can experiment easily with a number of backgrounds or flowers once created on separate layers. This is a good thing to keep in mind as you develop other compositions.

CHANGING A PHOTOGRAPH INTO AN INK PEN AND WATERCOLOR PAINTING

This exercise will demonstrate a good method for transforming photographs into paintings—a process known as *photopainting*. You'll be surprised how easy this can be considering the extent of the reinterpretation. If you're looking for an excellent way to get an illustration out fast (and have them wondering how you did it), try this out. The following illustration is the original photograph.

To Transform A PHOTOGRAPH INTO A PAINTING:

1 Open the file called compressor.tif.

2 Make a duplicate of the Background layer and select that layer. (The following technique demonstrates a unique way of outlining an image that you may find more convenient than Photoshop's stock Find Edges filter, which tends to find far too many edges and can't be adjusted.)

3 Choose Filter | Stylize | Glowing Edges. The Glowing Edges dialog box will appear. Adjust the parameters to get the best edge detail you can, then click OK. (It may look strange at this point, but bear with it.)

4 Choose Images | Adjustments | Invert. It should look better now.

5 Choose Images | Adjustments | Destaturate. This gives you a gray scale outlined version of the photo (see following illustration). To reduce the amount of extraneous detail, select Images | Levels. Use the sliders to adjust the detail. If you want to reduce it to pure black and white, choose Image | Adjustments | Threshold.

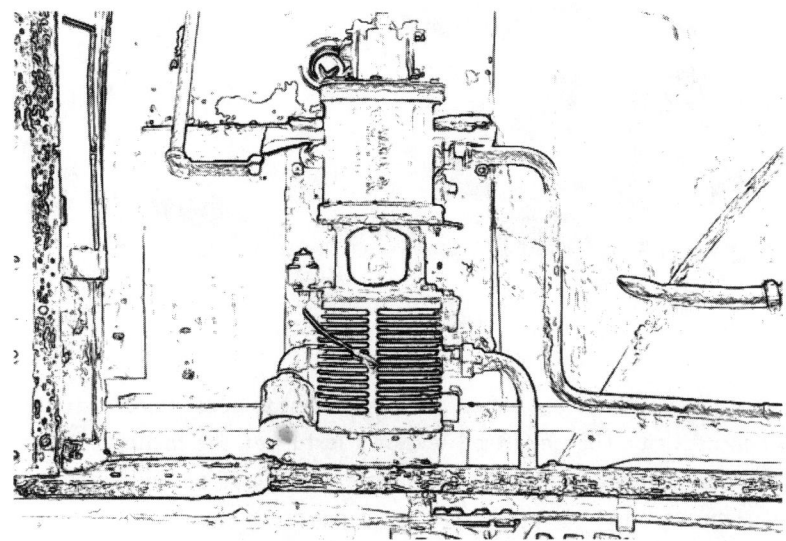

6 Change the Blend mode on the outlined layer to Multiply. You can now see the outline superimposed over the original photograph.

7 Create a duplicate of the Background layer just below the outlined layer. This will be used to paint in the washes, which will colorize the outlined image.

8 In the Layers palette, select the Background layer. Choose Windows | History. The History palette opens. From the History Palette menu, choose New Snapshot. Scroll to the top of the History palette and make the new snapshot active by clicking the square just to the left of the thumbnail. A small brush symbol will appear.

9 Choose the Art History Brush from the Tool palette. Adjust the settings to reflect the illustration shown here.

10 Hide the Background layer and then start painting in the new layer you just created with the Art History Brush. You'll notice that the brush mixes and blends the colors into a subtle wash as you paint. If you want more detail, reduce the brush size.

When you are through with the color washes, you might want to apply some texture to give it a look of authenticity. Choose Filter | Texture | Texturizer. The Texturizer dialog box will appear. Choose Sandstone and adjust the Scale at 50 to 55 percent with a Relief of 4. This simulates the texture of watercolor paper pretty well.

 ON THE VIRTUAL CLASSROOM CD-ROM In Lesson 7, "Original Art and Photopainting," some of the options available in the Brushes palette are demonstrated in live motion.

9

Special Effects

Photoshop can be used to create an endless variety of textures, lighting effects, brush and pen stroke effects, and photo effects, as well as effects we haven't even thought of yet. Since even a cursory discussion of all these effects would require a new (and badly-needed) book devoted to the subject, this chapter will spend its time showing you a few of the effects most useful in correcting problems that persistently plague photographers.

THE ART HISTORY BRUSH

Like the History Brush, the Art History Brush restores your image to a prior state based on your brushstrokes. However, the Art History Brush restores a "painterly" version of your image history. If you, for example, cut an object out of your image, then use the Art History Brush to return to that point, the deleted object will be restored in artistic brushstrokes. Figure 9-1 shows all the settings and options for working with the History Brush.

The Art History Brush is highly customizable in Photoshop 7, thanks to all the new options in the Brushes palette (see Chapter 8). Let's examine some of the adjustments you can make.

In the Options Bar:

▶ **Brush** The "look" of the brush–such as round, elliptical, patterned, etc.

▶ **Brush size** The diameter of the brush.

▶ **Paint Blend mode** With a few exceptions, these are the same as the Blend modes and determine how the "paint" reacts with the underlying image.

▶ **Opacity** The degree to which you can see through the paint, indicated as a percentage of *opacity* (the opposite of transparency).

FIGURE 9-1

The tools, settings, and options for using the Art History brush

- ▶ **Style** (the basic style, which is also influence by the Brush palette settings) Styles are: Tight Short, Tight Medium, Tight Long, Loose Medium, Loose Long, Dab, Tight Curl, Tight Curl Long, Loose Curl, and Loose Curl Long.

- ▶ **Area** The area covered in a single stroke of the brush. You can choose a small brush, but the area covered by the style can be much larger if you set the Area to a large diameter.

- ▶ **Tolerance** How much similarity in color between the paint color and the image color is allowed in order for paint to be registered on the image.

In the Brush Palette:

- ▶ **Brush Presets** The same choices seen when you choose Brush from the Options Bar. Choose from any of the preset and customized brushes that are presently loaded.

- ▶ **Brush Tip Shape** Lets you choose the size, diameter, feathering, shape of the ellipse, etc.

- ▶ **Shape Dynamics** Five settings, plus various pen controls for each.

- ▶ **Scattering** Three settings sliders, plus options

- ▶ **Texture** Three settings sliders, plus options

- ▶ **Dual Brush** Lets you use the Brush Presets palette to choose a second brush that will jitter (alternate) with the brush that's already chosen

- ▶ **Color Dynamics** 5 sliders, with pen controls on foreground/background colors

- ▶ **Other Dynamics** Only two sliders for Opacity and Flow jitter, with pen controls for each

- ▶ **Noise** Toggle on/off checkbox

- ▶ **Wet Edges** Toggle on/off checkbox

- ▶ **Airbrush** Toggle on/off checkbox

- ▶ **Smoothing** Toggle on/off checkbox

- ▶ **Protect Texture** Toggle on/off checkbox

To Use the Art History Brush:

1 If you wish to create a special effect to paint from temporarily, go to the Layers palette, duplicate your Background layer by dragging it to the New Layer icon at the bottom of the palette and then create the effect (such as a filter). Take a snapshot of the effect by clicking the Snapshot icon at the bottom of the History palette. You can now delete the special effect if you like. Or...

2 View your image and the History palette, and determine a restoration point for your Art History Brush to begin painting from.

3 Click the Art History Brush in the Toolbox and then click the state in the History palette you want to restore from (or the Snapshot you made when you created the special effect).

4 Use the Options Bar to adjust your brush to your liking. A certain amount of randomness is introduced as you drag your cursor through the painting. Note especially that the Area control lets you determine how much canvas is covered by your individual strokes.

5 Begin painting in your image. As you drag through the image, multiple strokes are added, rather than one long stroke.

> **NOTE** When you click the History palette with the Art History Brush to choose a restore state, make sure you pick a restore state before the point where you deleted, or else you'll be restoring blank canvas.

The illustration here shows an example of the Art History Brush in use. Here, the photograph was copied to a new layer and processed with the Fresco filter. The new layer was then tossed, and the image overpainted with the Art History Brush. Area was set at 25 pixels (the area that actually gets painted is independent of the brush size) and the Tolerance (range of colors that will be painted from the Snapshot) at 50 percent. In this case, one of Photoshop's default "Tight Short" Art History Brushes was used. The strokes were rendered over an existing image so that photorealism is blended with artistic strokes.

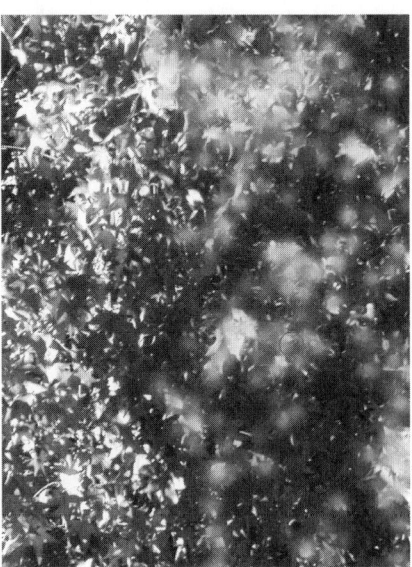

BLEND MODE OVERVIEW

Blend modes are found most prominently in the Layers palette, in the Layer Styles dialog, in the Fill dialog, and in the various brush Options Bars.

Blend Modes are actually mathematical formulas that determine how the colors of pixels on an upper layer affect the colors (and therefore the overall appearance) of the layers below. Normally, the images or drawings on upper layers will simply block anything beneath it. But Blend Modes change that. For example, the Lighten mode looks at colors of the upper layer and displays only the colors that are lighter than those on the layer below. The Multiply mode multiplies the color values of both layers, resulting in a darker color. Blend modes create fascinating selectively transparent and color-altering effects.

> **NOTE** The quickest way to understand what Blend Modes do is to look at them interactively, so you can quickly see how different modes applied to one layer affect those on the layer below. First, select the top layer in the Layers palette, then choose the Move tool. Now, press SHIFT-+ key several times in succession. Each time you do so, the image changes colors in different ways. By quickly looking at the Blend Mode menu in the Layers palette, you can see which Blend Mode is creating the current effect.

BLEND MODE EXAMPLES

As just mentioned, Blend Modes change the way colors in your layers interact with each other.

To Add A BLEND MODE TO YOUR LAYERS:

1 Overlap two or more layers in an image.

2 Select the top layer, and on the Layers palette, click the Blend Mode drop-down menu (it reads Normal because the default Blend Mode used is the normal blending method).

3 Choose any Blend mode you like. Experiment with several, repositioning the layers to achieve different effects.

USING LOCK TRANSPARENCY AND BLEND MODES

Let's say you have an image using a Soft Light fill with a layer set on Lock Transparency. There is a balloon and cloud in the upper left of the image and they are both on a separate layer. To make them appear to blend with the larger sky background, you can apply a gradient fill to the balloon and cloud layer using the same colors as the background sky.

To Do This, THERE ARE TWO IMPORTANT CONSIDERATIONS:

1 Don't replace the balloon and cloud with the color fill. Rather, the goal is to colorize the layer while retaining the layer contents.

2 Don't fill the entire layer with the colorization effect because that would affect the background image as well.

To Edit A LAYER'S CONTENT WITHOUT AFFECTING THE TRANSPARENCY SURROUNDING IT, CLICK THE LOCK TRANSPARENCY ICON ON THE LAYER PALETTE. HERE'S HOW TO RENDER THIS EFFECT:

1 Select the Gradient Tool and choose colors that closely match light and dark colors in the sky.

2 In the Options Bar, click the Mode drop-down menu, and choose Soft Light. (You may want to experiment with other modes as well, as each fill mode creates its own set of interesting colorizing effects).

3 Repeat this step for each layer in turn. Open the Layers palette and select each layer that contains a foreground object (in the case of this example, a kite). Click to toggle the Lock Transparency check box on. Drag the gradient so it fills with a lighter color from the top, to a darker color at the back. This gives the illusion of three-dimensional shape to the kites and makes their furthest parts seem farther away.

4 Apply your fill to the layer. The contents will be colorized, and the layer's hues will appear to blend in with the background. The end result can be seen in the illustration that follows.

USING THE LIQUIFY FILTER

The Liquify filter was called the Liquify command in Photoshop 6, but in version 7 it and the Extract command were moved over to the Filters menu, which is where the new Pattern Maker filter also resides.

Using the Liquify filter is fun and easy. It can feel a lot like finger painting, or resemble those Polaroid transfers in which the emulsion has been stretched into all sorts of interesting shapes. In fact, what it does *is* similar to the Polaroid technique, allowing you to move and stretch the pixels in the image in several ways.

To Use THE FILTER:

1 Select the layer you want to "push around."

2 Choose Filter | Liquify.

3 Your selected layer will appear in the Liquify dialog, as shown here.

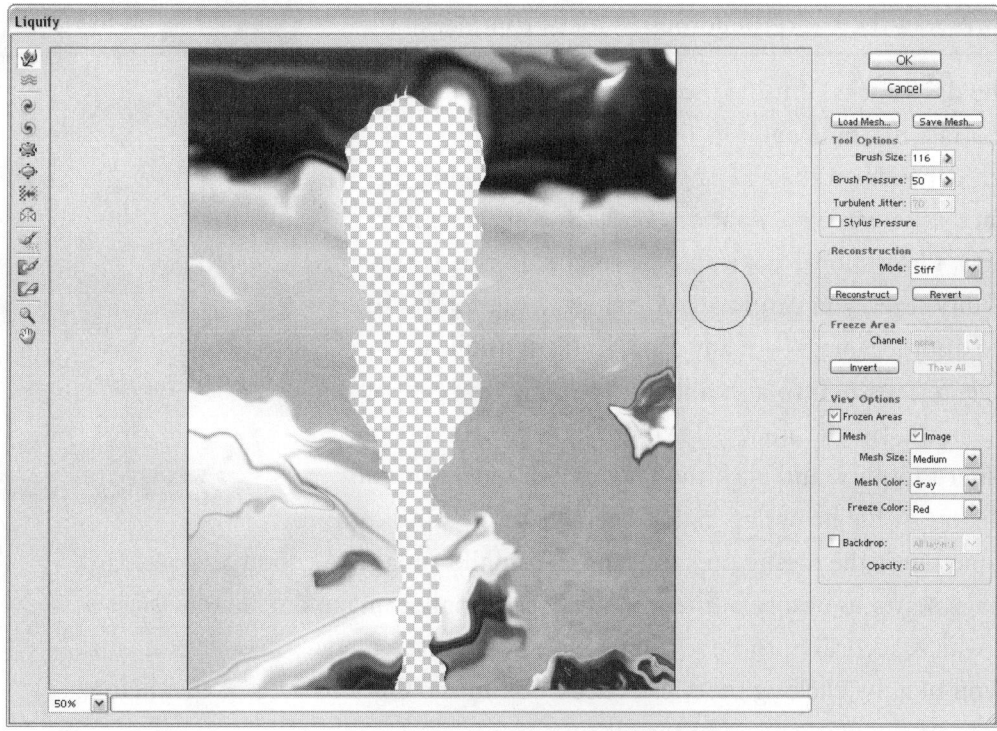

4 Now all you have to do is have fun. The first eight tools in the Liquify toolbox move and warp pixels in one way or another. You can push pixels, warp them, twist them clockwise or counterclockwise, make them pucker (suck in toward the center), bloat (swell outward), or shift in a variety of ways.

5 If you don't like the results you produced in an area, choose the Reconstruct tool and brush over the image to watch it slowly return to normal.

The two tools just above the familiar Zoom and Pan tools are the Freeze and Thaw tools. The Freeze tool paints a QuickMask-type selection that prevents the pixels within it from being moved. The Thaw tool erases that mask, making it possible to proceed with liquification.

In this illustration, the background was separated from the Love-on-Haight parking meter. It was then liquified, and the parking meter put back in place. This is an exercise that's an appropriate variation on the old throwing-the-background-out-of-focus routine.

> **TIP** The Liquify filter can be used in very subtle ways to resize portions of the image. It lets you make a person's eyes a little larger (or a lot larger if you're into cartoon characters), their waist smaller, or shape an object so it fits better with another object in a composite.

One of the drawbacks of using the Liquify filter is that unless you have a fast machine and lots of memory (how fast and how much depends on the size of your images), pushing the pixels exactly the way you want can be a slow process. But don't worry, Photoshop 7 comes to the rescue. In this version of the Liquify filter, you can save a Mesh and then load it to apply it to another image—of any size. You can duplicate your image and resize it to a smaller size and do your Liquifying in the smaller image. Then open the larger version, choose Filter | Liquify, and click the Load Mesh button in the Liquify dialog. A file browsing dialog opens, letting you locate the filename that's the mesh you saved for the smaller image. As soon as you load it, the image starts to liquify in the same way the smaller image did. The mesh is a grid that warps according to how you've manipulated the image's pixels. You can see it, if you like, by clicking the Mesh check box in the Options area of the dialog (to the right of the workspace) to turn it on.

USING THE PATTERN MAKER FILTER

One of Photoshop 7's magical new features is called the Pattern Maker. If you've ever had to make a seamless tile using the Offset filter and then laboriously clone out the overlap seams, you'll appreciate this feature.

The idea is to make it easy to either create a texture-tiled layer from any selected part of a photograph (well, a Photoshop layer, to be more precise) or add completely seamless tiles to Photoshop's pattern library. Using the Pattern Maker, you could make a whole CD full of patterns in only a few hours.

To Create A TEXTURE-TILED LAYER:

1 In the Layers palette, select the layer you want to make the pattern from. If you want to save the information in this layer, be sure to duplicate it before using Pattern Maker, because Pattern Maker is going to fill this layer with the pattern (unless you cancel out of it).

2 Choose Filter | Pattern Maker. The Pattern Maker dialog appears.

3 Choose the Rectangular Marquee tool. Drag diagonally to specify the area you want to turn into a pattern.

At the right side of the Pattern dialog's workspace is an Options area similar to those in the Extract and Liquify filters' dialogs. There are lots of settings you can experiment with, but the ones you're likely to find most useful appear in the following steps:

To Use THE SETTINGS:

1 Enter the values in the Width and Height fields to set the tile's size. (This has nothing to do with the size of the marquee you just drew.)

2 If you don't want the tiles to line up in a grid when you generate the pattern, specify that either the rows or columns be offset from one another by a specific amount. To do this, choose either Vertical or Horizontal from the Offset menu, and enter a percentage of offset in the Amount field (or drag the slider that appears when you click the button).

3 You can also change the Smoothness and Sample Detail levels, which can add even more variety to the samples you generate.

4 Click the Generate button. Depending on the size of your image, you may have to wait a few moments, but soon a preview appears of how the pattern looks when it fills the image. A sample of your new tile also appears in the Tile History. Most of the time, you'll want to keep the Update Pattern Preview box checked, too. If you like, keep clicking the Generate button. Each time you do, a new variation of the tile appears. The following shows the Pattern Maker dialog after the pattern has been generated.

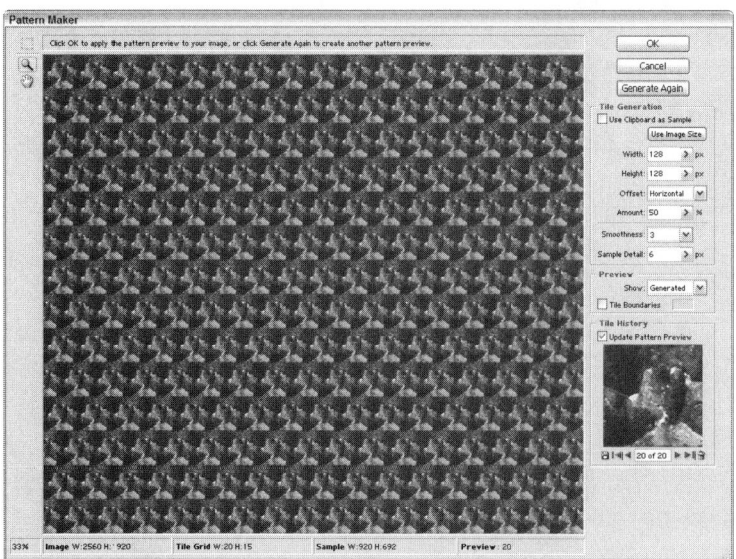

5 (Optional) If you want to save any or all of the patterns just generated, simply click the VCR icons to move to the tile you want to save, then click the floppy disk icon below and to the left of the Tile History preview window. A Save As dialog appears.

USING PHOTOSHOP'S NATIVE FILTERS

Photoshop comes with a set of over 90 subprograms that create special effects in a dozen different nominal categories. These can be narrowed down into a few functional areas:

▶ Artistic

▶ Focus (blurring and sharpening)

▶ Image distortions

▶ Noise

▶ Rendering

▶ Texturing

There's simply not enough room in this book (or in many others, frankly) to tell you everything there is to know about Photoshop's filters. It is, however, important to touch on a few that create special effects that affect the photographic outcome of an image. We'll learn how to create lens flares that give the impression the surface of the photo has been lit especially for exhibition, and how to texture a photograph so it looks as though it's been printed on a substrate (artist's material) other than flat paper. You should also know that the artistic filters have been largely covered in Chapter 8.

CREATING LENS FLARE

Sometimes, especially when you're using a wide-angle lens, you may see a little spot of light that intrudes on part of your image. Chances are, that spots resulted from the fact that the sun (or some other very bright light) struck the surface of the lens and created a reflection. You can make this accident look much more "on purpose" if you exaggerate this phenomenon by using Photoshop's Lens Flare filter.

To Use THE LENS FLARE FILTER:

1 Choose Filter | Render | Lens Flare. The Lens Flare dialog appears.

2 The image in your currently chosen layer will appear in the preview window of the dialog.

3 Choose from one of the three primary lens types by clicking its radio button. The preview will change accordingly, so you can see which type you like the best. Of course, if you're trying to be accurate, you'll want to choose the style of flare closest to the lens type you actually used.

4 Drag the small cross in the preview window to change the location of the lens flare's center-of-origin. When it all looks good to you, click OK. The effect will be rendered onto your currently selected layer.

LIGHTING EFFECTS

The Lighting Effects filter lets you aim any number of lights at the surface of an image. You can also insert another photograph to be used as a background texture.

The background texture can be any Photoshop-compatible file, or any one of three premade textures.

To Use THE LIGHTING EFFECTS FILTER:

1 Choose Filter | Render | Lighting Effects. The Lighting Effects dialog appears.

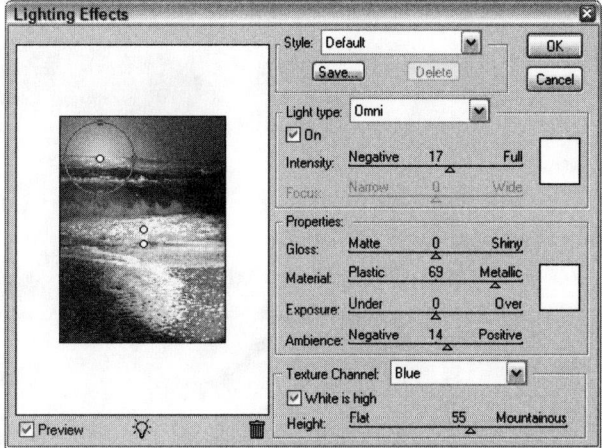

2 The style will be the default, but if you like, you can instantly choose from a number of preset lighting effects found in the Style menu. If you find a style that's appealing, all you need do to render it is click OK. It's more fun, however, to create your own lighting effect.

3 To add another light, drag the Light icon from under the Preview window onto the image until it's positioned where you want it. In this way, you can add a number of lighting sources.

4 You can change the light type from directional flood to omni-directional (bare bulb) to spotlight.

5 You can change the properties of each light in the Preview window by clicking the white circle that represents its center. That becomes the active light. Then you can drag any of the sliders in the Properties section of the Lighting Effects dialog to change the intensity of any of those properties.

6 If you want to introduce a texture, you can either use one of the existing channels in your photograph (the blue channel was used in the following example) or you can open the Channels palette, create a new channel, and paste in any photo you happen to presently have on the Clipboard. You could also fill the new channel with a pattern.

7 Once you've chosen the texture channel, drag the height slider until you see the embossing effect you want.

8 When you're satisfied with the overall effect, click OK. Shown here is a wavescape that has been lit and textured with the Lighting Effects filter.

10

Creating New Realities: Making Composite Images

Photoshop can create worlds that don't necessarily exist. You can place a car atop Mount Everest, or position an infant in the arms of a president. Photoshop provides tools for combining images, selecting image segments, blending those segments, and creating visual words that are as elaborate as your imagination can conceive. This visual sleight of hand is created primarily by carefully selecting objects, placing them on independent layers, and then carefully lighting and blending them so they create a whole new image.

WHAT ARE LAYERS?

Layers provide surfaces for adding new pixels or effects to your image. They rest on your image background like a deck of cards, each one a floating canvas, ripe for any type of editing. You can draw or add text to layers, copy images onto them and add color fills and special effects. Because layers (at least the portions of them not covered by images) are transparent, lower layers will be as visible as upper layers. For example, if you add text or draw a shape on a layer, everything around that text or shape will be transparent, allowing the content of the lower layers to show through.

CREATING A NEW LAYER

If you want to add something to your image that may need to be moved or resized later, you should create it on a new layer. If you want to add a drawing or image segment to your picture, while allowing part of the underlying image to appear underneath, you would add a new layer.

So how do you make a layer? Do one of the following:

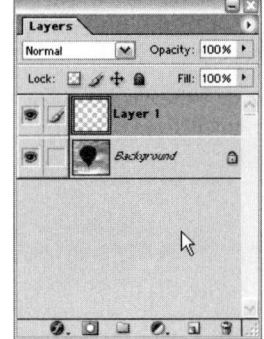

▶ Choose Window | Layers to bring the Layers palette into view, then click the New Layer icon at the bottom-right of the palette. This creates a new, transparent layer on top of the image background. The Layers palette displays a new layer thumbnail as well. Use this direct method of creating a new layer if you want, for example, to place a semitransparent gradient fill over the top of an image. The layer can be resized, moved, reshaped, recolored, or edited in any number of ways.

▶ Draw a shape over an image using one of the Shape tools (for example, the Ellipse, Polygon, or Custom Shape tool). The shape can be moved freely across the image background. It can also be recolored, resized, and blended uniquely with the background colors using a Blend mode.

▶ Type text over an image. This also creates an independently mobile layer.

▶ Create a selection in an image using one of the selection tools, then choose Layer | New | Layer Via Cut or Layer Via Copy. Layer Via Cut will leave a hole in the underlying image when you move the layer contents. Layer Via Copy duplicates the selection contents, so no hole is left when the layer is moved. Figure 10-1 shows a copied segment of an image promoted to an independent layer.

FIGURE 10-1

A layer created by copying a selection

▶ Paste the contents of the Clipboard onto an image. In Photoshop, pasting automatically creates a new layer.

▶ Dragging a selection or layer from another open image onto an image.

MOVING, TRANSFORMING, AND MANAGING LAYERS

In this section, you'll learn how to work with layers, moving and overlapping them, resizing them and changing their order, and otherwise manipulating them in any way you see fit.

SELECTING AND MOVING A LAYER

As previously mentioned, you can select a layer by clicking its icon on the Layer palette. However, unless your image has many layers, it's probably simpler to select it just by clicking the image.

To Select A LAYER:

1 Click the Move tool (or press the v key), and on the Options palette at the top of the screen, make sure Auto Select Layer is checked.

2 Click the layer to select it.

> **NOTE** A quick way to duplicate a layer is by moving it while pressing the ALT key.

You can then move it by dragging, or apply a filter, color adjustment, or any other type of editing. Once selected, a layer can be nudged by pressing an ARROW KEY, or nudged in 10-pixel increments by pressing SHIFT - an ARROW KEY.

TRANSFORMING LAYERS

Not only can layers be resized, but they can also be flipped, rotated, skewed, and shape-edited in many ways. To transform a layer, do one of the following:

▶ Press CTRL-T, and use the transformation options that appear on the Options palette:

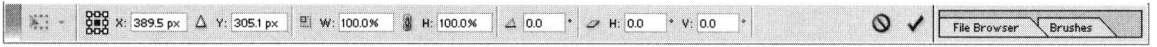

▶ Choose Edit | Transform, and select an option from the Transform menu. For example, select a layer and choose Edit | Transform | Scale, and the Options palette displays the layer's x and y reference points, Width and Height in percentages, and Rotation and Skew amounts. Type in a new number to change any of these parameters. After making a change, click the Check On The Options palette to confirm your change, or the No symbol to discard it.

After you choose a Transform option or press CTRL-T, the layer appears in a bounding box (see Figure 10-2), which facilitates manual resizing and shaping.

Drag on a handle or corner to edit the layer. Again, confirm or discard your change using the Options palette shown previously.

LAYER MANAGEMENT

As the number of layers in your image grows, you'll find it necessary to change their order, lock them in place once you are happy with them, and merge them

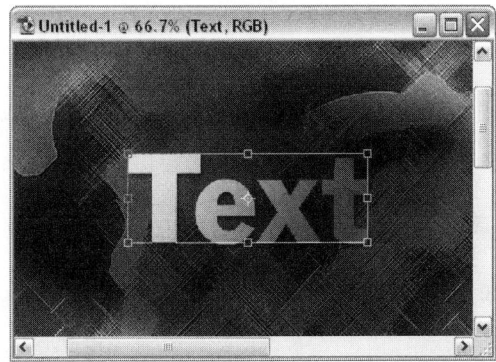

FIGURE 10-2
A layer in a bounding box, ready for resizing or reshaping

together when editing is no longer necessary. Also, at times, you'll want to flatten an image, merging all layers into the background. This can be necessary to save disk space, or simplify the act of dragging one complete image into another as a single layer in a completely different image.

CHANGE LAYER ORDER

To change the layer order, do one of the following on the Layers palette:

▶ Drag the layer's thumbnail to a new position on the Layers thumbnail list. The topmost layer thumbnail corresponds to the topmost layer in your image.

▶ Click a layer. Choose Layer | Arrange, and select one of the Layer Order options.

MERGE LAYERS

To merge layers, first select the layers you want to merge. Click one layer thumbnail, which will make it the current layer. A paintbrush will appear on the option selector, second from the left. That's one layer you'll be merging. To add others, click the second option selector on each layer you want to merge. A chain icon will appear, indicating that the selected layers are locked together. Then click Layer | Merge Linked. The selected layers will be merged.

FLATTEN LAYERS

To flatten all layers so they join the image background, choose Layer | Flatten Image.

LAYER STYLES AND EFFECTS

Layer styles and effects are more pertinent to text effects and will be discussed in more depth in Chapter 12. However, there are some aspects of layer styles that you will find useful in making composites.

ADVANCED BLEND CONTROLS

To Eliminate UNWANTED BACKGROUNDS, "SPECKS," OR FRINGES:

1 Note the gray or background color that you want to eliminate. Also, keep an eye on similar hues in your image that you want to keep. (You'll want to eliminate specks or edge pixels without discarding parts of your object.)

2 Drag the righthand control of the This Layer slider (see Figure 10-3) slightly towards the center. Slide it until the edge pixels or specks are not visible, but not so far that you discard wanted pixels. (To experiment with eliminating lighter or darker colors, drag the lefthand slider slightly towards the center as well.)

3 Click OK to confirm your edit, and close the dialog box.

> **NOTE** The Blend If controls do not erase information, but rather discard it according to the parameters you set with the sliders. Moving the sliders back to their original positions will restore the pixels to view.

The fireworks displayed on the layered image in this illustration were pasted from another image. The original fireworks image had a completely black background. So, was the background eliminated so that the fireworks appear as bursts of light on the layered image? When the fireworks were pasted in, the lefthand control of the This Layer slider was dragged inward, rather than to the right.

ADJUSTMENT LAYERS

We've discussed layers that contain pixels, image portions, and drawings that can be moved independently and edited at will. You can also create layers that adjust

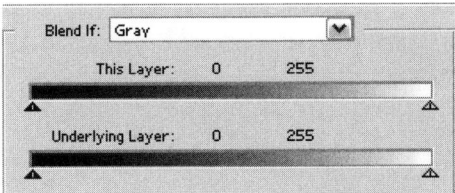

FIGURE 10-3
The This Layer slider in the Blend If control panel

the colors of layers beneath them. These are called Adjustment layers. They are created to darken, brighten, recolor, or change the saturation value of the image data directly beneath them.

Adjustment layers need not take up the entire canvas. You can create a selection, then change it into an Adjustment layer. The effects of the Adjustment will occur beneath your new layer, and nowhere else. Like other layers, Adjustment layers can be moved.

CREATING ADJUSTMENT LAYERS

To Create AN ADJUSTMENT LAYER:

1 Create a selection covering the area you want to adjust. You'll probably want to feather it so the effect tapers off, rather than having it end abruptly.

2 Click the Create New Fill or Adjustment Layer icon at the bottom center of the Layers palette. A list of layer adjustment types will appear. These will be familiar color adjustment tools, such as Curves, Levels, Brightness/Contrast, and so forth.

3 Choose one control type from the list. A dialog box will appear to specify the amount of the effect.

4 As you manipulate the effect, you'll notice that only the area under the Adjustment layer changes.

5 Close the dialog box to confirm your effect.

6 Move your Adjustment layer anywhere you like, and see how it affects the pixels beneath it. This layer will appear with all the other layers in the Layers palette. Its place on the list can be changed.

7 To later adjust the effect amount on the Adjustment layer, double-click the Slider icon that appears on the Layer thumbnail (see Figure 10-4).

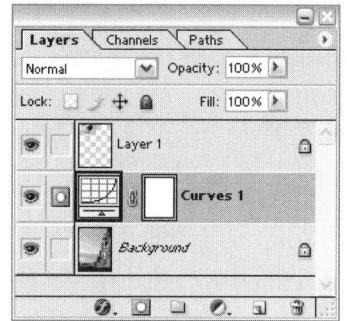

FIGURE 10-4
The Adjustment Layer slider lets you control the intensity of your color adjustment settings.

AN ADJUSTMENT LAYER EXAMPLE

The following illustration shows a practical example of an Adjustment Layer. The coming of dusk is limited to the left side of the street. Oddly, the people on the right still have enough light to read and enjoy the sun.

To Use AN ADJUSTMENT LAYER:

1 Use the Lasso tool to create a selection that encloses only the left side of the street. Before making the selection, set a Feather value of about 40 pixels.

2 Click the Adjustment Layer icon at the bottom of the Layers palette.

3 Choose Curves from the list, and when the Curve dialog box appears, drag the Input/Output graph line downward and to the right.

4 Click OK to confirm the effect. You'll see the left side of the street darken.

BACKGROUND REMOVAL TECHNIQUES

Now that you know a bit about how layers work, and can find your way around the Layers palette, let's talk about various ways to create photo montages and composite images. These always involve manipulating layers. Most of the work in creating photo montages involves removing backgrounds, or "knocking out" the portion of a layer that is not needed for your montage. Photoshop provides plenty of tools for getting rid of backgrounds. The tool you choose will depend on the intricacy of the background and how different its color is from the foreground— which is what you want to keep. For the rest of this chapter, we'll discuss how to create photo montages using various background removal techniques.

REMOVING A BACKGROUND WITH THE MAGIC WAND

We'll start with something simple. We'll take the background of an image showing Deborah holding a cat, and replace it with another background image, using pretty much only the Magic Wand tool. Figure 10-5 shows the finished product. The Magic Wand tool is up to such a task as long as the background being replaced is uniform, and doesn't share hues with the foreground.

To Use the Magic Wand:

1 To begin, select the Magic Wand tool from the Toolbox, or press the w key.

2 On the Options palette, make sure Contiguous is checked.

FIGURE 10-5
Creating a new background for an image

3 Click the background of your image at a point where the color is as different as possible from anything you see in the foreground.

4 Some of the background will be selected. On the Options palette, choose a Tolerance value that will select as much of the background as possible while leaving the foreground untouched. You may need to undo your initial selection and try again using a new Tolerance value. (I find that 15 works well.)

5 With the Magic Wand tool selected, click the Add To Selection icon on the Option palette (or press the SHIFT key), and click another section of background that has not been selected yet.

6 Repeat the previous step until as much of the background as possible is selected.

7 To clean up the small spots of background that remain, choose Select | Modify | Smooth, and indicate a Sample Radius of 4 pixels. (You may need to repeat this step.)

8 When the entire background is selected, choose Select | Inverse. What we want to do is isolate the foreground as a clean selection, and make the foreground into a layer.

After choosing Select | Inverse, the foreground is selected. We have a selection, but it has to become a layer.

To Change A SELECTION TO A LAYER:

1 Choose Layer | New | Layer Via Cut. The foreground is now a layer. If the Layers palette is not visible, choose Window | Layers. You'll see the new layer you've created on the Layers palette, and the background will remain as a layer of its own. The new layer will be called Layer 1 or Layer 2. If you like, you can rename it by clicking its name on the Layers palette and typing in something more meaningful.

2 Once our foreground is a layer, we can still clean it up a bit by getting rid of some of the tell-tale edge pixels. Click the thumbnail of the foreground layer to make sure it is selected, and choose Layer | Matting | Remove White Matte. (You may need to repeat this step.).

3 Let's clean out the background entirely, to clear the way for a new background image. Click the Background Layer icon on the Layers palette, and press CMD/CTRL-A. Then press the DELETE/BACKSPACE key. The background will vanish, leaving only the Photoshop transparency grid in its place.

4 Open a new image for the background. You'll have to change the image size so it's dimensions exactly match those of the foreground image. However, to avoid distortion, you'll want to choose an image that is roughly the same size as the first image.

5 After your second image is open, check the dimensions of the first image; these will be the target dimensions. With the first image selected, choose Image | Image Size, and note the Width and Height numbers in the Pixel Dimensions fields.

6 Close the dialog.

7 Click the second image, and again choose Image | Image Size. Change the width and height values in pixels to match those of the first image.

8 Press OK to complete the operation. Your images will now have the same dimensions.

9 Drag the second image onto the first, where it becomes a lower layer—essentially a background.

10 Click the first image, and on the Layers palette, click the thumbnail for the deleted background. This ensures that the pasted image goes into the background layer and doesn't obliterate the foreground.

11 Click the new image, and press CTRL-A, to select the entire image.

12 Drag the image onto the background of the first image. Use the mouse or the arrow keys to nudge it into place.

After pasting in the background and positioning it, you can also resize it, perhaps increasing its size to show any detail you would like to feature. For example, I increased the size of the displayed background image in order to highlight the man walking down the corridor. After enlarging it significantly, I dragged the image into place so the man could be clearly seen.

THE BACKGROUND ERASER

The Background Eraser is a great tool that makes it easy to selectively delete image backgrounds. It does a pretty good job of erasing areas behind such tricky items as bushes, hair, and other intricate objects. The Background Eraser is not automatic. You drag it through your image background, and it selectively deletes certain background hues while sparing the others.

To Use THE BACKGROUND ERASER:

1 Open an image with a significant amount of background.

2 In the Toolbox, click the Eraser Tool drop-down menu, and choose the Background Eraser. The Options palette will display settings for the Background Eraser.

Since you'll be doing lots of dabbing and dragging on your image, you should choose a rather large brush size—even as high as 400 pixels. The Background Eraser has a cross hair (as shown in Figure 10-6). The spot where you click the cross hair designates the background color. Thus (depending on how your Tolerance levels are set), even if the Eraser overlaps into nonbackground areas, it won't erase them.

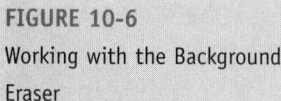

FIGURE 10-6
Working with the Background
Eraser

USING EXTRACT

The Extract command, found on the Filter menu, provides a separate dialog for tracing an object that you want to remove from its background. When the object is traced, you can fill it with a foreground color, which highlights areas you want to remove from the background and helps make sure you "got it all." When you click OK and leave the Extract window, the foreground is selected. The tool quite accurately extracts complex, intricate images—as long as you're willing to do a little practicing.

Before I take you into an exercise, you should understand a bit about how the Extract filter works. What it does is preserve transitional edges when it removes an object from its surroundings. *Transitional edges* are those that somehow graduate into their surroundings—such as fur, grass, and flying hair, and the transparent edges of glass. What Extract does is provide you with a way to designate the colors that you want to keep in the foreground and, conversely, to erase all the background colors that you want to throw away. The transitional area can vary in width, and is drawn with a felt-tip marker-type tool. Everything under the highlighter color is considered transitional, so whatever contains foreground color is kept, and whatever contains background colors is thrown away.

There is one problem with all of this. Sometimes there are foreground colors in the background, and vice-versa. If the foreground and background colors are distinctive enough, the extraction is likely to be amazingly realistic. Shots made against an evenly-lighted, solid-color background will work best. The greater the number of colors mixed into the background, the more likely it is that you'll have to do some (or a lot of) edge cleanup after the extraction.

To Extract THE FOREGROUND OF AN IMAGE FROM ITS BACKGROUND:

1 Open the image and choose Filter | Extract. The Extract window will appear, with the image displayed (see Figure 10-7).

2 At the upper left is the Edge Highlighter tool. Use this tool to trace the foreground object, enclosing it completely. If the image extends past the edges of the document, make sure the Edge Highlighter goes all the way to the edge—no gaps allowed.

> **NOTE** Use the Zoom tool to get a close-up view of the object's edges, or press CTRL-+ to zoom in, and CTRL-– to zoom back out. To make an accurate tracing around your object, zooming in will probably be necessary. To navigate around the zoomed-in image and complete your tracing, press the SPACEBAR. The cursor will temporarily change to the Hand tool.

FIGURE 10-7
Extracting a foreground object

3 After you've completely traced your object or the image segment intended for extraction, click the Fill tool at the upper left, and fill the interior of your tracing. The fill displays the extent of your extraction.

4 If the fill spills outside the highlight, there is a gap somewhere in your highlight. I recommend zooming to 100 percent and using the Hand tool to pan around the image until you find the gap. Then use the Highlighter to fill the gap. Now choose the Fill tool again and click inside the highlight to designate the foreground. The original fill will disappear before the new fill appears, so if it spills out again, you'll need to repeat this step until it stops.

5 Click the Preview button at the upper right. The result of your extraction appears in the Extract window.

6 A Cleanup Tool is provided for editing the extraction. To erase unwanted pixels to transparency, just stroke the image as though you were using an eraser. To add pixels to the foreground, press ALT while using the Cleanup tool.

7 When you're happy with your extraction, click OK. The extracted object will appear on an independent layer in Photoshop with all the extracted areas transparent.

> **NOTE** If your edges don't contain a lot of "fly-away fuzz," such as hair, check the Smart Highlight box to facilitate more accurate tracing. When Smart Highlight is selected, the Edge Highlighter will be just wide enough to cover the edge, regardless of the chosen brush size.

ADDING SPACE AND DISTANCE BETWEEN MULTIPLE LAYERS

The following illustration shows five balloons over an amusement park. The balloons were generated from a single balloon in another image. By duplicating and resizing each balloon as it appears on its own layer, you can create a rather believable, and crowded, sky. You can perform a similar effect with any type of object—for example, balls, people, or trees.

FIGURE 10-8
The balloon in its original image

Figure 10-8 shows the balloon in its original image, already selected and ready to drag into the amusement park image, where it will appear on its own layer.

To Duplicate AND RESIZE AN OJBECT:

1 Click the balloon and drag it onto the other image.

2 To resize the balloon, press CTRL-T and on the Options palette, type new digits into the Width and Height fields, making sure to click the Maintain Aspect Ratio chain-link icon first. Click the check mark, and the balloon will be resized.

3 To create another balloon, press v to turn the cursor into the Move tool, and make sure Auto Select Layer is checked on the Options palette.

4 Click and drag the balloon while pressing the ALT key. This creates a second balloon on a new layer.

5 You'll find this new layer positioned in front of the first. To change the layer order, click the new layer and choose Layer | Arrange | Send Backward, or press CTRL-[.

6 The balloon nearest the back needs to be resized to appear properly proportioned. Select the back balloon and press CTRL-T (CMD-T on the Mac). On the Options palette, reduce the W and H value to 80%. Click the check mark on the Options palette to confirm your resizing.

7 To add another balloon, click and drag the smaller balloon while pressing the OPTION/ALT key. A new balloon will be created. Again, the most distant balloon will need to be resized. Press CMD/CTRL-T and resize it as indicated previously.

8 Repeat the preceding steps to create as many new objects as you like. Next, arrange them against your background. Simply click each layer and move the balloons as you see fit.

We'll now move on and take a look at two tools on the History palette that you can use to restore your image to a previous state: the History Brush and the Art History Brush.

THE HISTORY BRUSH

The History Brush lets you restore your image to a prior state. Rather than simply jumping back to a previous image state on the History palette, you can use the History Brush to restore the image only in selected areas.

To Use THE HISTORY BRUSH:

1 View your image on the History palette, determining the point in its image history that you would like to restore it to.

2 Click the History Brush, and then click the specific restoration point on the History palette.

3 Adjust the brush size to suit your needs, considering that every spot you click on your image will be restored to that point.

4 Paint in the areas that require restoration. You'll see the restored pixels appear beneath your brush strokes.

There are many uses for the History Brush. For example, let's say you want to skew or distort a layer, but want to leave part of that layer unaffected. You can perform your layer edit, then paint with the History Brush over the areas that you want unskewed or undistorted. (See the example of the restored door in Figure 10-9.)

The History Brush is helpful for repairing image segments unintentionally altered by an edit. In Figure 10-10, when the gray from the building was deleted, it inadvertently deleted portions of gray from the Deborah's eye.

FIGURE 10-9
An image partially restored with the History Brush

FIGURE 10-10
The History Brush can fix Deborah's eye problem.

To Correct A PROBLEM BY USING THE HISTORY BRUSH:

1 Click the History Brush, and on the History palette, click the point just after the spot where the selection has been deleted.

2 Paint over only the eye. The eye's color will be restored, while the deletion of the building will remain untouched.

 ON THE VIRTUAL CLASSROOM CD-ROM In Lesson 8, "Making Composite Images," you get to see how a simple, everyday composite actually comes together in real time. We do the two things that photographers most often do with composites to make their photographs more attractive: substituting a more attractive sky for the pale blank sky that happened to be there when the photograph was taken, and adding a subject in the foreground that becomes the center of interest in the photograph.

11

Text Effects

In this chapter, you'll learn to apply text effects of various types. We'll begin with a quick overview of how to create text in Photoshop, so you'll understand a text object's characteristics as an editable layer. We'll explore a handful of text effects, such as warping, stylizing, and filling text with images. You'll see that some effects require changing the text into a selection or a bitmap first. In applying these effects, you'll have to "lock in" your font choices, such as letter spacing and typeface, before you can enjoy the effect. Thus, although it is desirable to always have the option to choose a new font or font size at any editing stage, many text effects require *rasterization*. This means you'll have to contend with resizing limits—how much you can increase your text bitmap before jagged edges begin to appear and so forth. Therefore, in this chapter, you'll not only learn some nice effects, but the plusses and minuses of various text effect editing options.

CREATING AND EDITING TEXT

We'll start with the process of creating text, selecting a font, specifying letter spacing, and other basic type tools.

To create text, first click the Type tool, and on the Options Bar, view the font, font style, color, size, anti-aliasing method, and other settings (Figure 11-1). Your initial typing will appear with these settings. You can then do one of the following:

To Create TEXT (FIRST OPTION):

1 Click in your document and begin typing. The text will continue towards the right as long as you type, even past the edge of the document's right border. Press ENTER to create a new line.

2 Click the check box on the Options Bar to confirm your text entry.

To Create TEXT (SECOND OPTION):

1 Click in the document and create a box for your text. Then click inside the box and type. The text will appear inside the box.

2 Click the check box on the Options Bar to confirm your text entry.

FIGURE 11-1
The Type tool and Options Bar

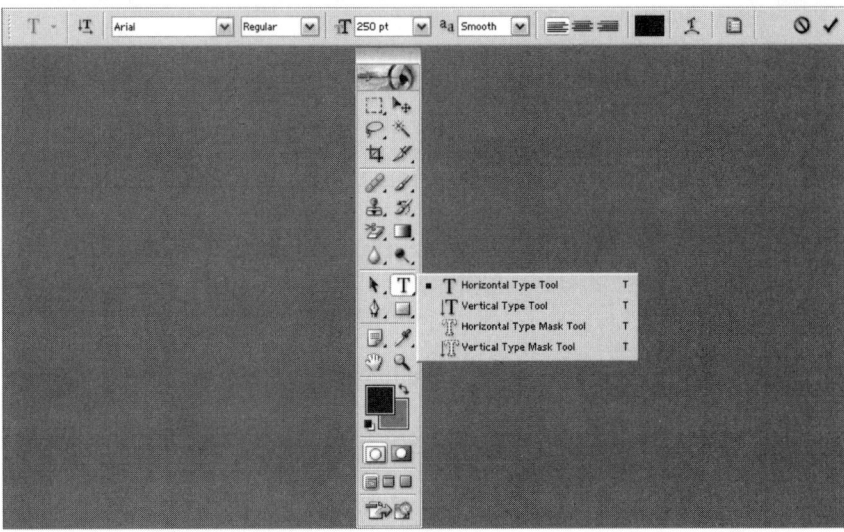

3 With the Type tool still selected, you can click and drag to resize the bounding box that the text appears in. This will change the size of the box, not the text. If you make the box smaller than the text, the text will overflow beyond the box, and not be seen. Drag the box to enlarge it again and the text will reappear.

4 However, if you choose the Move tool and click the Show Bounding Box check box, afterward resizing the box, the text itself will be resized. If you then want to resize the box, keeping the text the same size, you must again press the Type tool and drag the box boundaries.

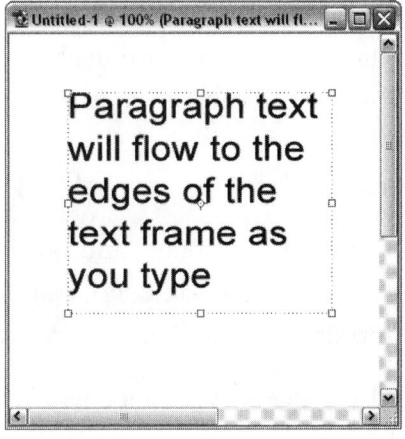

Using either method to create text, the text will appear on a new layer, and can be repositioned, moved, resized and blended just like any other layer (see Figure 11-2). For example, after creating text, you can fill the background and the text will be unchanged because the text is automatically on a new layer.

To edit text, drag across it with the Type tool to select it so you can then change its font, font size, style, alignment method, and so forth. You can also use the Character and Paragraph palettes to change text and line spacing, add indent parameters, and so forth in highlighted text. You can even use the Superscript feature on the Character palette to create words like O^2.

If the user wishes to have a type size larger than those given in the font-size menu, he can scale the text by selecting the Show Bounding Box choice from the Move

FIGURE 11-2
Text appears on its own layer

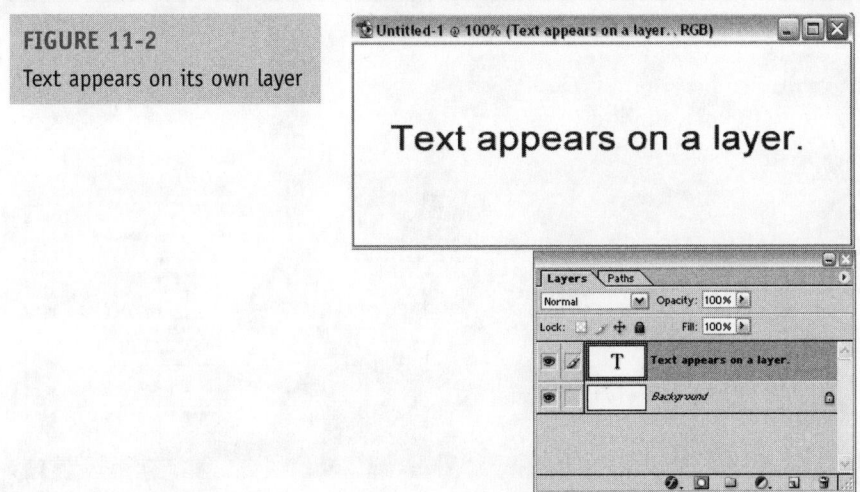

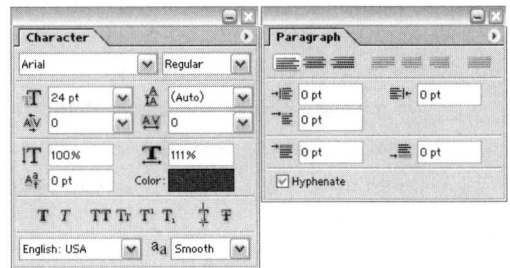

tool's Options Menu and scaling the text that way. This does not rasterize the text and (unless the SHIFT key is used) can give nonstandard type sizes. Also, typing a font size into the font size window will scale the text proportionally.

You can scale, rotate, and skew text by pressing CTRL-T or choosing Edit | Transform. The text will appear in a bounding box, ready for transformation.

Also, since text is on its own layer, you can change its Blend Mode using the Layers palette (see Figure 11-3).

To access other text creation tools, click and hold the Type tool on the toolbar. Additional Type tools will appear. You can create vertically-oriented text, as well as create a text mask, which we will explore shortly.

We'll now discuss text effects, beginning with text effects that do not change your text into a bitmap or selection, such as warping text, styles, text Actions, layering, and blend effects. You'll then learn about bitmap, selection-based, and path text effects.

WARPING TEXT

Text warping reshapes a text phrase, making it arc, bulge, inflate, squeeze, and such. This special effect does not rasterize the text (it doesn't make it into a

FIGURE 11-3
Overlaying text with other layers to apply Blending Mode options

bitmap). That means you can still change the font typeface, color, and spacing, after applying it.

To Apply TEXT WARPING:

1   Select text with the Type tool (not the Move tool), and on the Options Bar, click the Create Warp Text icon. The Warp Text dialog box appears (see Figure 11-4).

2   Click the Style drop-down menu and choose a Warp Type. You'll see the effect immediately rendered (Figure 11-5) to your text even before clicking OK.

3   Below the Style drop-down menu are sliders for editing the effect's Bend and Distortion values. They will change with each Style selection.

4   Click OK to confirm your warp choice. The effect will be rendered.

> **NOTE** You can change the font and other text settings on the Options Bar while you are choosing warp settings, even with the Warp Text dialog box open.

You can undo text warping by selecting the text, opening the Warp Text dialog box, and choosing None from the Style drop-down menu. You can also change the text and apply the warp to different lettering.

> **NOTE** Since text warping reshapes text in an exaggerated fashion, you may want to make sure you have Smooth anti-aliasing selected on the Options Bar.

LAYER STYLES AND TEXT

Layer styles are a quick way to apply fills, patterns, and blending effects to text. With quick access from the Layers Styles palette, you can apply, for example, a drop shadow and a preset pattern fill to text with a single click.

FIGURE 11-4
The Warp Text dialog box

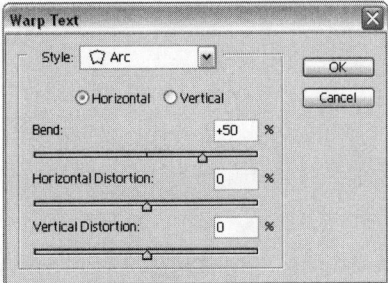

FIGURE 11-5
Applying various Warp Text
styles to text

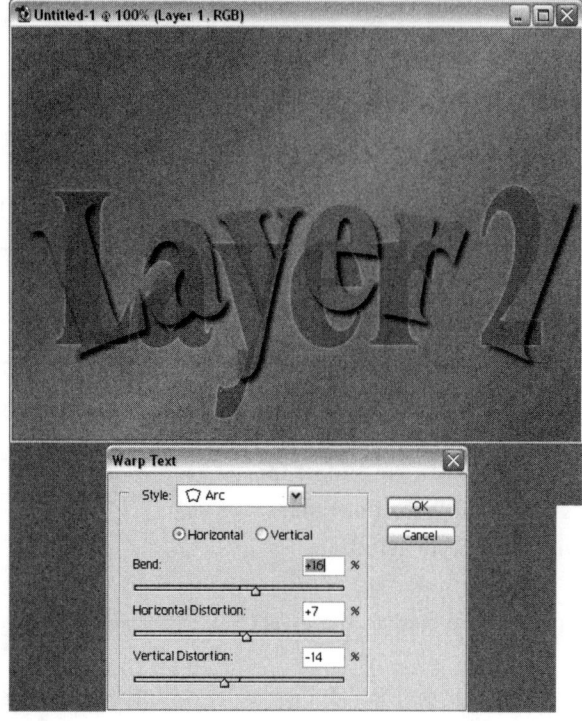

To Work with Layer Styles:

1 CTRL/right-click the layer containing the text you want to edit, and choose Blending Properties. The Layer Style dialog box will appear.

2 On the upper left, click Styles. A panel of styles will appear in the center of the dialog box.

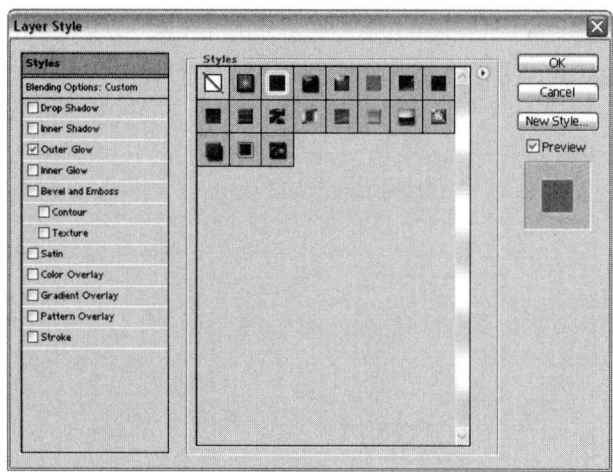

3 Click any style to apply it as a preview. While previewing, clicking any style will apply it over the previous previewed style.

4 When a Style is selected, click OK.

To view Style options, click the right-facing arrow at the upper-right of the dialog box. A menu of Style options will appear.

Here you can choose from a list of ten style types. Click a style type, and its thumbnails will appear in the Style Panel area (Figure 11-6).

APPLYING A STYLE TO MULTIPLE LAYERS

If you want to apply one style to more than one layer at a time, you can do so from the Layers palette.

To Apply ONE STYLE TO MORE THAN ONE LAYER:

1 Locate the layer with the style you want to apply to other layers. It will have the word Effects beneath the layer thumbnail (provided the collapsing arrow to the right of the thumbnails is turned down).

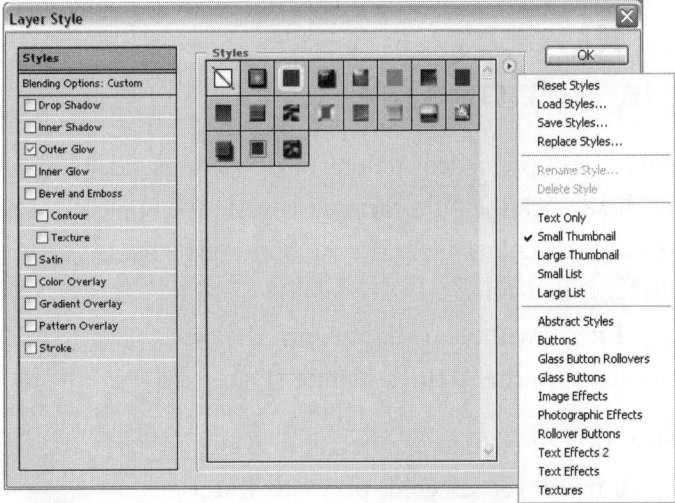

FIGURE 11-6
Choosing additional Style collections from the Style menu

2 Click the word Effects, and drag it to another layer in the Layer palette. To apply the effect to multiple styles, press the SHIFT key, then drag it to as many layers as you like— as shown here.

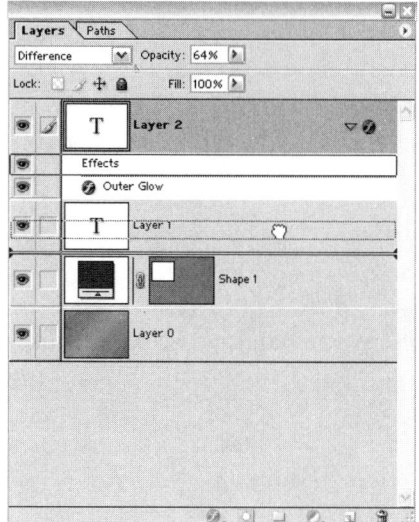

EDITING AND SAVING STYLES

To create and save a new style by adding Blending options (which appears on the left of the dialog box), choose the style you want to begin as your starting point, and add options.

To Create AND SAVE A NEW STYLE:

1 Click the New Style button. The New Style dialog box will appear.

2 Name your style.

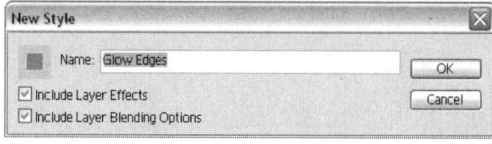

3 When saving your style, you can choose to include Layer effects, Blending options, or both.

4 Click OK and your style will appear in the Styles panel with the others.

CREATING REFLECTIVE TEXT USING THE ACTIONS PALETTE

Photoshop's default list of preloaded Actions in the Actions palette includes many text effects. To access these, click the right-facing arrow on the upper-right of the Actions palette, which opens the Actions menu. At the bottom is a list of Action collections. One Action collection, Text Effects, is a collection of 15 text effects. Select it, and the folder of Text Effects will be available with the other Actions currently listed in the Actions palette (Figure 11-7).

One Text Effect Action of particular interest is Water Reflections. With a text layer selected, play the Water Reflections Action, and a copy of the text will appear reversed and distorted, as if it were reflected in water.

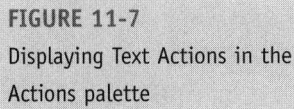

FIGURE 11-7

Displaying Text Actions in the Actions palette

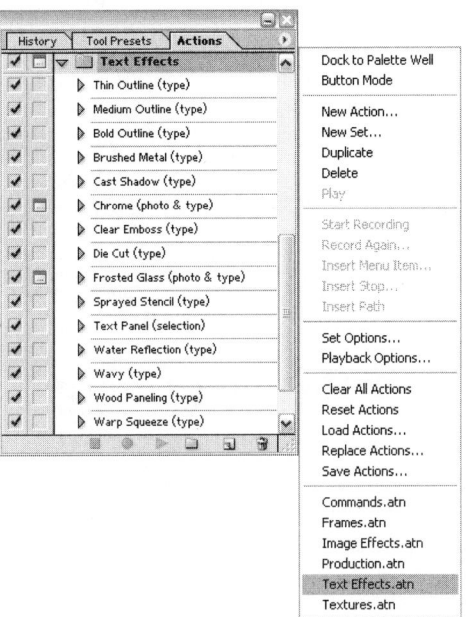

VARIABLE TEXT COLORATION USING AN ADJUSTMENT LAYER

If you add text to an image and later, after more editing, find that the text gets lost in the image, you can lighten or darken the edges of the letters, making them more distinct. Glowing letter edges is a common technique for adding more definition to text in composite images.

To Apply GLOWING LETTER EDGES:

1 Open a new image. Choose Edit | Fill. The Fill dialog appears. From the Use menu, choose 50 Percent Gray.

2 Create some text. The text will automatically appear on its own layer (as it always does).

3 In the Layers palette, select the new text layer.

4 Choose Layer | Layer Styles. The Layer Style dialog will appear.

5 Check the Outer Glow check box, then select its Name bar. When you select its Name bar, all the options for an outer glow will appear. Be sure to check the Preview box so that you can see the results that occur when you adjust the options. For the purposes of this exercise, set the options as I did in Figure 11-8—then feel free to experiment. When you are satisfied with your adjustments, click OK to render.

RASTERIZING TEXT

Some text effects require that you change your text into a bitmap first. For example, you cannot fill text, such as with a Pattern Fill, or use a Filter on text unless you first rasterize the text layer. To do so, Choose the Type tool and highlight your text, then CTRL/right-click the text layer in the Layers palette and choose Rasterize Layer, or choose Rasterize Layer from the Layers Palette menu. The text will still be on its own layer, completely mobile.

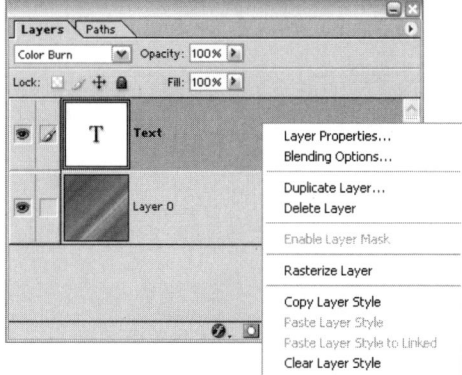

You can apply any fill or filter to it. Also, after rasterizing, you can add Perspective and Distort transformations to the text (choose Edit | Transform, as shown in Figure 11-9). However, you'll not be able to change fonts, change character spacing, or resize the text without introducing jagged edges. That's because the text is now a bitmap, and no longer composed of vector outlines.

FIGURE 11-8

The Layer Style dialog, showing my adjusted options

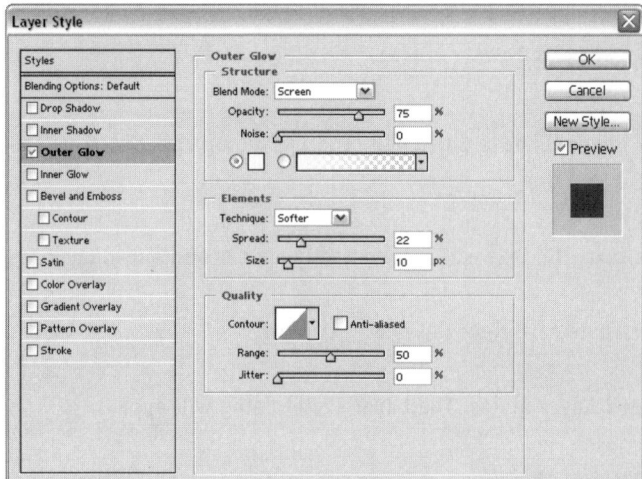

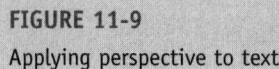

FIGURE 11-9
Applying perspective to text

CHANGING TEXT INTO A SELECTION

One way to fill text with photographs and patterns and resize it without introducing jagged edges is to change text into a selection, then resize it, then do your editing.

To Change TEXT TO A SELECTION:

1 Open an image in Photoshop.

2 Choose the Type tool, then click at the point where you want to enter some text. Be sure to specify the desired options in the Options Bar. Next, type your text. It will appear on its own layer.

3 Choose the Magic Wand tool.

4 On the Options Bar, deselect Contiguous and Use All Layers.

5 Make sure the text layer you just created is still the one selected in the Layers palette.

6 In the workspace, click anywhere inside the lettering. All the lettering will now be selected along its edges.

7 In the Layers palette, drag the text layer to the Delete Layer icon (trash). The Text Selection marquee will still be active, but the text and its layer will be gone.

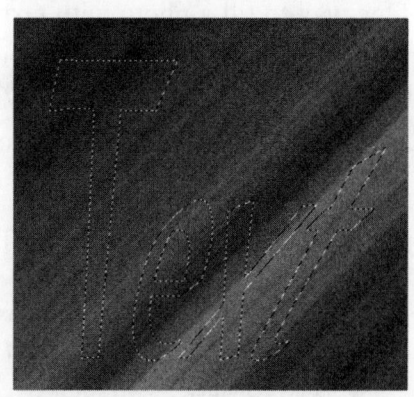

8 In the Layers palette, select the layer beneath. The text selection will now affect any layer you have selected in the Layers palette by clicking its name bar or any layer already highlighted.

9 To move or resize the text selection, press CMD/CTRL-T. Now you can use the Transform tools to freely reshape the selection marquee (not its contents).

10 When finished transforming your text selection, click the Commit check mark on the Options Bar.

Since the text is a selection, you can do any of the following (not to mention a few million other things):

▶ Fill the text with a pattern, gradient, or color

▶ Feather the text (choose Select | Feather)

▶ Apply a filter to the text

You can also place the contents of this selection on its own layer by any of the following methods:

▶ Choose Layer | Layer Via Cut, and the contents of the selection will be transferred to their own layer, while a hole will appear in the underlying layer.

▶ Choose Layer | Layer Via Copy (CMD/CTRL-J) and the contents of the text selection marquee will appear as a new layer, remaining in the layer from whence they came as well.

PASTING A MOVABLE IMAGE INSIDE THE TEXT BOUNDARIES

One way to fill a photo with text is to use Paste Into. After pasting a photo into text, you can drag the image around behind the text outline to decide how it should look after you paste it. What's more, even after continued editing, you can always return to the Layer controls and reposition the photo.

To Use PASTE INTO WITH TEXT:

1 Create an image with some text. You'll usually want your text set as a large wide font so that a maximum amount of image can be seen through the "keyhole" made by the text's shape.

2 Open the image you want to use inside the text. To copy it to the Clipboard, choose Select | Select All (CMD/CTRL-A). In the example that follows, an image of flame is used.

3 Return to the main image, then select the Text layer in the Layers palette.

4 Choose the Magic Wand tool. In the Option toolbar, make sure Contiguous and Use All Layers are toggled off (unchecked).

5 Using the Magic Wand, center the cursor over the center of one of the letters in the text and click.

6 Delete the text layer. The selection will still be active, and will create a selection on the layer beneath the now-deleted text layer.

7 With that bottom layer selected, choose Edit | Paste Into. The text will appear pasted into the lettering selection (see Figure 11-10). Also, the selected lettering and the pasted content will now appear on their own layer above the previous layer. On the Layers palette, look at the new layer created, and you'll see the text and the pasted image, linked by a chain icon.

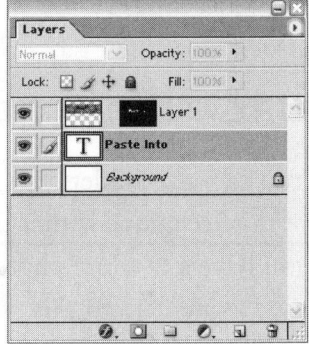

You can move both the text and the image inside the text, but to do so, you must first make the layer beneath it invisible, and remove the chain icon from the Text/Paste layer. This is done in the Layers palette.

To Move TEXT WITH AN IMAGE INSIDE IT:

1 In the Layers palette, click the layer beneath the text/paste layer, and then click the "eye" icon, which makes that layer invisible.

FIGURE 11-10
Applying the Paste Into command with text

2 In the Layers palette, click the Text/Paste layer, and then click the chain icon between the two thumbnails that appear on that layer. What you've done is made it so you can independently move the text, or move the image inside the text.

3 To move the image inside the text, in the Layers palette, click the image thumbnail of that Text/Paste layer, then click inside the actual image with the Move tool. The image inside the text will move.

4 To move the text around, in the Layers palette, click the text thumbnail on the Text/Paste layer, then click inside the image with the Move tool. The text will move.

When you are happy with the image and text position, you can again make the other layer visible, continue to add layers, and edit your image as you like. If you want to edit the pasted image position or text position at some other time, just make all the other layers invisible, and edit as you like.

CREATING IMAGE PATTERNS

You can also fill lettering with a photograph using Define Pattern. The advantage of this technique is that the pattern will be available in later Photoshop sessions. If you have a favorite photo fill you often use, keep it handy with Define Pattern. To use Define Pattern this way, you must first save the filling image as a pattern, then fill the lettering using it.

To Save YOUR IMAGE AS A PATTERN:

1 Open the image you want to fill text with.

2 Choose File | Define Pattern. The Pattern Name dialog box will appear.

3 You'll be prompted to name your pattern. A thumbnail appears with the image that will display in the pattern list, along with the pattern name.

4 Click OK to confirm your pattern. It will now appear with the preset patterns used to create Photoshop Fills.

> **NOTE** If you want to use only a portion of the image as your fill, first crop the image using the Crop tool so only the wanted portion remains. You do not have to save the image to use it as a pattern.

To Create TEXT AND FILL IT WITH THE PATTERN:

1 First, you'll create text in an image.

2 Use the Magic Wand tool to select the text. Before selecting, on the Options Bar, make sure that Contiguous and Use All Layers are not checked.

3 Delete the Text layer. The selection will remain, and will appear on the image background, or on the layer beneath the Text layer.

4 Click the text selection with the Move tool.

5 Choose Edit | Fill. When the Fill dialog box appears, choose Pattern from the Use drop-down menu. In the Custom drop-down menu, choose the pattern you created (see Figure 11-11).

6 The pattern will fill the text. Make this selection into a layer by choosing Layer | New | Layer via Cut or Layer | New | Layer via Copy.

CREATING STENCIL TEXT

Here's how to create a text mask, where the text cuts a hole in a layer, revealing the layer underneath.

To Create STENCIL TEXT:

1 On a new image, create a layer, either with an image background, a color, or a gradient fill.

FIGURE 11-11
Creating a text fill using
Define Pattern

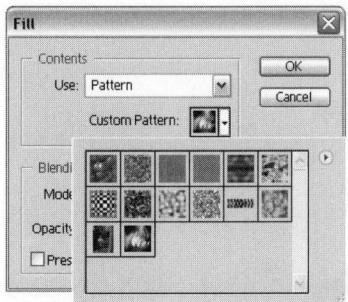

2 Create another layer on top of that one, again filling it with content in some way.

3 Click the Type tool, and choose Type Mask, either horizontal or vertical, whichever you prefer. A rose-colored mask overlay will appear over your image, indicating you are in Mask mode.

4 You'll be typing text against this rose overlay. Click the image exactly where you want the text to appear, starting from left to right. This is important because you won't be able to reposition your text after you begin typing.

5 Type some text. Your words will appear punched through the top layer, the bottom layer appearing through the hole left by the text. You can use the BACKSPACE key to delete text and start again, as well as change the font, font style, and so on. However, as soon as you are done typing, the mask overlay will disappear, and the cutout will appear.

6 Choose Edit | Cut to delete the top layer portion that fills the mask. The cutout text will appear.

7 You can move the top layer around, and you'll see the text change as it moves across the underlying layer.

To make your mask more mobile and interesting, you can use one of the Marquee or Lasso tools to select part of the top layer surrounding the text, and then make that selection into a new layer, as shown in Figure 11-12. You can also apply Blending modes, filters, and other effects to this layer as well. In the example that follows, the text was placed on a layer treated with the Spherize filter (Filter | Distort | Spherize). The text then matched the shape of the soccer ball layer beneath.

FIGURE 11-12
Text with a feathered layer background and a Blending Mode applied

After creating a text mask, you can perform effects such as cutting the text layer in half, (Figure 11-13), applying Adjustment layers or effects to only a portion of the layer, and so forth.

CREATING FROSTED TEXT

Here's how to use the Airbrush tool to paint the tips of letters in order to create a hand-painted, "frosted" effect. After applying this, your text will be a bitmap, and will not be editable as text.

To Create FROSTED TEXT:

1 Create a new image and fill the background with the desired text color.

2 Create your text phrase, using the font of your choice. It does not matter which color you use.

3 Use the Magic Wand to select the text, as we've done several times in this chapter.

4 Delete the text layer. The selection will now be on the background.

5 Select the Background layer.

6 Select the Airbrush tool, and using a very soft, large brush with a light yellow, gently touch the tips of the letters where you'd like the frosting to appear (see Figure 11-14).

7 Choose Layer | New | Layer Via Cut. Your text phrase will now appear on its own layer with the frosting touches as you placed them. The text may be indistinct at this point,

FIGURE 11-13
An effect applied to the upper layer of stencil text that was sliced in half

FIGURE 11-14
Applying an Airbrush to the tips of text that were turned into a selection

as it is the same color as the background, so you can replace the background if you wish. As shown in Figure 11-15, you can add a drop-shadow, a Bevel and Emboss, or other layer effect as you like (right-click the Layer with the text and choose Blending Options).

EDITING THE SHAPE OF INDIVIDUAL LETTERS

You may want to manually adjust letter shapes, changing a letter's appearance curve by curve. This is quite common when creating corporate logos based on two or three letters or symbols. Customizing each letter gives your text a one-of-a-kind appearance. This is done by converting letters to paths. You can use the Path Selection tools to stretch and pull any curve of any letter.

To Change THE SHAPES OF LETTERS:

1 Create a new image with a colorful background.

2 Add text, which will appear on a new layer above the Background layer.

FIGURE 11-15
Adding a drop-shadow and a Bevel and Emboss effect to a text selection

FIGURE 11-16
Creating a clip path by using an Action

3 Use the Magic Wand tool to fill the text, using the methods shown earlier in this chapter. On the Options Bar with the Magic Wand tool selected, make sure the Contiguous and Use All Layers options are deselected.

4 The text will appear selected. In the Actions palette, click the Make Clip Path (selection) entry, then click the Play icon at the bottom of the palette (Figure 11-16).

5 The selected text will be transformed into individual paths, one path for each letter. You can use any of the Path tools to edit the paths.

6 One or all letters can be moved and edited. Moving the path lettering will not carve a hole in the layer beneath.

7 After reshaping the lettering, change the paths back to selections by clicking the Load Path As Selection icon at the bottom of the Paths palette. The lettering can then be filled, treated with effects, Layer styles, and so forth.

NOTE You can also create paths directly from the text by choosing Create Work Path, found in the Layer menu (Layer | Type | Create Workpath). After creating the work path, the user can make the path permanent by choosing the Path tab and double-clicking the work path to rename it.

 ON THE VIRTUAL CLASSROOM CD-ROM In Lesson 9, "Text and Buttons," you will be shown more about layer styles and an easier way to place a photo inside of text will be demonstrated.

12

Photoshop, ImageReady, and Slick Web Tricks

Not all graphics are destined for print. An increasing number of designers are choosing Photoshop to illustrate, design, and prototype web sites. With this choice comes a new set of tools you can use to extend the reach of your imagination. In this chapter, we will be looking at how to extend Photoshop to allow you to export graphics for the Web. This will be done using the Save For Web option within Photoshop and then, later, you will be introduced to ImageReady.

ImageReady is most certainly the big gun in Photoshop's arsenal of web design tools. With ImageReady, you are not only able to control the format you export your images in, but it allows you to add interactive effects such as animation and JavaScript rollovers, but offers the capability to create instant photo albums as well.

If you have been using Photoshop for a while, you may be familiar with the Web tools that come with it. This chapter explains how to set up your Photoshop files to export them smoothly and cleanly to the Web.

Setting Up a File for the Web

The Web is a different medium from print, requiring that you make certain decisions relating to the technical characteristics of that medium.

In some ways, the Web is more forgiving than print. A web page is viewed through a computer monitor and does not require a resolution of more than 72- to 96dpi, whereas print typically requires a resolution of at least 300dpi. The resolution decreases still further when you develop graphics for web sites viewed through televisions and other Internet devices. The immediate advantage this gives you is that all image files are considerably smaller. Small files are a key success factor for web sites. Even today, nearly 80 percent of all households dial up to the Internet instead of using broadband solutions such as DSL and cable (Source: Forrester Research). The bottom line: images must be kept as small as possible in relationship to the level of quality acceptable for the use of a particular image. The bulk of web graphics are simply eye candy, and seldom made to be over one inch square. Even principal illustrations are seldom more than four inches square.

A second consideration you need to keep in mind with web graphics is your color palette. Typically, print images are converted to CMYK colors. Web graphics should always be created in RGB and only be converted from CMYK in instances where there is no RGB original since the RGB palette is capable of displaying a significantly wider *gamut* (range of colors and brightness).

There's another color mode that is extremely important to the preparation of web graphics. There are many instances when the most efficient file format is the 256- (or fewer) color, indexed-palette GIF format. Any time an image consists of text, logos, or hard-edged flat-colored poster-style graphics, you're better off using this format. Files will be much smaller (and, therefore, faster-loading). The graphics also look better because their colors translate more accurately, the edges are smoother, and flat-colored areas show fewer artifacts. About 90 percent of the time, you will want to index files destined for GIF output on the Web to the palette universally used by all web browsers. It is called the web palette and it ensures that the colors indexed to that palette are interpreted in the same way (give or take some differences in brightness) as the same color in all browsers.

It can be an enormously complicated undertaking correctly converting an image to be indexed by a web-safe palette, while simultaneously making sure the image colors match the web palette (especially if those colors were generated by means beyond your control—as is the case when dealing with photos). Of course, Photoshop makes it easy because, after all, it was made for pros whose time *is* money.

To Convert A PHOTO TO A WEB-SAFE PALETTE:

1 Duplicate your original image and then crop and resize it the way you want it to appear on the Web. It is VERY important you perform this first step.

2 Choose Image | Mode | Indexed Color. The Indexed Color dialog appears.

3 In the Indexed Color dialog, choose Local (Perceptual) from the Palette drop-down menu.

4 Choose Web from the Forced menu. This forces use of only web-safe colors.

5 If you plan to designate one of the colors as transparent when using the Save For Web command, be sure to check the Transparency box.

6 Choose Dither from the Diffusion menu.

7 If the Preserve Exact Colors box is checked, the dithering will attempt to imitate the illusion of having preserved the original colors.

8 Click OK to render the image.

You will notice that the result is usually quite a bit grainier than the original. This is because the program has intermingled pixels of the colors in the web-safe palette in order to create the illusion of having preserved the colors in the original image.

If you are going to use Photoshop to create an original web graphic from scratch, you should convert to indexed color before starting, and then load web-safe colors into your Swatches palette. This way you ensure you're painting with only web-safe colors.

To Ensure YOU'RE USING WEB-SAFE COLORS:

1 Choose File | New. The New File dialog opens.

2 Make sure RGB color is chosen from the Mode menu.

3 Enter your size and resolution requirements and then click OK.

4 Choose Image | Adjustments | Mode | Indexed Color. The Indexed Color dialog appears.

5 From the Palette menu, choose Web.

6 Choose None from the Dither menu and click OK.

7 Make sure you can easily pick web-safe colors to paint with. Choose Windows | Swatches. When the Swatches palette appears, choose Web Safe Colors from the Swatches Palette menu.

> **NOTE** You should NEVER create Photoshop images in CMYK for the reason stated earlier, and because some of the capabilities of Photoshop simply don't work in RGB color mode. You should only convert to CMYK when the image is going to be output to a reflected light medium such as the printed page. Even then, it is usually best to let an expert in prepress operations convert the image to CMYK. You will often want to convert to CMYK for proofing purposes, but you can easily do that from a duplicate of your image you don't end up destroying information in your original that you can't replace later. End of lecture.

You should carefully consider which type of graphic format your web image will have. Today there are three popular file formats (shown in Table 12-1).

As you can see, there are several considerations to mull over when creating a file for the Web. Fortunately, these can all be addressed when you start a new file.

To Create A FILE FOR THE WEB:

1 Select File New dialog box. From here you can choose how you want to format your default document. (See Figure 12-1.)

2 The first check you must select is the color mode. Change it to RGB.

TABLE 12-1 THREE POPULAR IMAGE FORMATS FOR THE WEB

JPEG (Joint Photographs Expert Group)	One of the most accepted formats for digital images on the Web is JPEG images (extension .jpg and .jpe). You can achieve some of the smallest file sizes when exporting to this image format. In addition, the JPEG format supports True Color, which allows for photographs to be accurately displayed.
GIF (CompuServe GIF)	CompuServe GIF images have been made infamous by banner advertising. Unlike JPEG images, GIF files can be stacked within each other to play back like a short movie. The final effect can be seen on almost any web site that supports advertising.
	In addition to supporting animation, GIF images can also have a transparent background. This allows you to design shapes, such as buttons, that appear to be irregular in shape. The GIF format only supports 256 colors. This makes it limiting for complex graphical designs. (See the earlier information regarding considerations for working in web-safe colors.)
PNG (Portable Network Graphics)	The PNG format is an open source format that addresses many of the needs graphic designers have for web graphics. The format supports the full 24-bit range of colors and can be animated in much the same way as GIF images. Another significant bonus is that PNG images support layer and opacity information in much the same way as a PSD file does.
	The only significant negative for PNG images is that the popular web browsers do not fully support the file format. 24-bit files are also lossless and, therefore, tend to be quite a bit larger than JPEG files. In addition, many older web browsers can't display PNG files without an extra plug-in, which many web users don't know how to find or install.

3 Name the file Project. This later appears as the title for your web page when you export the design.

4 The typical page layout size is 640x480 pixels, though as 17" monitors have gained in popularity, some designers today prefer to go up to 800x600. You should almost always work in pixels when designing for the Web. This is because HTML itself, particularly HTML tables, use pixels as the default measurement format.

5 Set the resolution to 72dpi. Select OK and begin working. It's as easy as that.

You can now begin to design the web page. Figure 12-2 shows a web page created in Photoshop.

FIGURE 12-1

The New File dialog box
allows you to format the
image for Web readiness

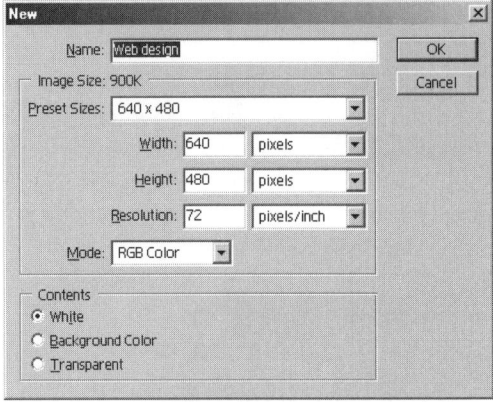

FIGURE 12-2

A web-formatted PSD file

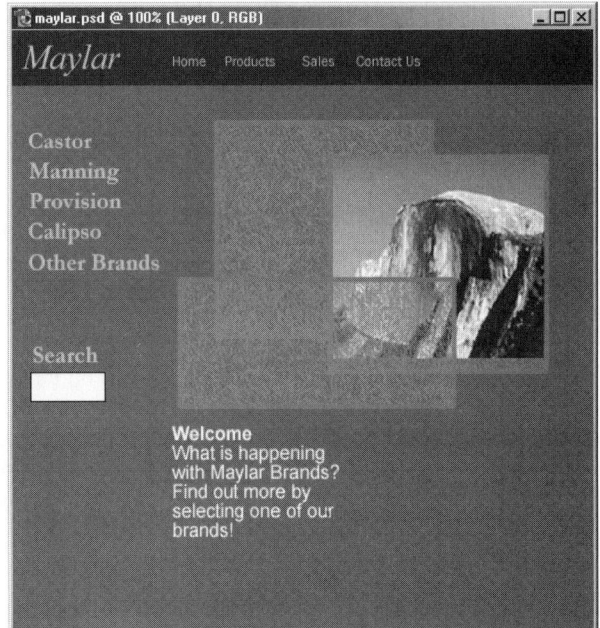

SIZING WEB GRAPHICS Most web graphics, because they are meant to occupy only a fraction of the web page, are much smaller than 640x480 pixels. Also, menus and borders take up quite a bit of available space, so the practical maximum image size will be about 550x400 pixels.

Under the Preset Sizes drop-down menu, Photoshop includes default file sizes for one web banner and three different web pages.

OPTIMIZING GRAPHICS FOR THE WEB

You have labored night and day to design your web page for publication. The catch now is that you need to export that file to the Web. To do this, you can simply select Save As... and choose either JPEG or GIF. This quickly exports the file in a format ready for the Web. Unfortunately, you have not optimized the file. In Photoshop-speak, to "optimize" means to make the most image-flattering compromise between image fidelity and file size (that is, download speed).

Photoshop allows you to tweak and curl every element you see on a graphic so it works perfectly for the medium you want it viewed through.

SAVE FOR WEB

Get it on the Web! These were the words bellowed at me at a conference in 1995. The speaker was talking about this new thing called "The Internet" (it came in quotes back then). Well, the same still holds true today. So far, Photoshop has been set up to create a web image, but up to this point has not actually done the image creation process.

To get it on the Web, you will have a much easier and more productive time if you choose either File | Save For Web (shown in Figure 12-3) or click the Jump To

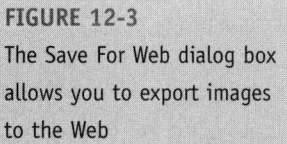

FIGURE 12-3
The Save For Web dialog box allows you to export images to the Web

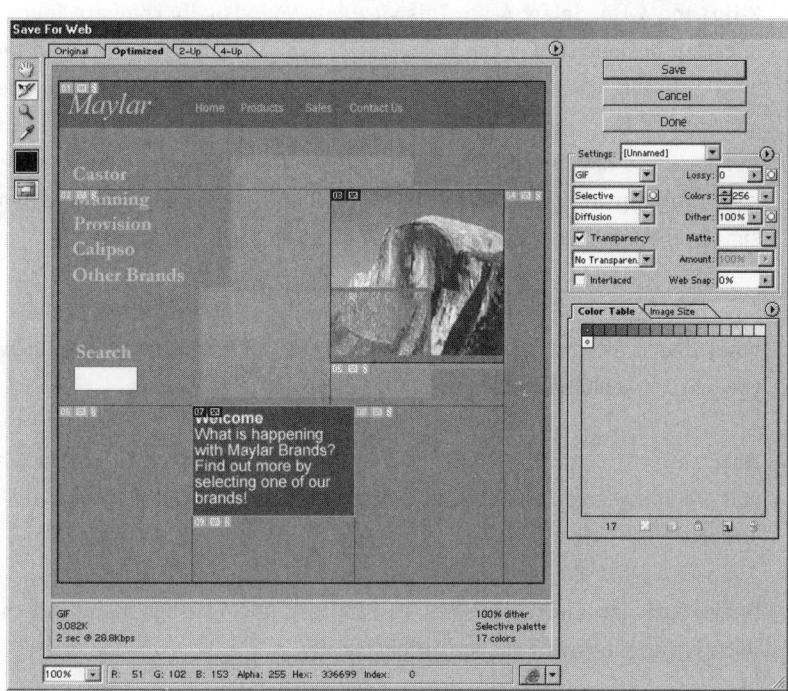

button at the bottom of the Toolbox to automatically move your image into ImageReady 7.0. In either case, you'll see your image in a workspace topped by four tabs: Original (only lets you see your original image), Optimized (only lets you see your image using the settings you've chosen to optimize it for the Web), 2-up (lets you compare the Original and one Optimized version), and 4-up (lets you compare the Original and three different Optimized versions of the image).

About the only difference between optimizing an image in the Save As dialog and doing the same thing in ImageReady is that ImageReady gives you a lot more control over the creation of GIF animations, rollover events, image mapping, and image slicing. Also, In ImageReady, the Optimize palette is a separate (but just as easily accessible) part of the interface. The following steps are virtually the same regardless of which way you optimize your image.

To Optimize AN IMAGE:

1 With your file still open, choose File | Open | Save For Web. The Save For Web dialog will open. Alternately, you can click the Jump To button at the bottom of the Toolbox and your currently active image will open in ImageReady.

2 Across the top of the workspace window, you will see four tabs: Original, Optimized, 2-Up, and 4-Up. Select 4-up. This view lets you visually compare four different optimization options so you can immediately judge when you've reached the best compromise between download speed (image data size) and image quality. The upper left quadrant of the 4-up view shows you the original image. Any of the other three views can show you any optimization settings you chose the last time it was your selected view. This capability to make a visual comparison between optimization settings seems simple enough, but it will save you endless hours of guesswork.

3 Select the upper-right optimization window. Your optimization options settings will now affect this window. You can look at it in the Optimize or 2-up views as long as you keep it selected before switching to one of those views.

4 Make sure the Optimize palette is in view (you don't need to bother with this step if you are using Save For Web—only if you're in ImageReady). If you don't see it, choose Window | Optimize.

5 Under Optimize, choose GIF Web Palette from the Settings menu. All the other optimization settings will change automatically.

6 In turn, select each of the other two windows and make a different choice for each from the Optimize Settings menu. (See Figure 12-3.) At the bottom of each of the optimized views, you can see the file size and upload time at 28.8 Kbps that will result from the setting currently chosen for that view.

7 Concentrate on the type of file format you're going to want to use as the result of what you've just learned and choose the same Settings menu choice for all three of them. Then subjectively experiment with the rest of the settings in the Optimize palette that can make slight variations in each of these files. As you experiment, note the difference in the performance for each window as well as the difference in the quality apparent in the file. When you find the setting that best suits the purpose of this particular graphic, click the Optimized tab.

8 If you're in ImageReady, choose File | Save As. A File Navigation dialog appears where you can name your file and navigate to the folder where you want to store it. If you're in Photoshop and using the Save For Web command, just click the Save button at the upper-right of the dialog. A Save Optimized As dialog will open, letting you name your file and navigate to the folder you want to save it in.

It's hard to write an exercise about Photoshop or ImageReady these days without finishing by saying "pretty cool, huh?" Well, at least, it's really nifty.

IMAGE SLICING IN PHOTOSHOP

Any image in Photoshop can be cut up with the Slice tool, something quite useful when dealing with web graphics. With the Slice tool, you can select different regions on the canvas and slice away. What happens when the file is exported is that Photoshop cuts up the main image and reassembles it in an HTML table. When the image is viewed through a web page, you see only the whole image. However, look at the files that are exported and you will see the image is created by a large number of smaller files.

When you slice, you can change the file format of that specific slice to be any web-safe image format, optimized in any way, and to any degree, allowed by that format. You will now slice up your image file.

To Slice AN IMAGE:

1 Select the Slice tool from the Toolbox. The cursor changes to a knife.

2 Click and drag the knife over the photograph. Release the cursor. The canvas is now cut up into different coordinates. Highlighted, as shown in Figure 12-4, is the Mountain. This region has now been sliced.

3 Using the Slice tool again, select and drag over the text at the bottom of the page.

That is all that is needed to slice up a page with the Slice tool. You will now take this page and begin optimizing each section for the Web. To do this, select each slice, one-at-a-time, and optimize it using the Optimization palette, just as described earlier. Experiment with the various settings. The whole idea is to create the smallest file possible consistent with acceptable image quality (only you can be the judge of this—and will depend upon your personal tolerance, the nature of the picture, and its context). Note that if you use the 2-Up and 4-Up tabs in the Save For Web or ImageReady environments, you will be able to make a side-by-side comparison between the original and either one or three alternatives for optimizations settings. Heck, they don't even have to be comparisons of the same file type. So you can compare the results of optimizing in either GIF or JPEG, side-by-side.

FIGURE 12-4
A region sliced with the Knife tool

ImageReady

As you've seen, Photoshop by itself is a powerful tool. However, the Web does demand more than Photoshop alone can deliver. What about animation? How about web buttons? And where do I make JavaScript rollovers? Enter ImageReady, the web graphics wing of Photoshop that comes in the same box.

When you open ImageReady, you'll notice it looks a lot like Photoshop. There are some differences, however. When you open a new file, you will not be asked to choose a color mode (only RGB will be allowed), and it is assumed that the dpi is going to be 72. If you jump directly from Photoshop 7 while using a large file destined for print, ImageReady's performance will seem very sluggish. You should immediately resize the image for the Web and the program's performance will return to something that seems much more normal. Actually, you should duplicate, flatten, and resize the file *before* you jump to ImageReady. Doing so will greatly reduce your chances of totally messing up your original.

ImageReady does come with a number of tools that make it a snap to get the impression you want on the Web.

Creating a Rollover Button

Rollover button effects are a great addition to your web site, and are very easy to create with ImageReady. To effectively complete this exercise, you will need ImageReady open.

To Create a Rollover button:

1 Choose File | New. In the New File dialog, enter 500 in the Width field and 400 in the Height field with pixels chosen as the unit of measurement (the default). This is just to give you plenty of room to practice in. Click OK to open the file.

2 Open the Layers palette. Click the New Layer icon to create a new layer.

3 With the new layer selected, choose the Ellipse tool and draw an ellipse on the canvas.

4 Open the Rollovers palette. The Rollovers palette allows you to add Rollover effects to an image. Select the Create Layer Based Rollover icon at the bottom of the Rollover palette (it looks like an exploding arrow). This slices up the page around the ellipse.

5 Automatically, the ellipse now has two states in the Rollover palette: Normal and Over State. Select the Over State and, with the Text Tool, write Click Me on the ellipse. Preview the page.

What has happened is that the page has been cut up and a second image is being swapped out with the original. Well done—your first JavaScript!

GIF Animation

You can create short animations in ImageReady by using Photoshop layers as frames. There are several procedures for going about this, but the one I recommend beginning with involves starting in Photoshop. One of the easiest ways to create an animation is to use a still camera that will shoot "motor drive" or time-lapse sequences.

To Create an animation:

1 Take each frame, in start to finish order, and place it on a separate layer in the same file. The easiest way to do that is to open all the frames as separate images. Then, in order of sequence, click each image to activate it, press CMD/CTRL-A to Select All, followed by CMD/CTRL-C to copy them to the Clipboard.

2 Next, click to activate the target animation image and press CMD/CTRL-V to paste the image last copied to the Clipboard. It will automatically appear on its own layer.

3 You will probably want the image to be positioned so it registers immediately above the previous image. Temporarily drag the newest layer's Opacity slider to about 50 percent so you can see the underlying layer through it, use the Move tool to reposition the top layer in the desired relationship to the layer immediately below it, and then move the Opacity slider back to 100 percent.

4 Repeat the first three steps until all the images are stacked sequentially on their own individual layers within the same file. Now choose the Crop tool and crop the image to the shape you wish for your web site. Usually, you'll want to crop it so all the layers appear to be the same size and shape. If you don't do this, each frame will appear to jump around (though this can sometimes be a desirable effect).

5 Now resize your whole image to the size you want it to be on the Web.

6 Click the Jump To button at the bottom of the Toolbox. Your layered image will appear in ImageReady.

7 In ImageReady, look for the Animations palette. If you don't see it, choose Window | Animations. The Animations palette should appear.

8 From the Animations palette menu, choose Make Animation From Layers. Instantly, the image on each layer appears in the Animations palette with the bottom layer as Frame 1 and the top layer as the last frame.

9 If you click the Play button in the VCR control icons at the bottom of the Animations palette, your animation will play—very rapidly if you have a fast computer. By default, the Animations palette sets each frame to play with no interframe delay. You change the timing for each frame individually by dragging on the arrow immediately to the right of "sec" just under the frame thumbnail. A timing menu will pop up, and you can either select from a list of preset delays, or you can enter your own custom delay. Longer delays between frames can be used to create a self-playing slide show.

10 To the left of the Animations palette you'll see a small menu called the Looping Options menu. It pops up to let you choose between whether the animation will restart and replay endlessly (loop), play once and stop, or replay a specified number of times.

11 To the right of the VCR buttons is the Tween icon. If you click the Tween icon, the Tween dialog appears. It lets you tween between frame (layer) position, opacity, and effects. You can specify the number of frames you want in the tween and you can add information to the tweened frames by using editing commands on each of the individual layers (anything you do to create new frames will also create corresponding new layers).

> **NOTE** A fast way to build an animation is with the Import tool. The Import tool allows you to navigate to a folder of images. These images are then brought in and formatted sequentially as a large animated GIF.

SUMMARY

As you have seen with this chapter, Photoshop is more than ready to meet the needs of the Web. With Photoshop itself, you can design rich, complex web pages that can then be optimized and exported to the Web. Throw in ImageReady and you have a *tour de force* suite of tools designed specifically to allow the designer to pass their vision onto a web audience.

13

Printing Your Photos for Print Presentation

Photoshop facilitates two types of printing. In the first, you send a print job to a printer attached to your computer. Tools are employed to make sure the colors onscreen reasonably match the colors of the hard copy, thus minimizing hit-and-miss printing and wasted paper. The second type printing is when you prepare your document for professional printing, meeting the specifications and formatting requirements of high-quality commercial printers. Typically, these two types overlap, because documents bound for professional printing should still be proofed—that is, printed on a desktop printer first in order to minimize expensive surprises later. In this chapter, we'll take a look at both tasks.

UNDERSTANDING COLOR MANAGEMENT

Photoshop's Color Management tools ensure that the colors you see on your monitor match the colors you print. This is important because you may want to correct, for example, a shade of magenta based on what your monitor displays, but when printed, you may find that no correction was necessary. Thus, if you had an idea of what your document would really look like when printed, your editing decisions might be entirely different.

UNDERSTANDING PROFILES

Though the preceding example applies to displaying output colors (as in printing), variations in color values also affect documents "going in" to Photoshop. Many scanners add a color cast to images. Because of a certain bias in the hardware, the scanned version of your document may have slightly different hues than the original hard copy you scanned. To correct for this, Photoshop lets you set up an automatic correction routine that adjusts every document coming in from that scanner, compensating for its color changes.

In order to ensure accurate color at every phase of your document editing and printing process, you require a way to correct for the bias of every input and output device you are working with. Photoshop lets you set up these adjustment routines, called *profiles*, for every device you choose.

This is important because customers, clients, employers, and anyone who asks you to work up a project will know when a color isn't quite what they expected. Your goal is to eliminate surprises at the end of the project, and be able to show your clients color-accurate examples of your work in progress, either onscreen, or on desktop printer hard copy. In your presentation, you want to avoid having to say, "This green will actually look a little darker on paper."

How can Photoshop be made to provide color accuracy at every stage of your image development? Through the use of color profiles. *Color profiles* are the automatic color adjustment routines you bring into play whenever you use a particular input or output device.

APPLYING COLOR PROFILES

Color profiles are applied three different ways. You can:

▶ Use the Color profiles Photoshop provides in the Color Management drop-down menus. These are actually very good and would be quite suitable for most needs, except in situations requiring the highest degree of color exactitude.

▶ Use color profiles provided by the manufacturer of your devices. Photoshop can read these, install them, and make them available via dialog boxes.

▶ Develop a customized Color profile for an individual device using calibration equipment. You would use a densitometer on printed matter or a spectrometer (for devices that use transmitted light, such as cameras, monitors and scanners) to measure the color output of a device, then record those values in Photoshop. Photoshop would then "know" the color range and limitations of that specific device, and deliver the most accurate possible color management.

Photoshop provides an all-inclusive system of color management. This global approach to identifying and accurately rendering color is very important to image editing. For example, monitors and printers display colors using completely different technologies. A computer monitor produces colors using the RGB color space, combining various percentages of red, green, and blue light to produce a large array of colors. Printers, on the other hand, use the CMYK color space. Print presses apply overlapping layers with varying percentages of cyan, magenta and yellow inks, and use black to strengthen colors and add definition.

PREPARING YOUR SYSTEM FOR COLOR MANAGEMENT

Before implementing color management, there are steps you can take to make sure the process works as you hope it will, especially when installing devices.

CALIBRATING YOUR MONITOR

Monitor calibration assures that the colors you see onscreen are faithful to those specified by you and Photoshop, allowing you to base your color editing decisions on genuine information. You don't calibrate your monitor inside the Photoshop program, however. Instead, Photoshop automatically installs a calibration applet called Adobe Gamma. During calibration, you'll be adjusting your monitor's color controls, brightness/contrast, and Gamma setting.

To Calibrate YOUR MONITOR USING PHOTOSHOP'S CALIBRATION PROGRAM:

1 Start the Adobe Gamma program.

2 The Adobe Gamma dialog box appears (Figure 13-1). You'll be prompted to create an ICC profile for your monitor. This profile then appears with others like it in Photoshop's color control dialog boxes and print options.

3 You can choose the Step-by-Step Wizard or the Control Panel methods for creating the profile. The wizard walks you through a handful of adjustments, mostly using onscreen sliders that adjust your monitor's hardware brightness/contrast setting. The process takes only a few minutes.

4 You'll be prompted to name your profile, and set it as the default if you wish.

The process is demonstrated visually in the Virtual Classroom lesson on this book's CD.

INSTALLING A PROFILE

Some device installations automatically install color profiles as part of their setup process. You'll find them with the other Device profiles in Photoshop, along with additional installed devices that use color management.

FIGURE 13-1
Adobe's monitor calibration program, Adobe Gamma

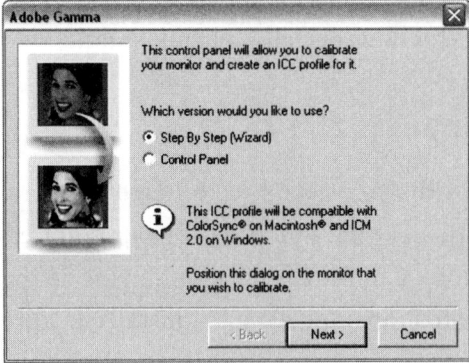

To Manually Install A DEVICE PROFILE AND MAKE IT AVAILABLE IN PHOTOSHOP:

1 Locate the .ICM file installed with that device. The file will have an ICM file extension.

2 Right-click the icon for the .ICM file and choose Install Profile (Figure 13-2), or copy the file into the Windows\system32\spool\drivers\color folder, or wherever the other .ICM files are stored. .ICM files are system files, and should be found in a subfolder beneath Windows.

WORKING WITHIN A RANGE OF COLORS

It is the job of Color Management to identify the color range, or gamut, of the color models and devices being used. A color gamut refers to all available colors in a color space. This process of identifying and interpreting the gamut is how Photoshop lets you correct colors with confidence.

At the top of the color range scale is the human eye, which can see millions upon millions of color shades and hues. The RGB color space, as applied through your monitor, can accurately re-create about 16 million of those hues. Since colors are created by varying phosphor intensities, the RGB color gamut is quite large. In contrast, the CMYK color space used by printers is based on overlaying four process color inks, and cannot reproduce as many colors as RGB. Therefore, its color gamut is smaller.

An RGB image must be converted to CMYK before being printed professionally. To do this, choose Image | Mode | CMYK Color. The question arises then: What happens to the colors that do not have an exact corollary in the smaller CMYK palette? In other words, what happens to colors that are "out of gamut" after conversion?

FIGURE 13-2
Installing a Device profile

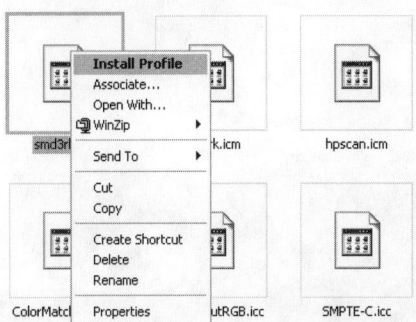

When you convert an RGB image to CMYK, Photoshop automatically finds the nearest corresponding color in the new palette. However, you may not want to be stuck with Photoshop's choices. To prevent this, you may want to view colors before converting, that will be out of gamut once you do so, and choose new colors manually.

To Identify OUT-OF-GAMUT COLORS:

1 Choose View | Proof Setup, then select the Device profile you want to match colors with, and identify colors outside the gamut.

2 Choose View | Gamut Warning. On your image, you'll see all colors outside the chosen gamut are highlighted with a "warning" fill (Figure 13-3).

3 Alter the image with colors viewable in the new color space, as specified by the profile.

COLOR MANAGEMENT WORKFLOW

Profiles are named after the devices they are profiling, and are listed in menus in several Photoshop dialog boxes. There are three points in your Photoshop workflow where Color Management is applied.

FIGURE 13-3
An image with out-of-gamut colors indicated by a fill

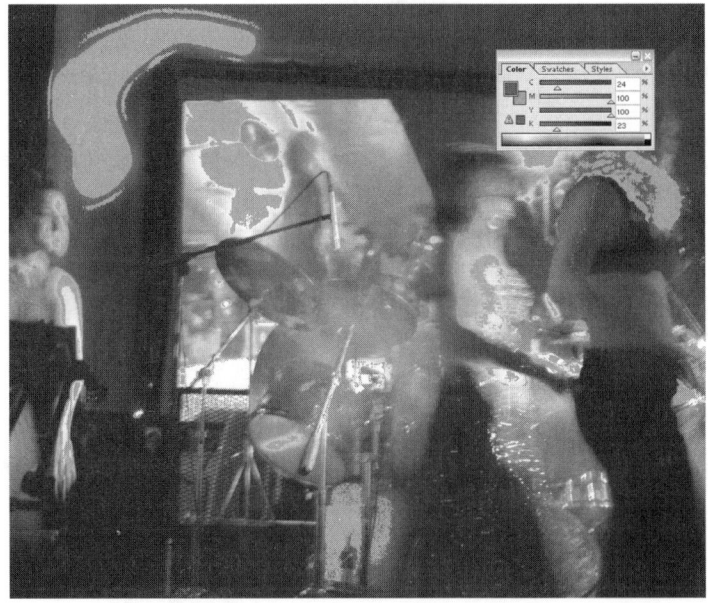

The first comes when creating a color workspace environment (choose Edit | Color Settings). The profile choices you apply here affect new documents, as well as documents that have no profile applied to them (referred to as untagged documents). Two working spaces are assigned this way: an RGB workspace for document editing, and a CYMK workspace for print proofing and making final edits before printing.

The second occurs when using individual document profiles (choose Image | Mode | Assign Profile). A profile is assigned to a document so the document displays the color gamut of that profile, rather than the workspace profile.

The third instance is when you apply Color Management and change profiles in the Print Preview dialog box. This lets you see how your document will look printed on various printers, or with various print settings.

We'll first talk about specifying Color settings, then we'll explore how to set up document profiles. Lastly, we'll discuss the print preview process.

SPECIFYING COLOR SETTINGS

You can set up color work spaces for new Photoshop documents (documents you've not yet created), and documents without embedded color management (that do not include an embedded profile).

To Set Up COLOR WORKSPACES:

1 Choose Edit | Color Settings. The Color Settings dialog box appears (Figure 13-4).

2 Use the Settings drop-down menu to choose or create a complete color environment (a collection of settings that include choices from all the options that follow). The drop-down menu includes defaults adequate for most printing needs. Choosing a particular default from this list will cause the options below to change appropriately. If a particular Color Settings environment is available, but is not seen in the drop-down Settings list, it may have to be loaded. To do so, click the Load button.

> **NOTE** The Color Settings dialog box is used to define RGB, CMYK, and Grayscale work spaces, as well as a Dot Gain setting helpful in print preparation. You can also specify Color Management Policies, which determine how to treat documents that already have profiles attached.

FIGURE 13-4

The Color Settings dialog box

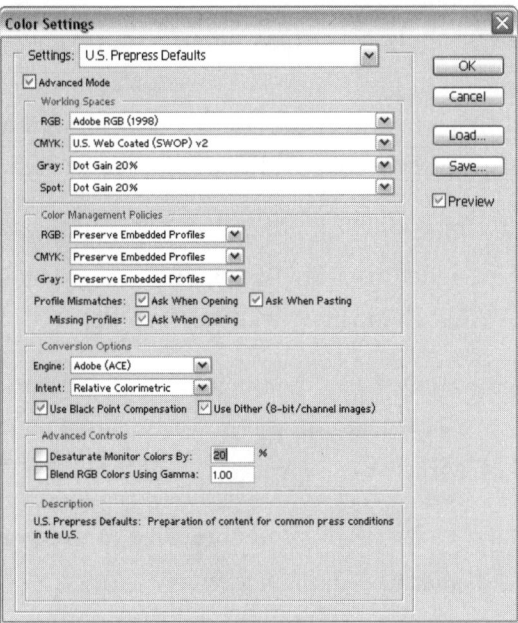

3 Click the Working Space drop-down menus to choose or create profiles for each color space: RGB, CMYK, Gray, and Spot. The combination of these settings creates a complete production color environment, from onscreen editing (RGB) to prepress and proofing (CMYK), to Grayscale and Spot color Dot Gain compensation settings (Gray and Spot). In the CMYK drop-down menu, you may want to select your own printer, if you'll be printing your documents directly, or choose the profile of a printer provided by a professional print service.

4 To customize the CMYK settings (if needed), just click the CMYK drop-down menu, and at the top of the list, click Custom CYMK. However, the only reason you'd need to do this might be because a professional printing service has provided you with their own printing press specifications. Unless you are an expert at this, you should ask your print house to provide you with a printer profile.

5 Choose a Gray or Spot option if needed. The Gray and Spot drop-down menus let you choose Dot Gain options according to your print hardware and paper output requirements. Dot Gain settings are also a product of paper choice, since dots spread much more on porous paper than glossy, for example.

6 Choose how to manage embedded profiles. The Color Management Policies drop-down menus let you choose to either leave documents alone that already have embedded profiles, or convert them to the current working space. You can specify to be prompted

(Ask When Opening), or when pasting a portion of a document from another profile (Ask When Pasting), as well as what to do about documents with profiles that aren't available.

> NOTE If you have a document open while creating Color settings, you won't see the results of your change unless you assign the profile to that document (choose Image | Mode | Assign Profile).

When you make changes to any setting, the Settings drop-down menu at the top of the dialog box will read Custom. You can then click Save, and save your customized settings for later use.

ASSIGNING PROFILES TO DOCUMENTS

You can assign profiles to individual documents. When you edit those documents, you'll use that profile's working spaces. A document's working spaces are the chosen color gamut used while editing onscreen (the RGB working space), and the color gamut that will be applied after converting to CMYK in preparation for printing. You would do this if your document is headed for numerous printers, not just one.

With the document open, choose Image | Mode | Assign Profile. The Assign Profile dialog box appears (Figure 13-5).

You have three options to choose from:

▶ **Don't Color Manage This Document** The image will have no profile attached, nor will it be affected by Photoshop's current Working RGB space.

▶ **Working RGB** The image will be displayed with the color gamut of the current RGB working space, which is indicated in the dialog box.

▶ **Profile** You can choose a profile for this document from the drop-down menu. All available profiles will be listed.

If you choose a profile for this image, it will be saved with the image. The next time you open the image, you'll be prompted to continue working with this embedded

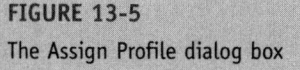
FIGURE 13-5
The Assign Profile dialog box

color profile, work with Photoshop's current working space, or discard Color
Management for this image completely.

MANAGING PRINT PREVIEW

The Print dialog box manages all aspects of the actual printing of your image. You
can preview the image, scale it to any size you like, print only a selected area, and
proof and manage your color choices.

To Use IT:

1 Choose File | Print With Preview. The Print dialog box appears (Figure 13-6).

2 If needed, use the Position panel to center or position your image as you like. With
Center Image unchecked, drag in the image area to move the image anywhere on the
page. You can also type in new settings in the Top and Left fields.

3 To scale the image, choose options in the Scaled Print Size panel. You can enter new
digits in the Scale, Height, and Width fields, and select a measuring system in the
Inches drop-down menu. To quickly resize the image to fit within the selected media,
choose Scale To Fit Media

4 Beneath the Print Preview area is a Show More Options check box. Click it to display
either Output settings such as calibration bars and registration marks, or Color
Management settings.

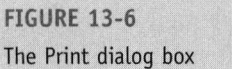

FIGURE 13-6

The Print dialog box

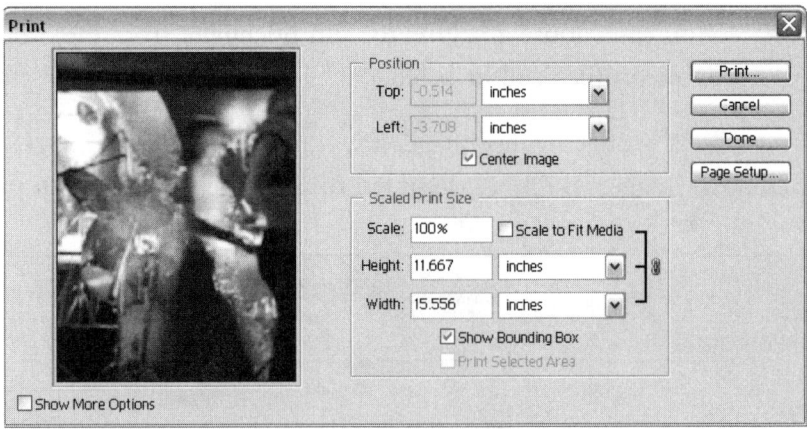

To Choose AND VIEW DEVICE COLORS WHILE PREVIEWING A PRINT JOB:

1 Make sure the Print dialog box is open and the Show More Options box is checked (Figure 13-7).

2 On the drop-down menu below the check box, choose Color Management. New options will appear at the bottom of the dialog box.

3 For your Source Space, choose either Document or Proof. Choose Document to display colors as interpreted by the currently assigned Document profile. Choose Proof to display colors used in the Proof profile, such as a printer or other output device.

4 Under Print Space, use the Profile drop-down menu to choose a Printer profile or other device profile. A commercial print shop may have provided specific settings for you to choose in this menu—for example, in the areas of Dot Gain amount or paper type.

5 To add calibration bars, registration marks, and other print-only features, choose Output from the Show More Options menu.

After choosing a Print Space profile, pick an Intent from the Intent drop-down menu. Let's talk briefly about setting a Rendering Intent.

When colors are converted to a different color space (such as moving from your monitor's RGB to your printer's CMYK models), there are choices to be made regarding scale and preservation. What type of conversion will make this document look best? After conversion, do you want the relationship between the colors to be the same, allowing the hues or saturation to shift, or do you want to preserve

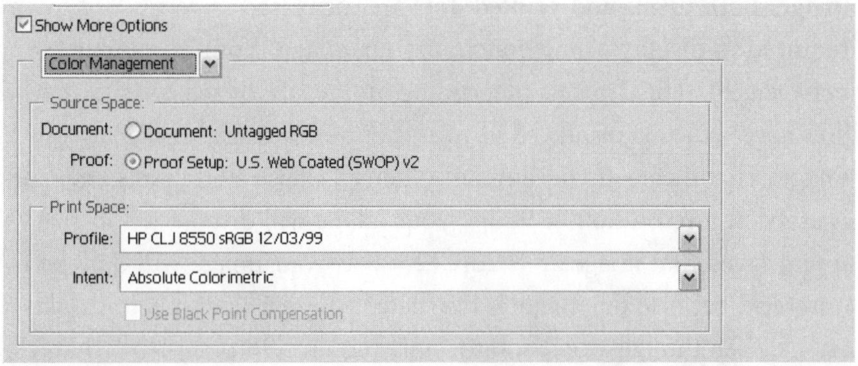

FIGURE 13-7
Viewing Print Preview's Color Management options

☑ Show More Options

Color Management ⌄

Source Space:
Document: ○ Document: Untagged RGB
Proof: ⦿ Proof Setup: U.S. Web Coated (SWOP) v2

Print Space:
Profile: HP CLJ 8550 sRGB 12/03/99
Intent: Absolute Colorimetric
☐ Use Black Point Compensation

color accuracy at the expense of the scale between the colors? What criteria should govern your Rendering Intent choice?

Here are the Rendering Intent choices, and suggested uses:

- ▶ **Perceptual** Preserves relationships between colors according to what looks natural to the human eye. Works well with photographs.
- ▶ **Saturation** When converting the source colors to destination colors, the saturation is maintained allowing the hue to shift. Works well with images requiring highly saturated block colors.
- ▶ **Relative Colorimetric** This is the default Photoshop setting, along with Use Black Point.
- ▶ **Absolute Colorimetric** Maintains color accuracy even if there are more colors in the Source color space than in the Destination color space.

Obtaining a Good Print

We'll now talk about the relationship between image size and resolution so you can resize your image for printing without losing print quality. We'll also discuss how to identify specific colors by name (a very important concept if you are editing a long distance project), and finally, how to accommodate a print shop that wants you to make adjustments to CMYK Color Separation settings.

Printing and Image Resolution

The smallest unit of measurement in your onscreen image is a pixel, and the smallest unit in your printed image is a dot. While they are not the same thing, the pixels on your screen do have a relationship to the number of dots in your printed image. Both pixels and printed dots are measured in terms of how many are required to display a single inch of your image. Your computer monitor requires between 96 and 72 pixels (depending on the size of the monitor and the resolution you have set to be displayed in your monitor settings) to display one inch of your image. That means if you have an onscreen image 960 pixels wide, and that image is saved at a resolution of 96dpi, your image will display ten inches wide. However, if you saved that image at 192dpi (2×96), your image will only be five inches wide onscreen, because the image is instructed to use 192 pixels to display a single inch of image, even though your monitor only requires 96 pixels (or whatever). That's why, when scanning images for the Web, you don't need a high-resolution scan, because computer monitors are limited to between 72 and 96dpi, so anything above that resolution is wasted.

A printer uses generally around 240 dots to display an image. That means hundreds of dots of ink are required to display a single inch of image. The same image that would stretch ten inches across your computer screen would only amount to three (or so) inches of printed width, depending on your printer's resolution. This is why images that look very large when displayed at 100 percent magnification on your monitor are not nearly as large when printed.

REFERENCING INDIVIDUAL COLORS

In printing, color accuracy is all-important, and a method to "call out" or refer to exact colors by name is required. For example, if you developed a logo that used a shade of blue, how would you identify that exact shade to someone you were on the phone with? The printing world has developed many color systems that assign names to each hue. In one system, known as PANTONE, color swatches are printed in a swatch book, with a name printed below the color swatch. Thus, two coworkers thousands of miles apart can each open a swatch book and refer to the exact same hue by name. Examples of these color systems used by printing presses throughout the world are, as mentioned, PANTONE, the popular TRUEMATCH, which color-matches more than 2000 computer-generated colors, FOCOLTONE, which helps solve certain prepress problems, and TOYO, which helps artists match inks used in Japanese printing.

NOTE The formula for the number of dots a printer displays is one-third of the printer's base resolution. That is because the resolution is based on the number of dots printed of each color. However, each pixel in the image must be printed by three colors (plus black for brightness) in order to produce its actual color. If the printer prints at 740dpi in one direction and 2880dpi in the other, the base resolution is only 740dpi. The extra dots in the other direction are *interpolated* (added according to a mathematical formula) by the printer to fill the spaces between dots and therefore produce a richer-looking and more continuous-tone image. However, those extra dots don't add one speck of additional image definition information. This is a fact that is very often misunderstood, but there you have it.

NOTE In Photoshop, pixels and image resolutions can be adjusted separately. However, they are interdependent. The ppi setting does not affect the size at which the image will print... only how many pixels (how much information) will be supplied to the printer in order to print at the specified dimensions. If the printer needs more information to print at its resolution than is supplied, it will simply *interpolate* (mathematically adjust) the pixels supplied with the pixels needed.

Photoshop digitally reproduces these systems so you can click a color in your image with the Eyedropper tool and identify it in one of the color systems. However, you can only use color matching for spot color. *Spot color* is used to print a specific area with a specific ink that exactly matches the color chosen from the color matching system. A good example of this would be the printing of a corporate logo that was required to be printed in a company's "branded" color. Think Coca-Cola red or IBM blue. The spot color ink(s) must be printed in addition to the four colors used to produce continuous tone. See the "Spot Colors" section later in this chapter.

CREATING COLOR SEPARATIONS

In CMYK printing, four color plates are used (cyan, magenta, yellow, and black); one color per plate. A clear film mask is applied in which various ink densities are used to create a wide color range when combined with the other plates. The masks vary dot patterns, which create varieties in ink densities called *color separations*. As each inked plate is pressed onto the stock (paper, vellum, or other medium), the original image is reproduced, using the overlapping pattern created by the four inks. Photoshop automatically creates color separations when you convert your image to CMYK. However, if your print shop requires you to make specific adjustments to separation settings and apply them to a customized CMYK color profile (choose Edit | Color Settings), click the CMYK drop-down menu under Working Spaces. Select the Custom CMYK option and indicate the separation settings required by your print shop.

GOOD RESULTS WITHOUT FULL-COLOR PRINTING

Full-color printing is hard on a budget, even a hefty one. You can print creative documents that hold the reader's interest without incurring the cost of a full-color print job. They are spot color, halftone, and duotone, printing.

SPOT COLORS

Sometimes, to add interest and detail in a single-color image, a spot color is used. A spot color is a shape, drawing, or application of an additional color into the detail of an image, usually a black or gray image that may need a little sprucing up. Use of a spot color is a happy medium between lackluster gray and the expense of multicolor printing, giving the project a little pizzazz without breaking the bank.

HALFTONE PRINTING

Halftoning is a printing process that creates the illusion of color shades by varying the size and pattern of single-color dots. There is no shading at all. It is often used to produce photographs and single-color documents like newspapers. Halftoning is what you do instead of grayscale. If you carefully look at a photograph in a newspaper, you'll see that only one color is used: black. The "shades of gray" in the photo are produced by simply varying the size and pattern of the dots used to print it.

The density and pattern of dots used to re-create the image is done through a process called *dithering*. Dots are arrayed in specific densities and patterns, done by photographing the image through a screen. The number of lines in the screen determine dot size and pattern, and is referred to as screen frequency. Generally speaking, the higher the screen frequency, the more detail in the resulting image. For halftone images, screen frequency is a corollary to image resolution. Photoshop lets you add screen frequency to your image's Final Print Output setting. However, if you add more line screens than your printer can accommodate, the dots will be too close together, and your image will appear muddy.

DUOTONES

Duotone is a technology used to increase the range of tones of a grayscale image. It is also used to add a tint of color to an image that otherwise uses only shades of black. In the digital world, a single-color image can use up to 256 shades of color. However, a printing press can reproduce only about 50 shades of a single color (for example, gray) per ink. A duotone image uses two inks to offer more range. For example, a black ink will be used to provide shadows and dark lines, while gray is employed for detail and lighter shading.

The following are some issues to beware of that are especially important in regards to halftone and duotone printing, as well as other nonphotographic print projects.

DOT GAIN

Professional printing measures ink and dot density very precisely. However, factors such as paper type cause ink dots to spread beyond their original dispersion, a phenomenon called *dot gain*. Since image color is based on a close reading of ink spread and density, dot gain is serious business. It is especially an issue with halftone, tritone, grayscale, and spot color printing. When printing images with these technologies, your print house will provide you with specific dot gain spread percentages. Dot gain settings are available as a profile option, and in the Color Settings dialog box.

CREATING COLOR TRAPS

When printing solid colors in a press, misregistration can occur. Small inkless gaps can be seen between color blocks. To prevent this, images with solid color often include small overlaps called *print traps*. Photoshop creates traps if you specify them. Your print shop will tell you if misregistration is a possibility with your project, and indicate proper trap values.

To Create A PRINT TRAP IN PHOTOSHOP:

1 Convert your image to CMYK mode if this hasn't been done already (choose Image | Mode | CMYK Color). Once changed, a Trap option appears at the bottom of the Image menu.

2 Choose Image | Trap. The Trap dialog box appears.

3 Indicate an appropriate trapping value and unit of measurement.

CHOOSING THE RIGHT PAPER FOR YOUR PROJECT

Although the print medium plays a huge role in the quality of final output, paper choice is often, unfortunately, an afterthought among digital artists. While designing your project, give due consideration to the paper your work will appear on. Paper comes in all types—porous, glossy, dense, thin, lightweight—and the choice of output will have a large effect on how your Photoshop design work is ultimately perceived.

Your choices include paper types and paper grades. Common paper types are as follows:

▶ Newsprint Thin and light.

▶ Offset Higher quality than newsprint, but inexpensive enough for general printing use.

► **Gloss** Highly reflective and great for continuous tone and full-color printing (especially good for photographs).

► **Matte** Absorbent, thick, serious looking, for work you want to keep around for a while.

When choosing a paper type, consider its effects on image clarity, definition, and color richness. Some papers are very porous and will absorb ink, thereby dulling the colors. Some paper types are bright, adding vibrancy and definition to your images. Because of this, you may want to spend some extra time prepping an image for its medium. For example, a photograph on matte paper could lose definition, and you may want to sharpen and brighten it up before printing.

You must also choose paper grade, which determines paper thickness and coating. This factor additionally affects image clarity and brightness. Paper grades available are

► **Book** A thickness range for printing books and magazines.

► **Cover** Thicker than book paper, suitable for fine art books, cards and placards.

► **Coated** Good for archival work, prints that will last for years rather than weeks or months. Coating types include gloss, dull, and lamination, which are applied after the image is printed.

Before choosing a paper for your project, you should also consider the following:

► **Ink coverage** The percentage of paper to be covered with ink.

► **Number of inks** A higher number of inks may require a thicker paper.

► **Output device** Different printers meet differing requirements, such as text clarity at the smallest font sizes, top-notch photographic quality, color accuracy, and image longevity.

► **Binding requirements** Some paper types bind better than others. Make sure you choose a good quality book grade paper for serious binding.

► **Budget** Paper costs are often a media project's number one budget-killer. Look for ways to shave off a few cents per copy—for example, buying at the price break, using front-and-back printing when possible, and moving down a paper grade.

Photoshop Actions

In this chapter, you will be introduced to how
Actions work and how to apply them to objects on the canvas.
Following this, you will learn how to create your own Actions.
The final section of the chapter will focus on extending the
Actions you have within Photoshop to those you can access
over the Internet.

In this chapter, you will learn the following:

▶ What an Action is

▶ How to apply an Action

▶ How to create your own Actions

▶ How to expand your library of Actions

You will find that Actions are fun and easy to use, with an end result that is often stunning. In this chapter, you will be transforming the following picture with just Actions. You can find the PSD file, called actions_original.psd, on the CD.

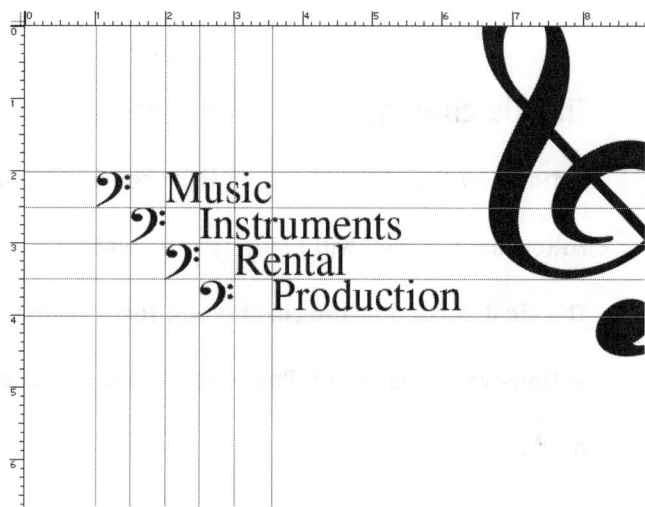

Photoshop 6.5 introduced a technology called Actions. Essentially, Actions save you time by letting you avoid having to repeat the same boring series of commands it takes to get a specific task done. Instead, you can just pick a menu item, choose a palette bar, or press a function key, and the Action will automatically execute the whole series of commands that you're recorded so that they affect whatever the current document is. All you have to do to create an Action is turn on an onscreen recorder that will capture a series of commands. Actions don't record the things you do with Toolbox tools because these would be different for every image (you'll want the brush in a different location and size, a different color of paint, etc.). However, you can tell the Action to stop when you want to use a tool and you can even enter instructions as to what the user should do when the Action stops.

After you've recorded an Action, events are replayed at the click of a button, key, or menu item (your choice). Actions will feel very familiar to those who have worked with Microsoft Word or Office macros.

USING THE ACTIONS PALETTE

The Actions palette is the interface for recording and playing back Actions. It can be accessed by choosing Windows | Actions.

The role of the Actions palette is to make it easier to automatically apply repetitive steps. This can be done three ways:

▶ Applying a default Action

▶ Downloading additional Actions from the Internet

▶ Recording your own Actions

An Action itself is made up of steps recorded in Photoshop. For instance, you may want to apply a drop-shadow text effect to a series of text objects on the canvas. Each step can be manually completed. However, it would be a lot easier if the steps to add, modify, and apply a drop-shadow could be recorded as a single step. This step could then be applied to any text by simply selecting the step and playing it back. This is what Photoshop Actions do.

Photoshop allows almost anything to be recorded as an Action. This includes layer effects, image effects, exporting, and batch conversions. No need to remember just how you performed that great Gaussian blur anymore—you can simply record the steps for the effect and save it as an Action, replaying it whenever you wish to repeat the end result.

Before we record any Actions, let's go ahead and apply some standard Actions to objects on the canvas. Then you can just watch what happens.

When you first view the Actions palette, you will see that the Actions are organized in sets, making it easier to find them. You can load additional Action sets by selecting the arrow icon from the top right of the Actions palette and choosing a set form the bottom of the pop-up menu, as shown in Figure 14-1. Sets also make it practical to record unlimited numbers of Actions, which can then be stored on

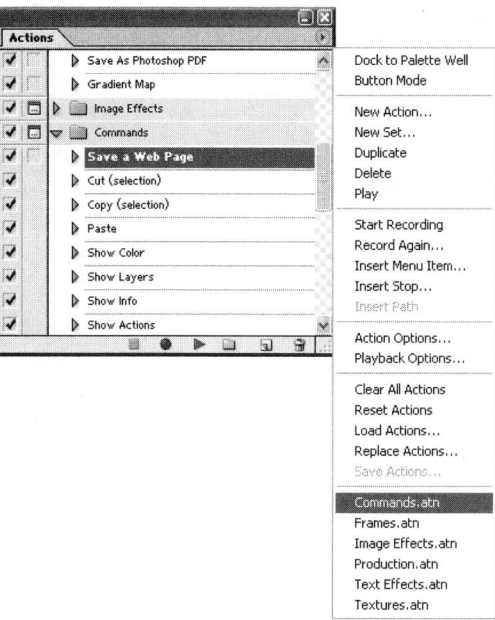

FIGURE 14-1

The Actions menu allows you to open additional groups of Actions.

CD-ROMs or other storage units outside your computer so there's no worry your system will run out of space.

LOADING ADDITIONAL ACTIONS

This exercise will allow us to load additional Action sets. Later, we will need these sets to complete the effects applied to the main image.

To Load ADDITIONAL ACTION SETS:

1 Choose Window | Actions to bring the Actions palette to the front.

2 From the Actions palette menu, choose Commands.

3 On the left-hand side of the palette, you will see that the group of Actions is loaded. The Command set is a series of basic tasks.

4 Repeat steps 1-3 to load the following sets.

- Image Effects
- Text Effects
- Production
- Textures

OK, the collection of Action sets looks impressive, but now we have to use them. So be sure to leave the Action sets you just loaded in the Actions palette. With this broad range of choices, you may want to put some thought into how you apply an Action. The following steps will demonstrate the range of tools that Actions give you.

To Use THE ACTION TOOLS:

1 Open an image.

2 In the Toolbox, choose the Text tool, and type some large text in the image. It will appear on its own layer.

3 In the Layers palette, select the Text layer you just created.

4 In the Actions palette, look for the category called Default Actions. Click the arrow to the immediate left of the category name. The category will expand to show the Action names available in this set.

5 Select and expand the Action called Cast Shadow (Type) so that you can see the individual commands that the Action will perform.

6 Expand the Gaussian Blur command. You will see that the blur radius is currently set for 2.8 pixels. Double-click the Gaussian Blur Name bar. The Gaussian Blur dialog will open and you can drag its slider to change the amount of blur.

7 Now you can run the Action and it will cast the shadow with the edge softness you preferred. To play the Action, click the Play button from the bottom of the Actions palette to apply the Action.

8 A dialog appears asking if it is OK to rasterize the current layer. Click OK. The Action is applied.

CREATING ACTIONS FROM SCRATCH

Actions are not difficult to create. You do not need to be a programmer to build an effective Action. If you are familiar with building Macros in Microsoft Word, then you will find that creating a new Action is very similar.

To Create AN ACTION:

1 Choose File | Create | New. Name the file Font Effect, with dimensions of 640x480. This will give you plenty of room to work in.

2 Select the Text tool and type This is some Text in the center of the canvas. We are going to apply a visual effect to the text. But first, we want to begin recording this process so we do not need to keep manually repeating it over and over again later. The recording will be completed by saving it as an Action.

3 Open the Actions palette. From the bottom right-hand corner select the option Create New Action. The New Action window opens. Name the Action Bold & Shadow Effect (Text).

4 Choose the Action to be saved with the Default Actions.atn set, as shown here.

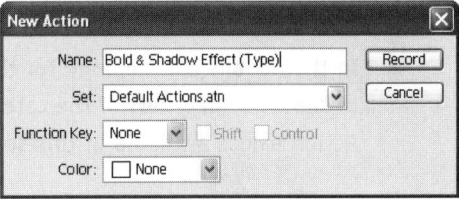

5 Press the Record button on the bottom of the Actions palette (it is the red circle). Every step we now take will be recorded.

6 Change the style of the text string to Bold.

7 With the Text Layer selected, choose the Layer style Drop Shadow.

8 Change the Opacity of the Drop Shadow to 45 percent, the angle to 124 degrees, and make the quality anti-aliased. Select OK. The Layer Effect is applied.

9 On the Actions palette, press the Stop button. The steps you have just taken have been recorded and can be replayed.

10 Open the file Actions_Wood.psd. Select the Text tool and type Where You are Our Life's Music on the screen.

11 With this layer still selected, apply the Action you just created, Bold & Shadow Effect (Text). Your image should look like Figure 14-2.

12 Save the file as Action _wood2.psd.

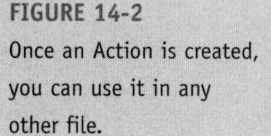

FIGURE 14-2
Once an Action is created, you can use it in any other file.

SHARING ACTIONS

When Adobe allowed users to create and share their own Actions, they may not have been fully aware of the massive impact that would have on the Photoshop community. The bottom line is that we all love to share the cool effects we have created with other people. Whether you are in a corporate workgroup and need to share specific tools, or you want to share your work with the Internet public, Adobe has made it very accessible.

In this exercise, you will take the Action you created earlier and format it so it can be shared with other users.

To Format AN ACTION FOR SHARING WITH OTHER USERS:

1 The first step is to move the new Action into its own set. Only a set can be exported. Open the Actions palette and choose New Set... from the Options menu.

2 The New Set window opens. Name the set My First Set. Select OK.

3 The Actions palette now has a new set named My First Set. Expand the Default Actions set. Select Bold & Shadow Effect (Text) created earlier. Drag the Action onto My First Set.

4 Expand My First Set. You will see your Action is now a member of this group.

5 Select the arrow in the top right-hand corner of the palette and choose Save Actions.

6 The Save As dialog window opens. The extension is saved as My First Set.atn. You can save the set anywhere on your computer. This .ATN file can now be sent through e-mail or over the Web to any Photoshop 7 user.

Any collection of Actions can be pulled together into sets and then exported as ATN files. Importing a set is easy. All actions must be imported as ATN files. A number of web sites allow you to download ATN files, the best of which is Adobe's Xchange site.

The Adobe Xchange is a centralized place where designers and developers can share plug-ins for any of Adobe's products. You will need to register to access the site, but the registration process is easy and, once in, you'll find a plethora of tools at your fingertips.

At Adobe's Actions Xchange for Photoshop, nearly 3000 Actions were listed as available for download at the time of writing. You can also search Google, Yahoo, and other web search engines for Photoshop Actions, and come up with an amazing number of sites.

IMAGEREADY ACTIONS

With Actions being so powerful and so useful within Photoshop, it is a nice surprise that Actions are now in ImageReady. Overall, ImageReady Actions are very similar to Photoshop Actions.

Many of the Actions in ImageReady were designed specifically for the Web, though some do allow you to apply visual effects.

In Figure 14-3, you can see the before and after appearance of the words Frozen Text, where the Frozen Text Action was applied to the text layer. The method of applying Actions is exactly the same as that used in Photoshop.

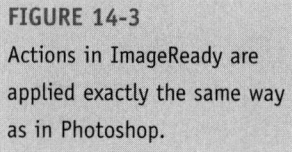

FIGURE 14-3
Actions in ImageReady are applied exactly the same way as in Photoshop.

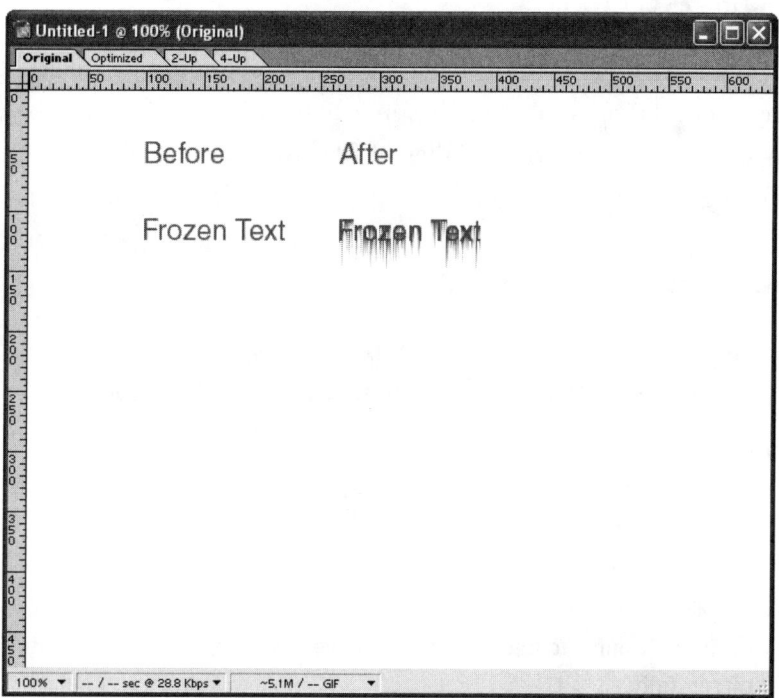

Additional Actions with ImageReady include the following:

▶ **2-State Button** This Action automatically converts an image into a button with a JavaScript roll-over.

▶ **Constrain to 200×200 pixels** This Action resizes the canvas to 200×200 pixels.

▶ **Flaming Text** This action adds flames to any text layer.

▶ **Multi-size and save** This exports the current file as a JPEG and GIF image.

▶ **Spinning Zoom In** Any text or image can be animated as though zooming into it.

▶ **Spin** Another animation that spins a selected layer.

▶ **Web Page Template** A new image 800×600 needs to be created for this Action to work. The Action adds a template, complete with text, effects, and slices that can be used for a web page.

▶ **Zoom In** A third animation sequence that zooms in on a layer.

▶ **Zoom Out** A fourth animation sequence that zooms out of a layer.

As with Photoshop Actions, you can download additional ImageReady Actions from Adobe's Xchange site.

BATCH ACTIONS

A final bonus that the Actions palette brings to designers is the ability to run Actions over a large number of files in a batch process. This can be something as simple as converting a large number of files to a specific file format, such as PDF, or changing the physical elements of an original file. It could just as well be a very complex series of commands that created a uniform look for a library of hundreds of illustrations for a Web site.

In the following exercise, you are going to change the Text layer of five files to add a drop-shadow effect to all of the text in each PSD. You will do this in Batch mode.

To Change THE TEXT LAYER AND ADD A DROP-SHADOW EFFECT IN BATCH MODE:

1 Open Photoshop. You do not need to have any files open for the Batch Action to run successfully.

2 Select File | Automate | Batch... as shown in Figure 14-4.

3 The Batch window opens. Choose Default Actions from the Set. The Action list will change. Select Cast Shadow (type).

FIGURE 14-4
The Batch process

4 For the source, select Folder. Press the Choose button and navigate to the Batch folder for this chapter on the CD, as shown here.

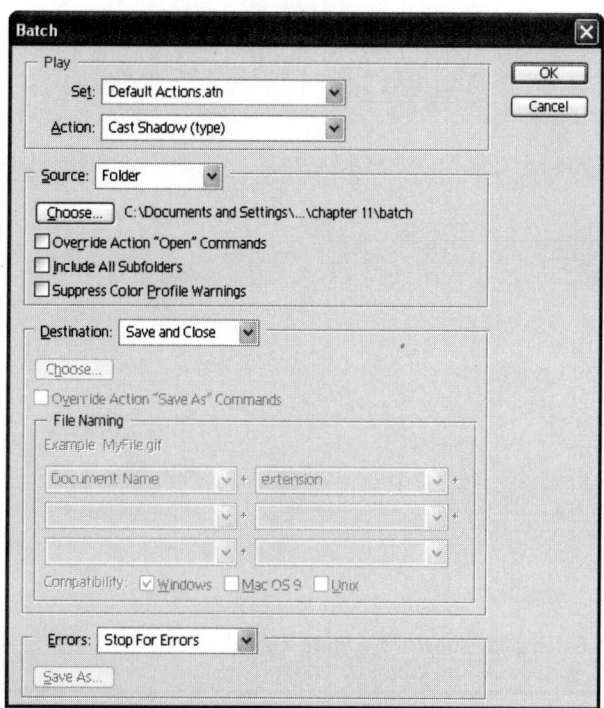

5 Select OK. The Process will now execute. All of the files in the folder will be opened and modified. When the process is complete, you can open the files to see the changes. All of the text layers will now have a drop-shadow.

The Batch Process makes it easy to apply global changes to a large number of files. The only caution I will add is that it is easy to ruin a large number of files. Once the process is run, there is no way to undo the changes. So, for instance, if you did not want a Glass Action added to every file, it may be a little too late.

Glossary

Antialiasing The process of graduating the shading of edge pixels from dark to light so they create the optical illusion of being smooth, rather than the pixilated "stair-stepped" edges we often see in sharp edges such as those in curved letters.

Artifact A part of the image that wasn't part of the original scene but was the result of digital processing. Artifacts are usually small blotches of color or "holidays" (blank spaces) in the image that may be a solid color. Artifacts resemble film grain but are usually considered *noise* (see entry for definition).

Aspect ratio The proportion of width vs. height. If you reduce an 8×10 image to 4×5, the second image is only one-fourth the size of the original but maintains the same *aspect ratio*.

Background That part of the image that is further from the lens then the main object or shape of interest. Also, in Photoshop, the Background layer is the primary layer in the image. In order to create transparent areas in the Background layer, it must be re-named so it becomes an ordinary layer.

Bezier curve A curve or line defined by its curve and angle of approach to, and angle of departure from, a control point. If you click the control point, control handles will extend from it. You can then control the shape of the approaching or departing curve by dragging the control point. All illustration programs use Bezier curves to define shapes (a.k.a. paths) and their fill patterns, colors, and gradients.

Bit depth The amount of data assigned to the interpretation of an image's color information, or to the definition of extra color channels (such as masks). An 8-bit image can contain up to 256 colors. A 16-bit image contains up to 64 thousand colors (most of the time, this is enough to fool you into thinking you're looking at a full color image). A 24-bit image can contain any of 16.8 million colors. 16-bit images make certain any visible color is recorded accurately in the image.

Bit The smallest piece of digital data. In the case of a photograph, one black or white pixel.

Brightness Another way of referring to the overall luminance of the image (or any chosen portion thereof).

Burn To use a tool that darkens a specific area as you scrub (repeatedly brush) over it.

Calibration Refers to premeasuring all the peripherals used for input and output of graphic images so that what appears on the devices accurately reflects what will be seen on another. Calibration is generally used most often in terms of choosing monitor settings that will accurately reflect the results seen on the monitor when sent to various output devices. Of course, the output devices generally require their own calibration for the complete scheme to work properly.

Clipping paths Bezier curve paths designated by Photoshop to be interpreted by illustration and page-makeup programs as a shape to be used for trimming the contents of the Photoshop file when it is incorporated into a page layout.

Color correction Can refer to many (and not always directly related) aspects of managing color for output to various devices such as printers, printing presses, and slide makers. However, it is most frequently used to mean the process of balancing color by using any of the myriad of controls that Photoshop makes available for that purpose. Command examples would be Levels, Curves, Auto Color, Hue/Saturation, and Replace Color.

Color management The process of creating calibration profiles for the variety of output devices that might be used by your photographs.

Color separation The conversion of an image into a set of primary colors according to the specifications defined for a particular screened printing process (e.g., offset printing, silkscreen printing, and lithography). So called because all the colors in the image are separated into separate colors for each layer in the printing process.

Compression Usually refers to a process wherein subtle changes in image color are digitally reinterpreted to be the same as their nearest neighbors. In this way, the amount of data needed to define the image colors can be made much smaller. There are two kinds of image compression: lossless and lossy. Lossy compression is so called because even (more or less slightly, depending on quality options) different-colored pixels are redefined as being the same, resulting in files that are typically one-fifth the size of losslessly compressed files. The higher the level of compression, the lower the image quality setting in the image compressing software and the greater the apparent loss in image quality. Conversely, lossless compression (such as TIFF or LZW) deletes and then mathematically duplicates only those pixels that are exactly the same color.

Contact sheet A term used by editorial and advertising photographers to refer to a proof sheet that is made by laying the original negatives atop a sheet of photo-sensitive paper and then placing a piece of heavy glass atop it to ensure the negatives are in perfect contact and alignment with the paper. The arrangement is then exposed to the light from an enlarger or contact printer and the paper is developed to produce a positive image. Today, many digital imaging programs—including Photoshop, of course—will produce the equivalent of a contact sheet automatically using all the images have been placed into a given folder. You can do many things that aren't possible with a conventional contact sheet, such as changing the names of files and specifying how or whether you want them labeled, what background color you want to use, and what size and margins you want to use for the images.

Context-sensitive (in-context) menus Menus that appear as a result of placing the cursor on any interface element (such as an icon, tool, or even the workspace background) and pressing a button or key. The in-context menu's commands always relate to what you can do in connection with that particular interface element or its contents. In Windows, in-context menus (if they exist for a particular interface element) will appear when you right-click the item. This is also true for Macintosh users who have two-button mice. If you're a one-button Mac mouse user, press Control-Click to get the in-context menus.

CMYK The four primary colors (<u>C</u>yan, <u>M</u>agenta, <u>Y</u>ellow, and blac<u>K</u>) in images that are reproduced for viewing by reflected light, such as digital and conventional printers and printing presses. Most of today's desktop printers, however, use RGB images as input files and these are automatically reinterpreted to CMYK by the printer software. Digital printers used for proofing and commercial printing presses almost universally require that images be converted to the smaller gamut (see *gamut* entry) of the CMYK mode.

Curves Usually an abbreviated way of referring to a Bezier Curve, also known as a vector image path. Also, one of Photoshop's brightness and color control commands that allows for precise control of the brightness of any color channel to any degree at any point or range of points in that channel's brightness spectrum.

Depth of field The distance between the closest and furthest points from the camera lens that are in acceptably (admittedly subjective) sharp focus. Shallow depth of field tends to focus viewer attention on a small part of the subject. Extended depth of field appears more realistic in landscapes because our eyes tend to see the entire scene as being in focus.

Dithering Digitally intermingling neighboring pixels so they create the illusion (because our eyes tend to blur them together) that there are colors in an indexed image that don't actually exist in that image's indexed color palette.

Dodge To use a tool that lightens a specific area as you scrub (repeatedly brush) over it.

dpi Dots-per-inch. The measure of image definition in a print. Not directly related to the number of *pixels-per-inch* (ppi) that defines the definition of a digital image.

Draw To create an image or graphic shape mathematically that is resolution-independent. In other words, to create Bezier curves. What you do in an illustration, CADD, or drawing program is draw. What you do in an image editing or painting program is called painting.

Edge smoothing Making an edge less pixilated than it would normally be at a given magnification. The process for creating this edge-smoothing is called *antialiasing*.

EXIF Exchangeable Image File. Information that can be generated by a digital camera so that it stays in that image's file header. An amazing amount of information is recorded this way: camera, model, aperture used, shutter speed (down to the smallest 1/1000th second) used, time of day taken, date taken, ISO rating used...and much, much, more.

File Browser Any program that shows your filenames as organized in your operating system's file folders. In Photoshop, the term refers specifically to a palette that shows all the image files in a directory as full-color thumbnails that you can open in Photoshop by dragging them into the Photoshop workspace.

Filters In Photoshop, filters are add-in programs that can be made to perform almost any imaginable special-purpose function. Hundreds (probably thousands) of special purpose filters made by third parties can be installed into Photoshop. Most will appear on the Filters menu.

Flat Photospeak for an image that displays an unattractive lack of contrast (i.e., a short range of tonal brightness).

Flatten To reduce the image's contrast so that it falls within a narrower brightness range—usually at the sacrifice of the lightest and darkest color. Also, to compress all the image's visible information onto a single layer.

Gamut The brightness and color range available to a color mode scheme or to an output device that is inherent in the image. The wider the gamut of an image or in a color scheme's limitations, the more colors can be displayed in that image. Colors that are beyond the range of a color scheme are called *out-of-gamut*.

GIF An indexed-color file format most often used for flat-color web graphics because the small file sizes and sharp color edges work especially well for the graphics used in logos, text, and buttons. GIF is an abbreviation for Graphics Interchange Format.

GIF animation A flip-page type of animation created by stacking multiple images in top-to-bottom order within the same GIF file. When that file is opened in a web browser (or any other program that is animated-GIF savvy), the animation begins to play automatically.

Gradient A smooth blend across one or more colors. In other words, there is no visible border between colors. Rainbows are full color-spectrum gradients.

Healing Brush A new tool in Photoshop 7 that automatically blends small portions of an image with the color and texture of their surroundings. So called because it can miraculously "cure" any skin or other small defect, this tool is useful for almost any kind of retouching.

Highlight The brightest portions of an image. Those portions of the image lit by the brightest lighting source(s).

History palette A Photoshop palette that places each action you take in its own Name bar, so you can return to any stage of an image as long as you haven't exceeded the number of steps allowed in your Photoshop Preferences settings. The default is 20 steps. You can also take Snapshots at any stage of an image's editing, then return to that stage at any point in the further development of that image, even if you've passed or deleted the step it was created in.

Image definition The degree of image detail and sharpness apparent in the image.

Image editing In the most limited sense, image editing refers to changing the color and brightness values in either the photograph as a whole or in specific parts of the photograph. The more modern definition could include almost any digital alteration one might make to a digital photograph, although the implication is that we are talking primarily about "digital darkroom" functions.

Image slicing Divides a web image into multiple images, each with a different sequential filename. Each of these individual images ("slices") can then be given an individual HTML link, JavaScript rollover effect, and can be optimized from all of the other slices that made up the original image.

Indexed color An image of 8 bits or less. These images must map (index) their colors to a specific position in each cell of a palette grid in order for it to be interpreted properly by other programs that read that image.

Interpolation The process of digitally reinterpreting the information in an image when its size is changed so that the added pixels blend between the original pixels in order to create the illusion that edge detail and smoothness have been maintained. Interpolation is usually fairly effective as long as the change in image isn't excessive.

Jaggies The stair-step effect caused when a bit-mapped image is enlarged without interpolation. In other words, pixels are simply multiplied to make them larger. In Photoshop, you can force jaggies to occur by using Nearest Neighbor interpolation when executing the Image Size command.

JPEG An acronym for Joint Photographic Experts Group, JPEG is the most popular file format for compressing images to save space on digital camera cards and maximize the efficiency of downloading full-spectrum images to web pages. All JPEG images use variably lossy compression. The lower the quality setting, the higher the loss of data in the image. Also, this lossiness is cumulative because it is recalculated each time the image is resaved.

Layer effects Interpretative combinations of Photoshop effects that can be automatically applied to any image layer. There are endless variations of the exact effects that can be applied, but these effects are mostly used to create surface and three-dimensional edge effects (such as bevels and drop-shadows) that are most effective when applied to text and shapes.

Layer mask A Photoshop mask specifically assigned to a given layer so it automatically controls the outside shape of what's visible on that layer. You can turn layer masks on and off at any time, move them, change their opacity, or transform them.

Layers Self-contained images stacked in top-to-bottom order within an image file. Layers can be assigned, in whole or in part, any level of opacity from 1-100 percent. To whatever extent a layer is transparent, the information on the layer(s) below them will be visible. Text, shape layers, and layer effects are all automatically created on their own layers.

Link A piece of computer code attached to a visible object (text, image, slice, and so on) with the result that clicking the object will automatically navigate you to another element of a web site or multimedia presentation (such as a PowerPoint page or Director movie). Links are usually made to change visually depending on the state of the mouse cursor in relationship to the link, so that, for instance, the link might change color or vibrate when the cursor is atop the link and might do something else (such as invert its colors) when the mouse button is clicked.

Mask A grayscale image that defines the degree to which Photoshop commands will affect the target image/layer. The blacker the mask is, the more opaque (command resistant). Conversely, the lighter the color of the mask, the more transparent. Completely white areas are totally unmasked.

Noise Grainy texture or odd color blotches that occur in digital images for a variety of technical reasons.

Optimization In Photoshop context, the process of making bitmapped images as physically small in bit size as is possible while maintaining an acceptable level of image quality. This acceptable level of image quality is entirely subjective and rests with the person doing the optimizing.

Options bar The bar that automatically appears beneath the Photoshop menu bar when you choose any Photoshop tool. The Options Bar for each tool is specific to the options available for that tool. If you place your cursor over an Options menu or icon, a Help balloon will give you an idea of what that option does.

Overexposure Camera settings have been miscalculated so there is little or no detail in the image highlights. This is usually accompanied by too little blackness in the shadow areas—or at least shadow areas that have an unbelievable level of detail for the subject and lighting conditions.

Paint In computer graphics speak, the opposite of draw. Images are made up by a matrix of individually colored pixels which can only be moved by editing as a group if they are first bounded by a selection (temporary mask).

Path See *Bezier curve*.

Pattern Any portion of a bitmapped image that has been preselected and defined to be used as a fill by choosing the Edit | Define Pattern command. Usually, textures taken from photos or bitmapped paintings are best used as patterns.

PDF Acronym for *Portable Document File*. An Adobe file format that will show predefined page layouts and fonts on any computer that runs the Adobe PDF Reader software, including most web browsers. This file format is so popular it has become almost universal across platforms, making it an ideal way to share published documents electronically with other computer users.

Pixel Short for picture element. A pixel is the smallest unit of a bitmapped picture. It consists of one square of a solid color in an overall matrix of colored squares (think of square tiles in a mosaic tabletop) that makes up the image.

Plug-in See *Filters*.

ppi Pixels-per-inch. The measure of image definition in a digital image. Not directly related to the number of *dots-per-inch* (dpi) that defines the definition of a printer's output.

Resolution The number of pixels in a digital image. The higher the resolution, the greater the number of pixels—and the more definable detail one can see in the image.

RGB Stands for Red, Green, and Blue. The color mode (three primary colors) used by all devices that display their images with transmitted light. This includes monitors and digital cameras. A newer mode, known as Lab color is used as the basis for many digital images and is becoming more popular.

Rollover Something that changes the appearance of a portion of an image map, image slice, or link depending on the current position of the cursor. Rollovers are also called mouse events. Typical rollover events (states) are so called because they are dependent on what the mouse is doing. States that can be assigned to rollovers are: Over, Down, Selected, Out, Up, Click, and None. You can specify that different things happen to change the appearance of the rollover when any of these states occur.

Rollovers palette The Rollovers palette is a part of the ImageReady interface that lets you create and see the effect of various rollover states in an image. It also lets you view and set options for those states.

Selection tools All of the tools that let you place a marquee around the part of the image you want to designate as being modifiable by Photoshop commands. If you converted the selection to a mask, the inside of the selection would be white (unprotected), the area outside would be black (completely protected), and any feathering in the border would be evenly graduated on each side of the marquee from white to black across the number of pixels specified for feathering. Any selection can be converted to a mask by saving it (so you can think of a selection as a temporary mask).

Shapes See *Bezier curve*.

Thumbnail A miniature representation of an image. These days, most operating systems' browsers (most notably Windows XP and Mac OS X) will let you view your image files as thumbnails or icons rather than force you to rely on choosing images from dozens (or hundreds) of similar filenames.

TIFF Tagged Image File Format. The most popular full-spectrum cross-platform file format for bitmapped images. TIFF images can also be saved to a lossless compressed file format known as LZW. The latest version of TIFF files can also be saved with independent, Photoshop-compatible layers. However, few image editing programs other than Photoshop can read these layered TIFF files.

Tool presets You can save the settings you've created in any tool's options bar, then recall them by choosing Window | Tool Presets and picking the desired tool from the Tool Presets palette or by clicking the Tool Preset picker (the down arrow just to the right of the current tool's icon) and choosing from the tool presets you've saved.

Transform To resize or relocate a graphical object. This includes rotating, stretching, scaling, perspective distortion, or corner distortion.

True-color Any image that contains 24-bits or more of color information—in other words, the full spectrum of visible colors.

Underexposed An image whose camera exposure was miscalculated so important parts of the shadow detail are hidden in total blackness. The brightest highlights usually contain so much detail they look unnaturally dark and dull.

White balance The color balance at which a plain white surface would, if it were part of the picture, lack any color tint other than pure white. When this is the case, colors usually appear to have the same overall color tint as they would if the scene were to be viewed by the human eye.

WBMP The file format used for displaying low-resolution images on PDAs and cell phones.

A

Absolute Colorimetric, 268

Actions, 275–286. *See also* Actions palette

    batch, 47–50, 284–285

    creating from scratch, 279–281

    defining, 276–277

    ImageReady, 282–283

    loading additional sets of, 278–279

    sharing, 281–282

    tools for, 279

Actions palette

    creating Actions, 280

    overview of, 277–279

    sharing Actions, 281–282

    text, editing letter shape, 241

    text, reflective, 230–231

actions_original.psd, 276

Add Noise filter, 84–85

Adjustment Layers

    creating, 209–210

    overview of, 113

    variable coloration, 231–232

Adobe Gamma, 10, 260

Adobe XChange, 282, 283

Airbrush tool, 239–240

airbrushing

    correcting skin defects, 82–85

    creating frosted text, 239–240

Aligned check box, Clone tool, 73

All command, Select menu, 144

Alpha channels

    masks as, 132

    Save Option, 35

    selection transparency, 142

Andromeda Software, 56

animation, creating GIFs, 254–255

Animations palette, 255

annotations

    Save Option, 35

    text, 39–40

anti-aliasing

    paint programs and, 3

    selections, 131

archival images

    photo collections, 44

    resolution of, 69–70

Art History Brush, 187, 190–192

As a copy, Save Option, 35

Assign Profile dialog box, 265–266

ATN files, 282

Auto-Color Correction, 14

Auto Levels command, 106

B

Background Eraser

    making knockouts, 158

    removing backgrounds, 214

backgrounds

    airbrushing defects, 83–85

    Blend If controls, 208

    cloning onto, 77–80

    depth-of-field, 100–101

    frosted text, 239–240

    Lighting Effects filter, 200–202

    painting, beginning with white, 181

    painting, photopainting, 186–188

    painting, setting, 185

backgrounds, removal techniques, 211–220

    adding space and distance, 218–220

    with Background Eraser, 214

    eliminating shapes, 97–98

    Extract command and, 215–218

    knocking out, 156–161

    with Magic Wand, 211–214

    replacing, 101–104

Superscript feature, Character palette, 225
Swatches palette, Web-safe color, 246

T

text, 223–242
  adding to images, 37–39
  annotations, 39–40
  changing into selection, 233–234
  creating and editing, 224–226
  frosted, 239–240
  glowing letter edges and, 231–232
  image patterns with, 236–237
  layer styles and, 227–230
  layers, creating, 204
  letter shapes, editing, 240–241
  pasting movable image inside, 234–236
  protecting, 20–21
  rasterizing, 232–233
  reflective, 230–231
  stencil, 237–239
  warping, 226–227
Text Effect Actions, 230–231
Text tool, 280
texture
  Lighting Effects filter for, 200–202
  paintbrush, 183
  photopainting using, 188
Texture dynamic, paintbrush, 183
Texturizer dialog box, 188
Thaw tool, 94, 196
thumbnails, 7–12
  choosing size of, 8
  previewing, 9
  renaming, 9–11
  rotating without resampling, 12
  turning off in Layers/Channels palettes, 30
tonal range. *See* exposure correction
toned images, 126–127

tools
  Action, 279
  color management, 216
  ImageReady, 253–254
  saving options for, 15–16
  selection, 134–141
TOYO, defined, 269
Transform options
  for layers, 206
  rasterizing text and, 232–233
  for shapes, 177–178
  for text, 226
Transform Selection command, 132, 148
transparency
  dithered, 22–23
  mapping/unmapping, 21–22
  in selections, 141–142
  using Lock Transparency, 194
Trap dialog box, 272
Trim command, 61–62
Trinitron monitors, 9–10
TRUEMATCH, 269
Turbulence Brush, 15
Twirl Clockwise, Liquify command, 93–94
Twirl Counterclockwise, Liquify command, 94
Type tool
  changing text into selection, 233–234
  creating text with, 224–225
  rasterizing text, 232–233
  stencil text, 237–239
  text warping with, 227

U

Ultimatte Knockout, 156
Undo levels, 29
Unsharp Mask dialog, 89
URL, 38
Use All Layers check box, Clone tool, 73
Use Filename As Caption box, contact sheets, 45

INTERNATIONAL CONTACT INFORMATION

AUSTRALIA
McGraw-Hill Book Company Australia Pty. Ltd.
TEL +61-2-9417-9899
FAX +61-2-9417-5687
http://www.mcgraw-hill.com.au
books-it_sydney@mcgraw-hill.com

CANADA
McGraw-Hill Ryerson Ltd.
TEL +905-430-5000
FAX +905-430-5020
http://www.mcgrawhill.ca

**GREECE, MIDDLE EAST,
NORTHERN AFRICA**
McGraw-Hill Hellas
TEL +30-1-656-0990-3-4
FAX +30-1-654-5525

MEXICO (Also serving Latin America)
McGraw-Hill Interamericana Editores S.A. de C.V.
TEL +525-117-1583
FAX +525-117-1589
http://www.mcgraw-hill.com.mx
fernando_castellanos@mcgraw-hill.com

SINGAPORE (Serving Asia)
McGraw-Hill Book Company
TEL +65-863-1580
FAX +65-862-3354
http://www.mcgraw-hill.com.sg
mghasia@mcgraw-hill.com

SOUTH AFRICA
McGraw-Hill South Africa
TEL +27-11-622-7512
FAX +27-11-622-9045
robyn_swanepoel@mcgraw-hill.com

**UNITED KINGDOM & EUROPE
(Excluding Southern Europe)**
McGraw-Hill Publishing Company
TEL +44-1-628-502500
FAX +44-1-628-770224
http://www.mcgraw-hill.co.uk
computing_neurope@mcgraw-hill.com

ALL OTHER INQUIRIES Contact:
Osborne/McGraw-Hill
TEL +1-510-549-6600
FAX +1-510-883-7600
http://www.osborne.com
omg_international@mcgraw-hill.com

LEARN FROM THE EXPERTS!

MASTER GRAPHICS SOFTWARE QUICKLY AND EASILY WITH MORE VIDEO LESSONS FROM BRAINSVILLE

CD Extras use the same easy-to-follow video presentation style as the CD included with this book. Each **CD Extra** is over an hour in length, with the author appearing on video throughout the entire presentation.

Adobe Premiere 6 CD Extra with Bonnie Blake

Bonnie shows you how to use edit tools, apply motion settings, use transitions, batch capture, create rolling titles, apply audio effects, and more!

Flash 5 CD Extra with Doug Sahlin

Create movie clips, gradients, motion paths, and special effects, animate multiple objects, use ActionScripts, and more...guided by a Flash expert.

Dreamweaver 4 CD Extra with Robert Fuller

Learn how to create styles, tables, links, Flash elements, and more from author and Web designer Robert Fuller.

Web Design CD Extra

Speed Web site development and improve design with Laurie's lessons on design tools, HTML basics, tables and frames, Web site critiques, and much more.

Name: Brainsville
Project: CD Extras

ORDER CD EXTRAS AT
Brainsville.com™
The better way to learn™